CANADA'S GAME

Canada's Game

Hockey and Identity

Edited by
ANDREW C. HOLMAN

McGill-Queen's University Press
Montreal & Kingston · London · Ithaca

© McGill-Queen's University Press 2009
ISBN: 978-0-7735-3597-8 (cloth)
ISBN: 978-0-7735-3598-5 (paper)

Legal deposit third quarter 2009
Bibliothèque nationale du Québec

Printed in Canada on acid-free paper that is 100% ancient forest free
(100% post-consumer recycled), processed chlorine free.

This book has been published with the help of grants from the Office
of the Vice President, Academic Affairs, the Dean of Arts and Sciences,
and the Departments of Canadian Studies and History, Bridgewater
State College. The editor wishes to thank Dr Anthony Cicerone for
his guidance and support.

McGill-Queen's University Press acknowledges the support of the Canada
Council for the Arts for our publishing program. We also acknowledge
the financial support of the Government of Canada through the Book
Publishing Industry Development Program (BPIDP) for our publishing
activities.

Library and Archives Canada Cataloguing in Publication
Canada's game: hockey and identity / edited by Andrew C. Holman.
Includes bibliographical references and index.
ISBN: 978-0-7735-3597-8 (bnd)
ISBN: 978-0-7735-3598-5 (pbk)
1. Hockey – Canada. 2. Hockey – Social aspects – Canada.
1. Holman, Andrew Carl, 1965–
GV848.4.C3C37 2009   796.9620971   C2009-902881-6

Typeset in Sabon 10.5/14
by Infoscan Collette, Quebec City

Contents

Acronyms

AAUC	Amateur Athletic Union of Canada
ACS/AEC	Association for Canadian Studies/ association des études canadiennes
CAHA	Canadian Amateur Hockey Association
CBC	Canadian Broadcasting Corporation
COC	Canadian Olympic Committee
CMC	Canadian Museum of Civilization
MLB	Major League Baseball
NHL	National Hockey League
NHLPA	National Hockey League Players' Association
NWOSHOF	Northwestern Ontario Sports Hall of Fame
SRC	La Société Radio-Canada
WHA	World Hockey Association

A Canadian lad in his Chicago Black Hawks outfit, Monkton, Ontario, c. 1949 (editor's collection).

Introduction

Canada's Game? Hockey and the Problem of Identity

ANDREW C. HOLMAN

In April 2004, the Association for Canadian Studies (ACS/AEC) held a one-day symposium at the Canadian Museum of Civilization (CMC) in Gatineau, Quebec, on the heady subject: "The Rocket." The scholarly event was timed to coincide with the grand opening of the CMC's exhibit on the life and times of the Montreal Canadiens superstar and Quebec nationalist icon Maurice Richard, a massive production that occupied a special exhibitions gallery for more than ten months (and probably would have continued to draw visitors had it remained there longer). Significantly, this event was the first time that the interdisciplinary (and normally scholarly) ACS/AEC had lent its mantle to the examination of hockey in Canadian culture. The symposium gathered scholars and reporters, poets and bureaucrats to the majestic glass-and-cement repository of national culture. Ice hockey and scholarship, once rarely considered in the same thought, were brought together in common interest. There were many offerings that day – scholarship, poetry, reminiscences – all of which made important connections between the sport of hockey and the slippery construction of identity in Canada and Quebec.[1]

Among the most interesting and telling exchanges that day was one that followed the presentation made by one Canadian media mogul, the executive producer of the iconic Canadian Broadcasting Corporation (CBC) staple "Hockey Night in Canada." One audience member inquired about the idea that perhaps the game that was happening on the ice was not wholly the game that everyone at home *really* saw and absorbed on television. After a longish preamble about the media, narratives, hero-making, and the tools of artifice, the question was posed: "If a hockey game is a spectacle that contains many stories, how did you choose which stories to show on television?" The producer responded, perhaps a bit tetchily: "What do you mean? We just showed the game as it really happened."[2]

AS IT REALLY HAPPENED: HOCKEY AND CANADIAN CULTURE

Until quite recently, a clear cultural divide existed in Canada when it came to discussing the perennial and overworked question: what does it mean to be Canadian? For generations of scholars of Canada in the humanities and social sciences, this search was a worthwhile but wild goose chase. Sparked by W.L. Morton's musings and the Symons Commission report about the Canadian identity and by a Centennial-era national awakening, scholars since the 1970s have searched for Canadian identities in "higher things": art and music, philosophy and film, ideology, and in the cultivation of a Canadian perspective in literature (Morton 1972; Symons 1975). A visit to virtually any Canadian Studies conference reveals this preference: colloquia on Kroetsch and Atwood, Keirstead and Innis, Arcand and Frye, and Charles Taylor and the Group of Seven. British litterateur Matthew Arnold would have seen "sweetness and light" in this project, one that still simultaneously motivates and consumes programs in Canadian Studies both in Canada and abroad (Arnold 1994). The evasiveness of the Canadian identity remains a motor for scholars of Canada, and the search goes on.

At the same time, this uncertainty about (or despair at) the evasiveness of Canadian culture, does not exist outside the academy. Oddly, it has been Arnold's "philistines" who knew (or claimed to know) what it meant to be Canadian all along. A visit to the local Legion or public library, to Rotary Club meetings or to more informal gatherings of ordinary Canadians yields responses that seem both more certain and ringingly familiar: To be Canadian is to be "not American." And "*hockey* is Canadian."

The Giller Prize-winning author David Adams Richards tells a humorous anecdote about this divide from his days as a writer-in-residence at the University of New Brunswick in Fredericton. It was in 1984, the day after Team Canada had defeated the hated Soviet national team 3 to 2 in overtime, and, a committed hockey fan, he was dying to chat with someone, anyone, about the great victory the night before. The first person he encountered was a young English professor, a good but perhaps pretentious scholar who had once been overheard saying that she could not see how anyone could *live* without having read Henry James. Despite her erudition, like Richards she was from small-town New Brunswick, and because of this, he thought, she *must* be a hockey fan. "Did you see the game last night?" No, she replied, "we don't have a television ... don't approve of it," but she continued on, saying that her husband had been eager to find out the result that morning on the radio.

"He's heartbroken," she said. "We were going for the Russians." Richards' face displayed his bewilderment at her treasonous statement. "Well we both hate Gretzky, you see." Her accent now turned slightly British ... "he's just such a Canadian." She smiled. He paused, uncomfortably, and then asked her: "You hate greatness ... or just Canadian greatness?" "In a way," Richards concluded, "Canadians have been asking this question all of their lives ... In a way [this] learned friend's stance embodies the notion of the intelligentsia that hockey is part of what's wrong with Canada." According to them, what is wrong with Canada is that its people find a sense of identity in a hopelessly plebeian pastime. The irony, Richards notes, is that in reality hockey is one of the very few things that Canada "got right" (Richards 2001, 12–15).

It would be difficult for Richards to make this claim as strongly today. In the decade since he published *Hockey Dreams*, scholarly disinclination towards reading hockey seriously as an emblem of Canadian culture has waned significantly. Resistance to earlier arguments by Bruce Kidd and John Macfarlane, and Alan Metcalfe for examining hockey as a scholarly subject has weakened, and the intelligentsia, it seems, has come around (Kidd 1970; Kidd and Macfarlane 1972; Metcalfe 1987). With the publication of Richard

Gruneau and David Whitson's synthetic study of the meaning of hockey to Canadian society and economy, scholars have carved out a fruitful agenda. First published in 1993, Gruneau and Whitson's book *Hockey Night in Canada* was remarkable as much for its pioneering analysis as it was for its renewal of a call for scholars of Canada to begin to "take hockey seriously as something suitable for social and cultural analysis" (Gruneau and Whitson 1993, 3).

The brilliance of Gruneau and Whitson's work is in its ability *problematize* hockey. To understand hockey in a scholarly way is to see it as a series of historical struggles that emanate from its central position in Canadian culture as national icon, as work and entertainment, as pastime, as enterprise, as privilege, and as a class-, race- and gender-based locus of identity. Scholars must recognize the game's ability to tell stories about Canada that reflect the country's uniqueness, strengths, and weaknesses. The importance of Gruneau and Whitson's book is that it urged scholars to look more critically at Canadian commonplace, to do more than just watch the game or play it; it urged them, in fact, to *read* it. And to read it, scholars need to understand the sport as a text that contains many narrative possibilities.

"As it really happened" has always depended on who was playing, who was watching, and, of course, who was relating the story. There is an old joke that when *Hockey Night in Canada* made the transition from radio to television in 1952, Canadian viewers were now blessed with not one, but two, hockey games: the one they saw with their own eyes and the one that CBC play-by-play announcer Foster Hewitt described! Accuracy in narrating the game was always a noble but impossible dream. The speed of hockey evades easy characterization; and language fails us. For scholars, the challenge of narrating hockey in a serious way involves much more than being concerned only about relating the game faithfully. It means, more importantly, that scholars must be aware of hockey's potential for multiple meanings. Hockey – like all sports – was and is a complex of stories, some that were never told; those that are being told come always from a variety of perspectives. (see Whitson and Gruneau 2006; *Sport History Review* 2006). Hockey reveals to Canadians stories about the ways in which they define and perform their multiple identities, as men and women, children and adults, whites and non-whites, francophones and anglophones, businesspeople and workers, and in other ways. As the scholarly quest for the Canadian identity continues, hockey can provide meaningful and useful texts for understanding who we are.

CANADA'S GAME

The chapters in this volume first took form as presentations made to a scholarly conference hosted by the Canadian Studies Program at Bridgewater State College and held in Plymouth, Massachusetts, in April 2005. "Canada's Game? Critical Perspectives on Ice Hockey and Identity" involved thirty-two presentations and about ninety scholars from Canada, the United States, and Europe. The chapters range widely in subject matter and disciplinary perspective, though they are bound together by scholarly rigor and a common consideration of hockey as a lens for understanding and articulating Canadian identity.

Canada's Game seeks to contribute to the interdisciplinary scholarly field – "hockey studies," perhaps – that Gruneau and Whitson carved out a decade ago and continue to define. To assert that hockey is Canada's game is to problematize the sport, to cast it as a phenomenon no less complex than the idea of a Canadian identity itself. The chapters in this volume address the problem of Canadian hockey in many different ways and belie the proposition held in the popular mind that hockey can be seen as a monolithic phenomenon interpretable in only one way: "as it really happens." In *Canada's Game* three themes are used to organize the multiple perspectives on hockey's meanings. In part 1, three chapters reflect how hockey has been employed (and misused) as an emblem of regional and national identities – identities that were subject to changing contexts over time. In part 2, analyses of fictional renderings of hockey occupy the stage. Here, three chapters examine how Canadian authors have characterized Canada and hockey's place in the country's makeup. In part 3, four chapters consider hockey's role as a commodity in modern capitalism, something to be sold and bought, consumed and internalized. These chapters debate the degree to which hockey, as a commercial spectacle, can be claimed by anyone, even Canadians.

Put together, these chapters skate the next shift in the scholarly study of hockey as Canada's game, and they challenge us to read it in ways that are new, revealing, and sometimes uncomfortable.

NOTES

1 The exhibit ran from 9 April 2004 to 20 February 2005. The symposium was called "Achievement and Legacy: Sports in Canada." Some of the presentations were published as essays in the ACS/AEC publication *Canadian Sports Studies* (March 2004).
2 This is a paraphrasing of the conversation.

PART ONE

COMMUNITY, REGION, NATION
Hockey and the Contexts of Identity

Canada's silver medal men's hockey team (Port Arthur Bear Cats) at the 1936 Olympics, Garmisch-Partenkirchen, Germany. The Canadian Press Picture Archive.

1

Big Liners and Beer Gardens

The Port Arthur Bear Cats, Shamateurism,
and the Selection Controversy Surrounding Canada's
1936 Olympic Hockey Team

GREG GILLESPIE

Rather than dreaming of Olympic gold, the 1936 Port Arthur Bear
Cats dreamt of big transatlantic ocean liners and overflowing
German beer gardens. Their dreams came from a sense of compla-
cency after more than a decade of Canadian dominance in Olympic
hockey. Beginning with the Winnipeg Falcons in 1920, the Canadian
Olympic hockey team won every Olympic gold prior to 1936 and,
in numerous cases, dominated its international competition. The
Bear Cats, from the small, close-knit Northern Ontario community
of Port Arthur, had every reason to feel confident, even convinced,
of their impending gold medal at the 1936 Olympic Games in
Garmisch-Partenkirchen, Germany.

Given their bumpy road through the Canadian Amateur Hockey
Association (CAHA) in 1935, the team had little reason to feel over-
confident. After all, the Halifax Wolverines, only months before,
defeated the Bear Cats in the senior amateur championship of
Canada.[1] This meant that that Wolverines, not the Bear Cats, laid
claim to the Allan Cup (symbolizing senior amateur excellence) in
1935; and, because the following year was an Olympic year, tradition
held that the Wolverines would represent Canada and advance into
international Olympic competition. As the Olympics neared, the
CAHA contacted the manager of the Wolverines to begin preparations

for an Olympic training camp. Subsequent discussions with representatives from Halifax revealed that, due to player movement to
professional teams after the championship game, the Wolverines
were unable to lace up a representative squad (a CAHA requirement).[2]
Rather than waiting for Halifax to pull a team together, the CAHA
invited the Bear Cats, the team defeated in the championship game,
to represent Canada in place of the Wolverines. This decision gave
rise to, at the time, an unprecedented controversy in the history of
amateurism and professionalism in Canada. To add national injury
to Maritime insult, the Bear Cats advanced into Olympic competition and promptly lost to Great Britain, resulting in Canada's first
silver medal in Olympic hockey.

In addition to this tough-to-swallow development, a series of other
controversies hounded the 1936 Canadian hockey team. Issues
regarding the eligibility of Canadian players on the British team led
to the questioning of Canadian sportsmanship by the assembled
international hockey community. Accusations of "shamateurism"
(the bending of amateur rules) and allegations of broken-time payments (payments for missed work shifts) to players followed the
team before, during, and after Olympic competition. The controversies that followed the 1936 Olympic hockey team provided the final
straw in a long-standing amateurism-professionalism dialogue in
hockey between the CAHA and its ally, the Amateur Athletic Union
of Canada (AAUC). (Morrow 1989; Howell 2001; Gruneau and
Whitson 1993, 76–7). In the spring of 1936, just months after the
Olympic Games, the CAHA broke once and for all with the AAUC.

Two recent articles by historians Mark Savoie (2000) and John
Wong (2003) examine the 1936 Olympics and the Canadian Olympic
hockey team specifically. Savoie's research examines the CAHA's decision to invite the Port Arthur Bear Cats to take the place of the
Halifax Wolverines and the subsequent selection controversy that
ensued in the Maritimes. Claiming central Canadian bias, Savoie
focuses on the perspective of the Maritimes and the Halifax Wolverines.
Employing sources weighted towards the perspective of the Maritime
provinces, his work fails to contextualize the overall controversy and
the responses of all parties involved. For example, despite its team's
loss to Great Britain, the community of Port Arthur, part of the

amalgamated city of Thunder Bay since 1970, enshrined the Bear Cat players native to Northern Ontario (Nummy Friday, Alex Sinclair, Bill Thompson, Jakie Nash, Arnold Deacon, Gus Saxberg, Ray Milton) and their coach Albert Pudas in the Northwestern Ontario Sports Hall of Fame (NWOSHOF) in 1987. For Port Arthur, the Bear Cats meant more than a group of simple hockey players: they were a team that was representative of Port Arthur and that reflected its community values and small-town identity (see Bouchier 2003). With this team went the aspirations of a Northern Ontario community.

Savoie's article does provide an excellent overview of how the selection controversy played out in the Maritimes. There were indeed disgruntled team officials, and no doubt this contributed to broader feelings and a sense of disenfranchisement among Maritimers and their general relationship to Canadian Confederation. However, the archives examined for this paper from the NWOSHOF, and in particular the excellent scrapbook of Port Arthur head coach Albert Pudas, fail to demonstrate any sort of sustained effort through which central Canada and the CAHA sought to alienate the Maritimes and Maritime hockey. Although Maritimers perceived the selection controversy as a snub of the Halifax Wolverines and eastern Canada generally, the central issue rests with the regional negotiation of shamateurism, particularly in relation to representative players and broken-time payments, in amateur hockey across Canada in the 1920s and 1930s, which culminated in the selection crisis in amateur hockey prior to the Olympics in 1936. No doubt, regional differences between central and eastern Canada likely played their part, but I suggest that these differences emerged from local understandings and negotiations of shamateurism between the Maritimes and central Canada. Situating this debate and controversy merely within a desire to exclude eastern Canada or eastern Canadian players from the Olympics simply fails to address the complexity of the situation.

Wong's work examines the period that immediately followed the CAHA's break with the AAUC and the new organizational relationships in hockey that developed in the wake of that important event, particularly in relation to the meeting and discussions that took place with the CAHA and the National Hockey League (NHL) (Wong 2003; Metcalfe 1992; Metcalfe 1983). Only four months after the break with the AAUC, the CAHA and the NHL came to an agreement regarding the organization and regulation between amateur and professional hockey in Canada. This established that the NHL would discontinue pinching players from the teams in the CAHA; however, in turn, the CAHA agreed to work as a feeder system for the NHL. In doing so, the CAHA made a great mistake in the history of amateur hockey: it gave the NHL a beachhead, or stake, in Canadian amateur hockey – one the NHL never relinquished (Kidd 1996; Field 2002). Although the CAHA loosened its relationship with the professional NHL, it tightened its relationship with international leagues and amateur associations, including the British Ice Hockey Association, notorious for its penchant for playing Canadian players whom the CAHA had deemed ineligible.

THE SELECTION CONTROVERSY AND CANADA'S 1936 OLYMPIC HOCKEY TEAM

Prior to meeting the Halifax Wolverines in the CAHA championship, the Port Arthur Bear Cats defeated the North Battleford Beavers in the western Canadian championship in 1935. After its victory over North Battleford, the small community of Port Arthur held a joyous celebration for its team, which included a short parade from the train station to the reception led by the local MacGillivray Pipe Band (Pudas 1935–36, 3 April 1935). Community boosterism for the Bear Cats found expression in other areas, such as newspaper articles and poetry. One spectator immortalized the victory over North Battlefield as follows: "A game apiece, now watch their smoke, / As they turn on the heat, / Those fighting Bear Cats have gone bugs, / They don't know when their [sic] beat! / The coach said Out and Check'em boys! / And then there was some fun / (The final bell). The Bear Cats four, the Beavers only one'" (5 April 1935). Even before the 1935 season took place, those in Port Arthur knew that an invitation to represent Canada at the Olympic Games, which most considered a shoe-in for Olympic gold, rested in the balance. The Port Arthur community liked its chances, having previously won the senior amateur championship of Canada three times between 1925 and 1930 (8 March 1935). "Those Tickets to Berlin," wrote a local newspaper, "thrown into the Allan Cup this year by the Canadian Amateur Hockey Association, had … [the] … Port Arthur Bear Cats dreaming of big liners and beer gardens today as they prepared to continue their struggle for the Dominion title" (17 April 1935). Having defeated North Battleford, the Port Arthur squad looked forward to meeting the Halifax Wolverines in the CAHA championship game.

While en route to the Canadian championship to face the eastern Canadian champion Halifax Wolverines, the Bear Cats practised at Maple Leaf Gardens and then attended the Stanley Cup final between the Toronto Maple Leafs and the Montreal Maroons (Pudas 1935–1936, 5 April 1935). New York Rangers manager Lester Patrick watched practice and scouted the western Canadian amateur hockey champions (9 April 1935). Upon reaching Halifax, the Bear Cats found that the facilities left much to be desired. The Port Arthur newspapers complained about the ice and the rink, referring to the conditions as "loathsome and repulsive" (17–18 April 1935). The "rink" was more of an agricultural building, with no washrooms for the seven thousand spectators in attendance. The public "just went indiscriminately under the stands and the smell, just as bad for the following day's practice, prompted players to ask each other if they had brought their gas masks." The dressing rooms provided little comfort. They had "a little stove in the corner, no toilet, no running water, no water to drink, no showers, a bench to sit on while putting on their skates. Cows and horses have often been cared for in better places" (17 April 1935).

The Wolverine squad ultimately outgunned the younger and less-experienced Bear Cats in the first two games of a three-game series. The Bear Cats represented an amalgam of players strictly from the remote community of Port Arthur, who averaged a mere twenty-three years of age. In contrast, the Wolverines put forth a group of cagey veterans averaging twenty-six years of age – a non-representative "all-star" team put together from across the country and hailing from places ranging from South Porcupine, Ontario, to New Glasgow, Nova Scotia (Pudas 1935–36, 15 April 1935). The newspapers nonetheless praised the sportsmanship displayed by the Bear Cats, which, in turn, reflected on the community of Port Arthur: "The

Port Arthur team did full credit to their city and lived up in every respect to examples set for them in sportsmanship and fair play by previous Port Arthur squads" (18 April 1935). Even the Bear Cat players offered kind parting words. After losing to the Halifax team, forward Jimmy Haggarty stated exactly what they had lost: "The Wolves have our best wishes for the Olympic series [in Germany]."

However, after the CAHA championship game, the majority of Wolverine players left Nova Scotia for other amateur and professional teams in Canada and the United States. When contacted to begin training for the Olympics, Wolverine officials stated they had no team to field. Once the CAHA realized that that Halifax was unable to provide a team for the Olympics, CAHA president E.A. Gilroy called a two-day long meeting with Halifax team officials in November 1935 to discuss the issue. This special emergency CAHA session, held behind closed doors, resulted in the generation of four possible alternatives: (1) the Bear Cats should take their place; (2) the CAHA should restore the Halifax Wolverines with new players; (3) an all-star all-Canadian team should be created; and (4) the Bear Cats and the Montreal Royals should play a two-game series, with the winning team to represent Canada (Pudas 1935–36, 22 November 1935).

The CAHA executive, harassed by the representatives from the four semi-final teams (Port Arthur, North Battleford, Halifax, and Montreal) held a vote during a second closed-door meeting. The vote resulted in an invitation to the Port Arthur team sent by CAHA president Gilroy. Newspapers hinted that, even though the team would hold the Bear Cats name, there was mutual agreement among the committee members to confine the selection of players to the four semi-final teams from the 1935 season (Pudas 1935–36, n.d. December 1935).

Gilroy offered a statement that summarized the events of the closed-door meetings and the decision to invite Port Arthur. The meeting, he wrote, included the CAHA executive and P.J. Mulqueen, chair of the Canadian Olympic Committee (COC); J.E. Wry, president of the Maritime Hockey Association; and J.H. Conn, president of the Halifax Wolverines. The CAHA and the COC desired to give additional time to the Halifax club. However, due to the number of players who had left the area following the championship game, the CAHA was forced to invite the runner-up Port Arthur Bear Cats to take the place of the Wolverines. Gilroy's telegram to Port Arthur officials read: "Halifax being unable to go, CAHA invites your team to represent Canada at Olympics. E.A. Gilroy, President, CAHA" (Pudas 1935–36, 22 November 1935).

The Port Arthur newspapers tried to make sense of this shocking decision for their readers. One paper ran the following headline: "Halifax Is Unable to Get a Team Together." The paper wrote: "The invitation came when Halifax was unable to field a representative team." And: "The Halifax wolverines, cup-winners, could not muster their playing strength, Wolverines have broken up in the off-season, some players moving to other centres and several signing pro contracts" (Pudas 1935–36, n.d.; 10 December 1935). The Port Arthur newspapers noted that the Halifax Wolverines, as the rightful champions of senior amateur competition through having defeated Port Arthur, held the right to represent Canada at the Olympics and deserved the opportunity to go to Germany. They also tried to sum up the unique nature of the situation: "The plight in which the CAHA found itself for the selection of a team with the breaking up of the Halifax wolverines was unprecedented in the annals of amateur hockey." The Montreal Royals senior amateur hockey team (which the Wolverines had defeated in the eastern semi-final competition prior to meeting Port Arthur) joined in the uproar against the CAHA in selecting the Bear Cats to represent Canada at the Olympic Games. They claimed that they provided a better level of competition against the Wolverines than did the Bear Cats, and Montreal team captain Ralph St Germaine challenged Port Arthur to a two-game series to determine who should represent Canada. The Port Arthur newspapers argued against this and suggested that the CAHA wanted to "select a team that has played and shown its form rather than to select a group of all-stars who might or might not be welded into a workable combination" (23 November 1935).

Although the situation presented problems, the invitation to represent Canada in Germany provided an opportunity to retain several budding young Bear Cat players who threatened to migrate to a professional team in Baltimore. The local paper wrote that "any lingering ideas of this kind have been chased out of their minds now that the Cats have been definitely given the nod [for the Olympics]. Only one player, Robillard, who left the team in defiance of a suspension on players leaving for the states brought down by the Thunder Bay Amateur Hockey Association, was deemed a declared professional and outside the boundaries of amateur play" (Pudas 1935–36, 23 November 1935).

The newspapers hinted at the coming additions to the Port Arthur team and intimated that, although the team would retain the Bear Cats name, it would, over the coming weeks, likely take the shape of an all-star team.

> Once the invitation to represent Canada at the Olympics is accepted the Port Arthur team, although it will continue to be generally spoken of as such, becomes, actually, the Canadian team and passes into the management of the CAHA and the Olympic committee. That committee will, therefore, have charge of its affairs and will be responsible for any additions or alterations to the line-up that may be deemed advisable in order that the strongest possible team may be iced in the competition which will this time be more severe than ever before.
> (Pudas 1935–36, 22 November 1935)

Just one day after the selection controversy announcement, local newspapers in Port Arthur ran a story that identified four players from the Halifax Wolverines whom the CAHA planned to add to the Olympic team. The four represented the remainder of the team that had defeated the Bear Cats for the Allan Cup months earlier. Gilroy himself recommended the inclusion of the four remaining Wolverines who had helped the Maritime team to the Canadian championship the previous year (Pudas 1935–36, 23 November 1935).

By early December 1935, thirteen players – seven from the western champion Port Arthur team (Saxberg, Sinclair, Thompson, Deacon, Friday, Milton, Nash), four from the Canadian champion Halifax Wolverines (Mosher, Ferguson, Lawlor, Bubar), and two from the Eastern finalist Montreal Royals (Neville and Murray) – gathered in Port Arthur (Pudas 1935–36, 12 December 1935). Port Arthur coach

Albert "Puddy" Pudas was to coach the Olympic team, and Malcolm Cochran was to serve as team manager (ibid.). The newspapers reported: "It seemed only right that four remaining Halifax players should be given consideration, and consequently invitation was issued to them. They accepted and will report in Port Arthur next week. Somewhat of a surprise followed with the extending of invitations to Neville, a brilliant forward, and Murray, a defenceman, of the Montreal Royals, to join the squad" (Pudas 1935–36, n.d. December 1935).

Just as the team appeared set to begin training for the Olympic Games, the CAHA dropped another bombshell on Canadian amateur sport and Maritime hockey. It expelled the four Halifax Wolverines from the Olympic team and replaced them with four new players selected from teams across Canada. The CAHA ejected the four Wolverines because they had allegedly sought financial remuneration in the form of broken-time payments (i.e., pay for missed work shifts). The four players from Halifax each denied the charge, but the association was unconvinced. The CAHA selected P.W. Moore (Port Colborne), Hugh Farquarson (Montreal Victorias), Walter Kitchen (Toronto Dukes), and Jimmy Haggarty (Port Arthur Bear Cats) to replace them (Pudas 1935–36, n.d. December 1935). Days later, the CAHA added Montreal Royals captain Ralph St Germaine to the Olympic team (ibid.).

The CAHA withheld immediate details of the dismissals from the public. However, the particulars of the situation did come forward at the CAHA annual general meeting six months later, well after Port Arthur lost the gold medal at the 1936 Olympics to Britain. Over that six-month period, Gilroy faced intense pressure from Maritime newspapers, the Maritime branch of the CAHA, and, especially, Jack Conn, president of the Halifax Wolverines, whose version of the dismissals presented them as based on central Canadian bias, thus fanning the flames of discontent in the Maritimes.

To clear his name, Gilroy released the telegrams exchanged between Conn, James Wry, and himself between October 1935 and January 1936. In response, Wry, president of the Maritime Hockey Association, released to the press sworn affidavits by the four players that the CAHA had expelled from the Canadian Olympic team (Pudas

1935–36, n.d. April 1936). So gripping was the issue that Canadian newspapers published the telegrams verbatim. In the wires, Gilroy related his desire to have the Province of Nova Scotia pay some sort of broken-time payment to Nova Scotia players, but he made it clear that the CAHA could not, in any way, support players' families. The affidavits from the players indicated that they never demanded money from the CAHA.

A review of these critical telegrams provides fascinating insight into the selection controversy that shook Canadian amateur hockey. The telegrams began on 26 October 1935, with one from Jack Conn, president of the Wolverines, to Gilroy, president of the CAHA. Conn wrote: "Must know immediately where I fit re: Wolverines' trip to Olympics. How much money is available for trip? Who will handle finances on trip? Will all trip expenses of team be looked after by Olympic committee? What provision will be made for players to care for their families while they are away? Imperative I have this information as quickly as possible." Gilroy replied: "Olympic Committee pays all trip expenses fourteen men which includes manager of team. Olympic Committee representatives will handle finances. Olympic Committee does not provide for families of players while away" (Pudas 1935–36, n.d. April 1936).

Gilroy received only silence from Conn, so he wired again on 28 December 1935: "This wire confidential. As per our understanding that Olympic Committee would not provide for families of players while they were at Olympics, are not city of Halifax and province of Nova Scotia looking after families of Halifax Players? Rush Reply" (Pudas 1935–36, n.d. April 1936). Again no response came from Conn. Gilroy wired again on 1 January: "Situation one that hockey reputation of Dominion of Canada is affected. As executive member of the CAHA it is your duty to reply to my wire of Dec 28." Wry replied on 2 January 1936: "When decided that Wolves were not to go as a team, all arrangements fell through. Have been trying to get information re: arrangements made before players left. To date unable to get anything concrete. Wire particulars of present situation." Later the same day, Gilroy replied to Conn: "Maritime players demanding three months salary. Demand cannot and will not be granted by committee. If their threat is carried out it will be necessary to replace them. Naturally reason for doing so will have to be made public. Their action would cast unfavourable reflection on Halifax and the Maritimes." Almost a week later, Conn wired Gilroy: "Halifax and local government interested. Expect decision hourly. Will advise" (Pudas 1935–36, n.d. April 1936). But Gilroy received no reply from either Conn or Wry.

The CAHA executive met in Toronto on the night of 6 January 1936, and the four Halifax Wolverines players were dropped from the team. For some reason, Wry did not want Gilroy to release these telegrams to the press. He even went so far as to bring forth a motion to prevent Gilroy from making the telegrams public knowledge. When they were brought publicly forward, Wry released the sworn affidavits from the players as a rebuttal. Gilroy tried to calm Wry, who responded with the following statement to the papers: "Now he [Gilroy] gives the telegrams to the papers. In fairness to the players their side of the story should be told as well. After these see the light of day, I am through with the entire proposition." Notably, all four affidavits swore that Gilroy himself and Olympic team manager Malcolm Cochran brought up the question of caring for Wolverine families through broken-time payments. One of the players quoted Cochran while en route to Toronto as having said: "Ernie, everything is OK. Mr Gilroy has put everything in my hands and I am to make my own arrangements." The four Wolverines also stated that they had discussed the matter directly with Gilroy. "There were five of us there, including Gilroy," the affidavit related. "He [Gilroy] asked if any preparation had been made for our families at all. We said no. He said Port Arthur is looking after the Port Arthur Bear Cats and Montreal is looking after their boys and it is no more than right that Nova Scotia should look after you fellows" (Pudas 1935–36, n.d. April 1936).

At that time, the premier of Nova Scotia, Angus L. Macdonald, perhaps still stinging from the previous controversy, which had led to the CAHA's invitation to Port Arthur, "informed us that he could, under no condition, give the money to individual players, but if the team had gone over as a unit the $1000 [for the whole team] would have been given" (Pudas 1935–36, n.d. April 1936). Later, the same player quoted Gilroy as having said: "If we don't get you fixed up

I am not going to permit you to go overseas." The players stated that Gilroy himself suggested $100 each, to which they agreed. The players then heard of their dismissal through a Toronto newspaper. Mosher concluded his affidavit: "I further say that at no time did I ever mention the matter of remuneration or family expenses to any-body connected with the Olympic hockey team or Canadian governing sport bodies. Where the matter was introduced it was always [from those] in charge of the team" (ibid.).

A downcast newspaper editor considered the selection controversy in light of the future of Canadian Olympic hockey at the next Olympic Games: "It's highly probable that CAHA officials will change their methods when the next Olympic year rolls around, and that instead of sending the Allan Cup winners of the preceding year, will send over an all-star outfit, selecting the cream of the season's amateurs. Of course much can happen in four years and perhaps there won't be enough good amateurs left to form even a good all-star team. At the rate they've been leaving and the numbers expected to leave next fall, this night prove true" (Pudas 1935–36, n.d. April 1936).

Despite the amateur orientation of his sport, Gilroy himself asked for $100 in reimbursements for expenses on the trip to Germany. And amateur rules did not keep Head Coach Albert Pudas from taking endorsements. Pudas worked as spokesman for Crown Brand Corn Syrup in 1936. One advertisement read:

> Selected as Canada's Best, The Olympic Hockey Team Coach recommends "Crown Brand." Albert Pudas, distinguished coach who is responsible for the condition of the team which will represent Canada at the Olympics says, "I heartily endorse CROWN BRAND Corn Syrup as an energy food for athletes. It quickly restores the energy expended in strenuous games. [If you mail in label Edwardsburg Crown Brand Corn Syrup you get a free team poster]." (Pudas 1935–36, n.d. April 1936)

After returning to Canada, a number of Bear Cat players faced accusations that, following the Olympic Games, they engaged in a money-making, barn-storming tour of Europe. Norman Friday, captain of the Port Arthur Bear Cats, explained the situation. The team did indeed play; however, instead of making money, Friday observed, the trip cost Bear Cat players money from their own pockets. He also rebutted the rumours that each player came home with $500 or $1,000 generated from the tour. All told, the Bear Cats played fourteen games following the Olympics (including two each in Munich, Nuremberg, Hamburg, Paris, and Amsterdam; three in Berlin; and one in Dusseldorf). Friday claimed he was told that the CAHA was trying to meet expenses by holding the tour. He observed: "Going over on the boat we were told the CAHA was $3,200 or $3,700 in debt on account of the trip before we left Canada and they had all the expenses in Europe and Germany to pay." And he continued:

> What did the players get? All we got was an allowance for expenses over and above the hotel, travelling, and other major items. The allowance was to b[u]y tea, coffee, and milk which we had to pay for extra. The allowance amounted to $2.50 per day, Canadian money, but that didn't go very far in paying also for cigarettes, taxis, theatres, and other such expenses. One package of a well-known brand of cigarettes cost eighty cents and the other forty to fifty cents. Some of us had to use our own money or go without.

When asked if anyone made any money out of the tour, Friday claimed that the team members were supposed "to get an allowance of 100 marks, $40 each from the German Government as a complimentary contribution to our entertainment while in that country, but I never got that and don't know who did. It cost us money to make that trip." The newspaper reporter asked Friday, "Did the CAHA make anything?" Friday replied, "I can't see where they lost" (Pudas 1935–36, n.d. April 1936).

A series of scandals and controversies followed Canada's 1936 Olympic Team. The first centred on the CAHA's decision to invite the Port Arthur Bear Cats to take the place of the Halifax Wolverines, the rightful representatives as 1935 champions of senior amateur hockey in Canada. Following this, the CAHA's decision to expel four members of the Wolverines over allegations of broken-time payments further clouded the team's prospects and fuelled the flames of discontent in the Maritimes. These controversies created an environment the likes of which Canadian amateur hockey had never seen. It brought to the public forefront issues of shamateurism that existed, to a greater or lesser degree, in all corners of amateur hockey in Canada (see Cosentino 1973; Lansley 1971). Despite the numerous crises and their dramatic nature, the most important issue rested with broken-time payments. Ironically, this formed part of the CAHA's decision to break from the AAUC (see Macdonald 1992; Morrow and Wamsley 2005, 70–86).

Unfortunately, we will never know what might have happened if the 1936 Port Arthur Bear Cats had focused on their goal of Olympic gold instead of on transatlantic ocean liners and overflowing German beer gardens. Numerous problems and public relations nightmares plagued the initial formation of the team as well as their Olympic run. The eligibility crisis raised by Canadian officials regarding Canadian players on the British team who were deemed ineligible by the CAHA resulted in Canadian sportsmanship being questioned internationally. The Canadian team assumed a dual-elimination scenario and fully expected to meet the British team again in Olympic competition. After learning that their single loss to Great Britain eliminated them outright, they claimed the rules had been changed to remove them from the gold medal round. Nevertheless, Canada would have to "settle" for the silver medal in 1936 – its first in international Olympic Competition.

NOTES

1 The senior teams that comprised the Canadian Amateur Hockey Association during the 1935 season as listed by the press included: Kimberley Dynamiters, Vancouver Cubs, Edmonton Superiors, Coleman Canadians, Weyburn Beavers, Yorkton All-Stars, Prince Albert Mintos, North Battleford, Winnipeg Falcons, Manitoba Deer Lodge, Fort William, Port Arthur, Kirkland Lake, Sudbury Frood Mines, Hamilton Tigers, Toronto All-Stars, Acton Intermediates, Sherbrooke Maple Leafs,

St Jerome, Montreal Royals, Ottawa Senators, Île Maligne, Three Rivers Lyons, Smith's Falls, Chesterville, Ottawa Canadiens, Royal Air Force, Halifax Wolverines, and New Brunswick Intermediates (Pudas Scrapbook).

2 Team members had to be residents of the communities in which they played by the May before the hockey season.

2

Are Americans Really Hockey's Villains?

A New Perspective on the American Influence
on Canada's National Game

CRAIG HYATT AND JULIE STEVENS[1]

INTRODUCTION

A great deal of discussion within Canadian academic and popular
press forums addresses the impact of American interest upon hockey.
Since the 1970s, academics have noted that many Canadians feel
threatened by what they perceive as a growing negative American
influence upon the sport that many consider to be the heart of
Canadian culture and identity. Theorists have examined changes
such as the National Hockey League's control over Canadian amateur hockey (Kidd and Macfarlane 1972), hockey becoming more
commercialized within the global marketplace (Gruneau and
Whitson 1993), the relocation of a Canadian NHL team to an
American city (Silver 1996; Scherer 2001), and the NHL's commitment to American television networks (Mason 2002) as American
threats to Canadian hockey.

Each of these criticisms builds a collective sense of blame and
demonstrates that, overall, Canadian hockey fans view Americans
as villains whose aggressive changes to "our" game show that they
care little for the importance and meaning of hockey within Canadian
culture. Specifically, a majority of Canadian popular media and
academic commentaries critique the American influence upon
Canadian hockey according to the negative impact of capital and
executive actors. However, little work has been done to incorporate

the American hockey fan's perspective into the larger debate about the United States' aggressive takeover of Canada's national pastime. Consequently, this chapter critiques the notion that Americans are hockey's villains and Canadians hockey's victims by presenting two arguments. First, stories about the lived experiences of American Hartford Whalers hockey fans are utilized in order to reveal that American fans can sympathize with Canadian fans over the capitalist impact upon the sport. This situates the American hockey fan, rather than the American hockey capitalist, within the context of Canada-US hockey relations. Second, the nature and origin of Canadian power and capital that has influenced hockey during its history is examined in order to demonstrate the role of Canadian, as opposed to American, elites in undermining the cultural value of hockey in Canada. We argue that Canadian hockey enthusiasts, be they the public or media, should focus blame for the commercialization of hockey less upon American corporatists and more upon their Canadian counterparts.

LITERATURE REVIEW

Canadian academics have examined the impact of American influence on the game of hockey for more than a generation. From the end of the Second World War until 1967, the NHL consisted of two Canadian-based and four American-based franchises. In the late 1960s, the league doubled in size by adding six new American teams, thereby making Canadian-based franchises one-sixth of the league instead of one-third. It was during this expansionist era that Kidd and Macfarlane (1972) argued that hockey had been sold to Americans and suggested that the creation of a Canadian-based professional hockey league was the best strategy to return control of the game to its rightful owners.

After a period of relative stability during the 1980s (with no teams relocating or entering the league via expansion between 1982 and 1991), the NHL added five teams in the early 1990s. Besides the Ottawa Senators, the league placed the remaining four teams in cities located in the non-traditional hockey markets of California and Florida. It was during this period that Gruneau and Whitson (1993) stated that the Americanization of professional hockey was part of broader trends that threatened the distinct Canadian national culture. As the league sought to put teams in world-class facilities in world-class markets, "many of the traditional connections between cultural practices and national identities threatened to be lost in the process" (246).

As the 1990s progressed, two Canadian-based NHL teams relocated to the United States. In his account of the Winnipeg Jets' relocation to Phoenix, Arizona, Scherer (2001) made mention of a *Winnipeg Free Press* article that noted the frustration many Jets fans felt when they realized that "New York lawyers" were to blame for stealing part of Canada's cultural heritage. In another telling of the story of the Jets' departure, Silver (1996) alluded to the idea that NHL executives – namely, Gary Bettman, the NHL commissioner – were American and, as a result, had little understanding of the cultural significance hockey played in the identity of Canadian communities. Silver concluded his book by stating, "as the NHL's new marketing-oriented, US Sunbelt strategy takes effect, Canadians are losing a part of our heritage" (176).

It was also in the 1990s that the league signed a lucrative television broadcast deal with the Fox network, which ensured league exposure throughout the entire United States. When the US-based Fox television network introduced a technologically advanced glowing puck as part of its hockey telecasts, many Canadian fans again felt that American big business was changing the game for the worse, with little concern for Canada's hockey heritage (Mason 2002).

Evidence for this concern with corporate America's increasing influence over hockey can also be found in the columns, opinion and editorial pieces, and letters to the editor in Canadian media sources as well as on Canadian-based internet fan websites. Over the last decade, the NHL's labour strife of 1994–95, the relocation of the Québec Nordiques and the Winnipeg Jets, the league's new marketing initiatives, and the league's 2004–05 lockout have all been catalysts for anti-American sentiment among Canadians. The following quotations from these sources show that, although the catalyst for the sentiment has changed over the years, the blame has remained constant:

Despite much gnashing of western (Canadian) teeth, the fate of the small-market teams will not be decided in Toronto. The power in the NHL has slipped under the border ... Rightly or wrongly, hockey has been the one thing we could boast we invented, mastered, and successfully exported. Alas, the game has turned out not to be a game at all; it's a business, and commerce is, of course, America's forte. If nothing else, the lockout made that clear to even the most naïve among us. (Tim Falconer, "The Only Sport Left Is Bashing Toronto," *Toronto Star*, 10 January 1995, A13)

With the loss of the Jets, a part of us has also left. The Jets represented the province of Manitoba. They also represented Canada as a team which has now been taken over by the Americanized league ... The Jets, who will be called the Phoenix Coyotes next year, will rarely have true hockey fans attending their home games. Instead, they will have corporate bigwigs and wealthy businessmen filling the stands. (Rempel and Van Leewan 1996)

Once again, our great game of hockey is threatened. This time, instead of it being from the Russians of 1972, it's the Americans of 1998. National Hockey League President Gary Bettman wants to change the rules, take out the red line and move the nets forward. If we Canadians remain our usual complacent selves, we could lose forever the game of hockey as we know it. (Angus Stewart, "Change Hockey Rink Size, Not the Rules," Letter to the editor, *Toronto Star*, 8 February 1998, F2)

But, as league commissioner Gary Bettman might tell you (from his office at NHL headquarters in New York), professional sport is a business ... American greed gobbled up our national treasure (Wayne Gretzky) in 1988 and since then Canadians have watched the long, slow demise of professional hockey in Canada. (Purdon 2000)

The thought occurred to me that because of the lockout the emphasis has been on the multi-billion dollar pie and the multi-million dollar athletes ... I can see hockey going the way of the dodo within our lifetime. I think it will dry up first in the

US and we may once again have a six or eight team league of Canadian teams only. Hockey is Canada's game. It's as simple as that. The US are in it only for the money, as an investment opportunity. The reason that hockey is in the dire straits it is today is because of the US and TV. Almost every change made in the game over the last several decades has been made for the sake of TV and the US market. This whole bigger is better, the slick marketing techniques and especially the greed have been instilled into the game by the US. They have attempted to turn the sport into big business and treat it solely as an investment opportunity (Bobknows 2005)

Given these commentaries, there appears to be no shortage of incidents that prompted Canadian academics, journalists, and fans to express concern over the demise of Canada's influence within hockey over the last generation. Although the incidents change from year to year, the conclusion remains consistent: greedy Americans who care nothing about what hockey means to Canada are stealing the Canadian game.

RESEARCH BACKGROUND

Twenty-three American Hartford Whalers fans were interviewed in-depth between 2002 and 2003. The Whalers played eighteen seasons in the NHL before relocating to North Carolina in 1997, where they became the Carolina Hurricanes. From April 2002 until April 2003, twenty-four fans (twenty-three American and one Canadian) of the ex-Hartford Whalers were interviewed face-to-face and one-on-one. The interviews were part of an interpretive study to ascertain what it was like to become a Whalers fan, to be a Whalers fan, to live through the relocation of the franchise, and to live life in a world without the Whalers. Fans were found through word of mouth, through having fans refer others, through joining the Hartford Whalers Booster Club and asking their members to participate, and through a solicitation posted on the Booster Club's website. Nineteen men and five women participated. The sample varied in age (from twenty years to sixty-three years with an average of thirty-four years), education level, income, and geographic location.

Because the research was positioned within the interpretive paradigm, we used inductive theory generation rather than deductive theory testing. This grounded research approach enabled new perspectives and ideas regarding a fan's experience to emerge from the data. In keeping with the tenets of the interpretive research paradigm, each fan was given great latitude to lead the interview in whatever direction he/she wished. This resulted in four fans' discussing hockey with respect to Canada, even though none was asked questions on the topic.

FAN PERSPECTIVES

Without any prompting, four fans indicated they sympathized with Canadian hockey teams/fans either due to an understanding of how much hockey means to Canadians or due to an understanding of Canada's significant place in the history of the game. These comments were found to be relevant to a new category: "American sympathizers." These data question the popular label that Americans are oblivious to hockey's significance within Canadian culture, and they provide an opportunity to re-examine the Canadian-American hockey relation according to a new perspective. The following section presents the fan commentaries verbatim. Pseudonyms are used to ensure confidentiality.

Fifty-seven-year-old Ed has been a Whalers fan since the team first arrived in Hartford as part of the World Hockey Association in the mid-1970s. A season ticket holder during the WHA era, he kept his season tickets when the Whalers, Edmonton Oilers, Québec Nordiques, and Winnipeg Jets jumped to the NHL in 1979 and held them until the Whalers relocated. Ed remains active in the team's Booster Club. The Booster Club arranges bus trips to NHL cities to watch live NHL hockey, and these trips remain very popular with the members. One of the most popular destinations is Montreal, and Ed's mentioning of his continued interest in travelling to Montreal prompted him to discuss the issue of Canada with respect to hockey:

> I love going to Montreal. I'm more of a fan of theirs than I've ever been now that the Whale has left – I like to see Montreal do well. I like to see any of the Canadian teams do well. I think

it's a sad shame that these teams are leaving Canada and coming down here – *nobody* should lose their team. And especially up in Canada. I mean, that's their sport. It would be like the New York Giants going to play in Canada or something. Or the Yankees moving to Puerto Rico, or something similar. People would be devastated. Baseball's our game. Football's our game. Hockey's their game. And for them to lose their team. Quebec – as much as I feel for the Whalers – the people from Quebec, I think, got the worst deal ever in the NHL. These people filled *Le Colisée* – sixteen thousand seats – game in, game out – didn't matter the weather. Team was terrible – constantly terrible. They would put people in the seats. They wanted a new building, the government people said, "We're not building you a building. You have to do it privately." So that's when they moved to Colorado. Those fans got the royal screwing. No two ways about it. They followed their team. They supported their team. They would come down here – Quebec would come down to play the Whale and there'd be four bus loads that would come down from Quebec to watch – this was when the WHA was playing. This was when the Whale was still in the WHA. They'd be down. And better fans you wouldn't want than Quebec fans. And they got screwed. They got their team taken away from them through no fault of their own. They supported their team. (Emphasis his)

At various points throughout the interview, thirty-one-year-old Dan indicated that he now has very little rooting interest in any hockey team, even though he cared very deeply about the Whalers when he was a season ticket holder. When asked how he was a sports fan now, Dan replied:

Well, no rooting interest in hockey. I'll have to say that. Except during the [2002] Olympics. I did watch and rooted for the States, although at the beginning I rooted for Canada, but I was so appalled by how Wayne Gretzky handled the media and the teams, and Pat Quinn – that I just couldn't bring myself to root for Canada at that time. And I liked the players on the US team; I liked Herb Brooks. Even though I knew it meant a lot more to

Canada to win, and in the end, I'm glad that they did. That was the last time that I rooted for a team in hockey.

When Dan first met the interviewer, he presented him with a handful of oval bumper stickers that read "WHA." When asked if he was a fan of the WHA Whalers, Dan replied:

Not so much while they were here – I kind of heard *of* them in school, but I never really got to see much of them. I knew that they won the AVCO Cup when they were in Boston. And that the league existed. I think the appeal of the WHA is a nostalgia that I didn't quite get to experience but I just respect the roots that it represented. And the teams that followed, and the teams that have moved, like Quebec, and Winnipeg as well, there's some sort of kinship with those cities, even though I never – well, I've been to Quebec – haven't been to Winnipeg, haven't been to Edmonton – but we're all in that same boat: small town, and at times, pretty passionate about hockey. And probably deserve another chance, but as things are the way they are now, it's just a lot tougher. So – no, I didn't really get to experience it first hand, but the stickers are just a way to remember back, and encompass more than just Whalers fans, but the entire scope. Because I feel bad for the Nordiques fans especially. They were the best in the league, *bar none*. They were nutty. I mean, I remember the trumpet player – you always see him. They dressed in white almost all the time. They were just so passionate. Even when – I think the Avalanche just played an exhibition game [in Quebec] this past year and they sold it out. They are just really intense. They certainly, above all – even more so than Hartford – deserve the team back. But that will never happen, thanks to the Canadian dollar, and it's really just a tourist town up there for the most part. So, the WHA thing is also to show kinship and solidarity with other cities that have lost their teams, regrettably. Because they didn't deserve it. Winnipeg – same boat. (Emphasis his)

Twenty-six-year-old Andy mentioned that, although he did not root for the Carolina Hurricanes, he still considered himself a fan of the Hartford Whalers. Because the interviewer was familiar with fan loyalty theories and definitions from the sport marketing literature that indicate that a loyal fan has a positive attitude towards his/her favourite team and directs a certain amount of behaviour towards that team, he was curious as to what behaviour Andy directed towards the Whalers six years after their departure. When asked, "Are there other things that you do tangibly as a Whalers fan?" Andy stated:

And you know, I played hockey in high school and now play in a men's league and occasionally I will wear my Whalers jersey [pause] – and there are a few Canadians actually that I play with who grew up playing hockey in Canada, and I frequently talk with them about – one guy is from Alberta, and I talk with him about the tenuous situation of the Flames and the Oilers, and so I think that as a Whalers fan, that's something I see. Because I don't want them to lose their teams, and I don't want Canada to really lose any more hockey teams than it already has. I'd be very interested in knowing your thoughts on that subject as a Canadian. But, so I guess the Whaler fan in me kind of is also an Oilers fan and a Flames fan and a fan for those other teams that are maybe kind of on the brink there.

Finally, Julia, who was forty years old and the only woman to offer data that fit the "American sympathizer" category, had been following the Hartford Whalers since the mid-1980s. In response to the probe, "How are you a sports fan now?" Julia commented:

Sports fan – a lot of things have happened. You've had baseball strikes and lockouts and I've soured a lot. It took me a while before I went back to a baseball game. I don't watch it as much as I used to, because I used to watch baseball and hockey. I watch the hockey, but [pause] – even that is starting to sour on me a little bit. I umm – just doesn't feel the same. You've got this impending – you don't know what's going to happen next year between the players – you've got the ahh – what is it – the collective bargaining agreement – whatever they call it – I think

it's that. You know – I *don't* like the commissioner. I just –
I think he's hurt – you've got teams leaving Canada left and
right, and I think, you know – there should be more teams in
Canada, because that's really where hockey – in my opinion –
started, and I think there should be more teams. I know
Phoenix has done well, but they had some problems after they
moved, and that was the Winnipeg team. They went too far
south. And it's just like all the other sports, I think Bettman –
coming from basketball – tried to make hockey more like
basketball, when it should have stayed like hockey.
(Emphasis hers)

DISCUSSION

These excerpts from the stories told by American Hartford Whalers
fans indicate sympathies for Canada and Canadian hockey fans. In
the case of Dan and Ed, the sympathy was motivated by an understanding of how much the sport means to Canadians in general.
Julia's sympathy was based on her understanding of the significant
role Canada has played in the history of the sport. However, it
remains unclear as to why Andy does not want Canada to lose any
more hockey teams. It is interesting to note that Andy sympathizes
with fans of any NHL hockey team that might be "on the brink"
of relocation.

One of the larger themes found in the investigation of the lived
experience of Hartford Whalers fans concerns the presence of sympathies towards other sports fans. Although the focus of this chapter
is on Canada, it is interesting to note that Whalers fans often
expressed a bond with other cities, teams, and fans who reminded
them of the Hartford Whalers or of themselves as Whalers fans.
Based on these stories, and on those of the other nineteen Hartford
Whalers fans who were interviewed, sympathetic bonds emerged
with regard to six areas: (1) Canadian fans, (2) fans of small-market
teams in any professional sport, (3) fans of any team in any sport
left behind by franchise relocation, (4) fans of current teams threatened with relocation, (5) hockey fans in cities that share a World
Hockey Association legacy, and (6) great sports fans of any kind in

any city. In numerous cases, there is a complex interrelationship among many of these points of attachment, and it is difficult to separate one point from another. This phenomenon is most clearly seen in the second quotation from Dan, in which he comments on his kinship with specific cities, teams, and fans. Overall, Dan feels connected with passionate small-market hockey fans.

The "American sympathizer" category offers a different perspective on the long-held argument regarding the negative impact of American interest upon Canadian hockey. The notion that American hockey fans sympathize with Canadians about the declining sense of hockey's Canadianness challenges the traditional "us" versus "them" distinction that exists within Canadian popular sentiment. This new perspective recognizes the universality of franchise loss. Hockey fans can be segmented according to those who have and have not survived franchise relocation or according to those who support a small-market team under the threat of relocation and those who do not. In other words, franchise mobility, not nationality, may be one way of defining contemporary hockey passions.

The data from the Hartford Whalers fan interviews also raise the subject of Canadian hockey centrism. Much of the hockey literature, within academic and popular spheres, presents Canadians as well-intentioned guardians of the game. However, this understanding is self-serving and fails to criticize the impact of Canadian culture and business upon hockey. This type of critique raises many key questions. First, do Canadian fans feel a kinship with American fans or is there a bias in popular Canadian sentiment that holds that only Canadian fans have suffered from the commercialization of the game? Second, does a false sense of victimhood apply beyond Canadian fans to include corporate and executive Canadian hockey actors? That is, are Canadian hockey capitalists really the well-intentioned keepers of the game they are portrayed to be? Finally, if the Canadian notion of victim is dispelled, then what has been the larger Canadian impact upon the globalization of hockey? Each of these questions is discussed in greater detail in the final section of this article.

Canadian fan sympathy towards American fans is an area rarely discussed in Canadian hockey media or explored in academic research. The findings from the Hartford Whalers fan interviews suggest that there is a need to examine the Canadian centrism argument by exploring whether Canadian hockey fans have any sympathy towards American fans who have experienced franchise loss. It would also be interesting to examine whether American fans from stable markets that have not experienced any threat of franchise relocation are sympathetic towards Canadian hockey fans. The goal would be to determine the nature and extent of hockey fan kinship. Is there a sense of kinship between fans who have suffered franchise loss regardless of nationality or is such kinship isolated, with fan affinities generally being defined according to nationality?

Our critique of the "us" versus "them" distinction is further advanced by examining the contemporary mobility of capital. Previous discussion about the professionalization of men's hockey highlights a shift from community, or local fan, allegiances to national loyalties. Thus, the Americanization of hockey debate is clearly founded on whether one is a Canadian or an American. However, the data presented in this study suggest that nationality may no longer be a dividing line between those who respect the game and those who exploit the game. Although Whitson and Macintosh (1993) examine how the mobility of capital transforms the relationship between mobile businesses (e.g., the connection between professional hockey franchises and governments), we suggest that the mobility of capital translates into universal franchise mobility, which affects both Canadian-based and American-based teams and fans.

According to this view, it is evident that some American fans have the same contempt for the exploitation of the sport by the capitalist elite as do Canadian fans – a circumstance many Canadians fail to recognize. Does the Americanization of the game argument hold when the American corporate hockey elite is exploiting American fans? Silver (1996, 11) writes about how the "up-cost and down-south" movement of hockey meant the game could not survive in many Canadian cities. However, he fails to acknowledge that American-based teams were also at risk during this period. For example, the Minnesota North Stars relocated in 1993, and the Hartford Whalers were on unstable ground at the time, ultimately relocating in 1997.

Given that the view of Canadian hockey fans as victims is narrow and ignores the plight of American hockey fans, the portrayal of the manipulative hockey capitalist as American may also be a misrepresentation. Although popular Canadian sentiment holds that American capital has exploited, and continues to exploit, the game, it does not acknowledge that the Canadian corporate elite is just as exploitative. Before the creation of the National Hockey League in 1917, Canadian men's professional hockey teams were managed by civic boosters (Stevens 2003; Gruneau and Whitson 1993). The boosters were either rink owners who supported a men's amateur team in order to ensure they had a stable supply of talent for the facility or local businesspeople who supported a team to demonstrate community involvement. However, over time, the civic boosters were replaced by corporate owners, whose investment in a professional men's hockey team was strictly a means to generate wealth. The NHL was originally an all-Canadian league and was founded by a group of Canadian, not American, businesspeople who had been operating the professional National Hockey Association. Cruise and Griffiths (1991, 31) report that these owners were motivated not by a "vision of the future but by a desperate desire to get rid of the argumentative owner of the Toronto Arenas, Eddie Livingstone." The National Hockey Association was rendered ineffective when team owners opted to create the NHL but to leave Livingstone and his team out of the new enterprise. By 1926, the NHL became the only men's professional hockey forum after the demise of the Pacific Coast Hockey League and the Western Canadian Hockey League. Even though the league included five American franchises by that time, control rested in Canada, with league headquarters in Montreal. As a result of this, credit for laying the foundation for a profit-driven professional men's hockey entertainment spectacle can be given to these early Canadian profiteers.

Following this period of early development, the NHL soon came under the control of another Canadian capitalist, James Norris. By the mid-1940s, Norris controlled three of the six NHL franchises, although two of these were driven by a desire to invest in the facility rather than in the teams. Although Norris and his fellow owners, including Toronto Maple Leafs owner Conn Smythe, a Canadian, engaged in a power struggle for years, the frequent feuds rarely infringed upon the profits owners ultimately sought. With the authority and business savvy of Norris, NHL owners were able to reap great rewards during this very lucrative era in the league; however, with the focus upon profit, they failed to better the game itself.

By the 1970s, Alan Eagleson, another Canadian, was the opportunist of the time as he held various hockey positions, including executive director of the National Hockey League Players' Association (NHLPA), owner of a hockey enterprise that represented individual players, and board member of Hockey Canada, an agency that managed the Canadian men's national hockey team. Through these multiple roles, Eagleson was involved in critical decisions that furthered the commercial exploitation of the game while, at the same time, inhibiting the development of the sport in Canada. For example, from the 1940s and 1950s, the NHL paid the revenue-starved Canadian Amateur Hockey Association (CAHA) for the right to establish a country-wide NHL farm system. As a result, the CAHA lost its independence from the NHL and a culture of bought hockey talent, or what Kidd and Macfarlane (1972) refer to as "child buyers," was planted within the Canadian minor hockey system. Eagleson became the leader of the NHLPA in the early 1970s, and, under his watch, the association failed to amend this situation. In addition, he colluded with NHL owners to ensure that players remained on a tight rein, thus hobbling progress related to salaries, benefits, and players' rights for two decades. Finally, Eagleson extended his hockey empire into international ranks when he used his position with Hockey Canada to control major events such as the 1972 Canada-Russia Series, the Canada Cup, and other international challenge series between NHL players and European teams. His efforts alienated the CAHA and undermined its role as the national sport federation that managed hockey in Canada. This left the CAHA struggling to justify its existence to Canadians, and it left the public unaware of the developmental mission the association served.

Although historical accounts chronicle the political and economic development of men's hockey, there are also recent examples of Canadian owners trying to manipulate Canadian hockey in order to make money. For example, Gruneau and Whitson (1993) suggest that regional elites pursued ownership of major sport franchises as a growth strategy for western Canadian cities. Although they focus primarily upon the use of professional hockey franchises to demonstrate the world-class status of a city, their discussion provides a modern-day account of Canadian hockey profiteers in action. In his account of the relocation of the Winnipeg Jets to Phoenix, Arizona, Silver (1996, 13) identifies how Winnipeg's corporate elite, who could have provided the money needed to keep the NHL franchise in the city, simply "[were] not there." Despite the fact that the hockey public within and beyond the city limits desperately wanted to keep the franchise in Winnipeg as a symbol of Canadian hockey culture, the local corporate powers acted as businesspeople, not boosters, and opted out of the franchise because owning it simply was not in their best economic interest.

Each of these examples demonstrates a trend rarely recognized by scholars, hockey media, or the Canadian hockey public: Canadian hockey capital serves its own interest just as much as does American hockey capital. In fact, the negative impact of Canadian businesspeople upon hockey may be more pronounced than that of American businesspeople given that, over time, the former have made many of the key decisions related to the commercialization of men's hockey. Quite simply, Canadian capitalists allowed several decisions about the development of hockey in Canada, and abroad, to be left to the marketplace, where hockey was just another commodity.

Finally, given this account of negative Canadian influence upon hockey, it is important to discuss how this, in turn, has influenced the globalization of the game. Triggered by an appetite for televised international men's hockey spectacles, the past few decades have witnessed a movement towards one single hockey vision. In 1972, Kidd and Macfarlane (1972, 69) recognized this trend, pointing out that

> not very many Canadians play the game we call our national sport. Despite the soaring teenage registration of the CAHA, there are just two kinds of hockey in this country: the hockey we play for a brief few years during adolescence, and the

hockey a few hundred professionals provide as a televised spectacle. Left out are hundreds of thousands of Canadian who ski and curl, play golf and tennis, who love hockey as much as they did when they were kids but who have been relegated to the sidelines as spectators. We play hockey to win, we play hockey to make money, but we have forgotten what it is to play hockey for fun. That, more than anything else, signals the death of hockey.

In addition, Gruneau and Whitson's (1993) analysis of international men's hockey recognizes that globalization has led to the greater flexibility and power of capital. Specifically, Whitson and Macintosh (1993, 233) argue that "capital is freer to move ... to move to other places or, increasingly and crucially, to move into other kinds of more profitable investment." When this concept is developed along with Kidd and Macfarlane's notion of hockey driven by market-based decisions, the need to expand the critique of capital's influence on hockey from a Canada-US axis towards a global context becomes clear.

A recent embodiment of the growing threat of international capital to the Canadianness of hockey may be seen in the pursuit of star Canadian amateur Sidney Crosby during the summer of 2005. As he was one of the most anticipated amateurs to become available to the NHL in a generation, both the league and the league's fans eagerly awaited his draft day as the labour dispute wound down. By mid-summer, rumours surfaced that the new collective bargaining agreement would contain a clause limiting rookie salaries to US$850,000 per season. Rumours also had the Swiss club Lugano offering Crosby a three-year contract for US$10 million (W. Scanlan, "NHL's Party Would Be Spoiled without Crosby," *Montreal Gazette*, 10 July 2005, C5). These rumours spawned internet postings in fan chat rooms on the part of Canadian fans who were contemplating a bleak future in which Canadian star players would sign large European contracts instead of playing in North America. Although many fans thought it unrealistic to believe that the NHL could ever lose its standing as the world's premier professional league, one fan thought it possible that professional hockey could soon mirror professional soccer, with multiple leagues based around the world, all fighting over the game's elite players (LaRose). The Canadianness of hockey could be more strongly threatened by this kind of international competition than it was when the Americans were seen as the sole rivals.

CONCLUSION

The purpose of this chapter is to challenge the popular Canadian portrayal of Americans as hockey villains intent on taking the Canadianness out of hockey. Placing blame for the commercial changes in the sport solely on American hockey executives may be criticized as an exaggerated position that is easy to debunk. However, very little of the work that counters the "Americanization of hockey" claim includes the perspective of American hockey fans. We believe that incorporating the American fan's view offers a novel interpretation of this issue. Further, we criticize the "blame the Americans" stance by scrutinizing Canadian hockey elites, and we reposition the negative influence of commercial forces upon the game as an issue recognized by many hockey fans, regardless of nationality. In other words, American hockey fans can sympathize with Canadian fans who feel a sense of loss and betrayal.

Based on the stories reported here, Canadian fans should reconsider the notion that Americans do not care about the game's significance to Canadians. At least in the case of Hartford Whalers fans, who lost their favourite team through franchise relocation, American fans express sympathies for and kinship with their Canadian counterparts. If Canadian fans want to continue to blame corporate actors who are perceived to be ruining the game in their pursuit of profits, they should blame all such actors: American, Canadian, and international. Amateurs have given way to professionals on the worldwide Olympic stage, foreign ownership of major professional sport teams has become commonplace in the world's biggest leagues, and star NHL players are being offered more and more lucrative contracts to play in Europe. Consequently, framing the problems of professional men's hockey in Canada as an "us" versus "them" nationalistic debate is an outdated perspective.

NOTE

1 The authors appreciate the feedback of Dr Stephen Hardy and Dr Lucie Thibault on earlier versions of this article.

3

Confronting a Compelling Other
The Summit Series and the Nostalgic (Trans)Formation of Canadian Identity

BRIAN KENNEDY

INTRODUCTION

The issue of Canadian identity came to the forefront in the 1990s in a series of beer advertisements that have gone well beyond their intention to sell a few suds. The "I am Canadian" campaign, premiered by Molson, features a young man standing in front of the camera "passionately inform[ing] Canadians as to what distinguishes them from Americans and renders them unique as celebrated Canucks" (Manning, EP1).[1] The ad created a popular culture phenomenon and spawned a merchandising spin-off campaign that featured the slogan emblazoned on everything from T-shirts to bedroom slippers.[2] In one of the more recent versions of the ad, "Joe Canadian" stands on the moon, smiling guiltily after shooting a puck that has cracked the visor of the space helmet worn by an American astronaut who, it appears, believes *he* has just laid claim to the place in the name of the United States. The commercial ends with the two saluting each other by clinking together their beer bottles, followed by the American banging his up against the glass of his helmet as he raises the drink to his mouth. The Canadian emits a laugh, but one more of embarrassment for the other fellow than anything else. His levity symbolically differentiates him from the American, who, one imagines, would be anything but so kindly self-effacing were the situation reversed.

The commercial highlights two important components of Canadian identity: hockey as a locus of shared experience and the tendency to construct the national self-definition as an inverse of a visible "other."[3] Thinking of the contemporary situation, one might imagine that, for Canadians, the other is their southern neighbour, which plays the role Britain might have taken in earlier days. In fact, however, the other that created contemporary Canada for many of its residents is to be found neither in Uncle Sam nor in Mother England but, rather, in the likeliest of unlikely places: the hockey arena, in the form of a group of Soviet amateur players and their coach,[4] who came to Canada to play the first four games of the Summit Series of 1972 and then retreated to Russia to host Team Canada for another four.

By quite unexpectedly threatening Canadians' presumed mastery over the sport of hockey, the Russians created a situation that came to have lasting symbolic value. Thus, it might be argued that the events of September 1972 helped to create the Canada of today through giving a generation of people a touchstone moment with which to mark their participation in a shared culture. Perhaps this is why the series is still commemorated both in popular culture – through its continued mention during hockey commentary, in casual conversation, and through the production of kitsch – and in popular history.[5]

The resulting identity construct was not easily formed, however; rather, it involved a process that, at first (i.e., before the series) entailed no sense of a compelling other, then (i.e., during the series) entailed a growing recognition of the other as not-us, and, finally (i.e., in the years since the series), entailed a sense of the other that had lost its cultural specificity as the series was turned into an epic event. I conclude by indicating some of the ways in which the series might be deployed in a negative sense in an era of an increasingly multicultural Canada – that is, a Canada that is not what it was in 1972 but, rather, is increasingly populated by people for whom neither the series nor hockey has any cultural resonance.

THE THEORY OF IDENTITY FORMATION

In a recent article, Stephen Frosh (2002, 393) points out that "there are now a number of converging theoretical approaches that give primacy to the notion of the other as formative of the self," including those forged upon the thought of Levinas and, especially, Jean Laplanche. Frosh says that contemporary psychoanalysis understands that the "functioning of the unconscious as an 'internal other' radically disturbs the rather homely sense that each of us is 'master' of himself or herself, and in doing so it opens the way to a collapse of confidence in the self, to a sense that however robust it might seem, it has already been infiltrated by something subjectively inexplicable, something that the 'self' is not" (394). Discussing an introduction to Laplanche's (1999) *Essays on Otherness*, Frosh comments that "awareness of the extent to which what is other dominates our existence is too painful, too terrifying, to be maintained; instead, both the subject and psychoanalysis itself 'wander' back from the momentary vision of this truth, to the fantasy of completeness, of narcissistic selfhood" (396).[6]

With this in mind, one might ask whether a similar construct could work on a national level with regard to the creation of identity. In a recent study of Inuit (Aboriginal "Canadian") identity, André Légaré (2002, EP2) suggests a definition reminiscent of Laplanche: "[Identity] is, in its essence, a social construct: one's own conscious identity is a product of one's meeting with different forms of others' identities." Moving to the group level, he indicates that both a sense of territory and the existence of cultural symbols are necessary to the creation of identity. His claim is that "certain cultural or regional symbols are established through which the people learn the distinctiveness and uniqueness of their region. These symbols canonize certain features to distinguish the region from all others" (EP6). Yet symbols do not preexist the people, nor are they impervious to change; rather, "they are forged in social context and are continually reinvented," though they begin in fact not fiction (ibid.). According to Légaré, "symbols create a sense of belonging, a sense of purpose, and a sense of continuing tradition" (EP6). To add Laplanche to Légaré might yield something like this, then: To say "I am Canadian" and to achieve a degree of cultural assent at a level past the individual might be to say, "I share the belief with a group of people I am labelling 'Canadian' that we are who we are because we can collectively identify an 'other,' having experienced that other through symbolic action."

In the Canadian context, one might argue that a cultural moment such as a series of hockey games has the power to create cultural identity, and many have done just that. It has been said that "the Canada-Soviet hockey series in the fall of 1972 was one of the most memorable events in Canadian sports history ... Most of Canada, or so it seemed at the time, followed this series on television" (Macintosh and Greenhorn 1993, 107). The series, according to another critic, "has become an enduring folk memory, a cultural text. For once, disparate notions of class, ethnicity and gender were welded into a rare Canadian moment" (Earle 1995, 108). For Canadians, the 1972 Summit Series provided both a visible other through which they as individuals could create a sense of self-identity and a set of cultural symbols that would come to bind them together as a group. However, it was anything but an instantaneous process, nor was it one that remained fixed as time passed in the aftermath of the events.

THE SERIES AND THREE PHASES OF IDENTITY CREATION

Canadian identity before the Summit Series

Michael A. Robidoux (2002, 209) comments on the irony that "hockey, known for its ferocity, speed, and violence, would come to serve as Canada's primary national symbol," given the way Canadians are presumed to act in the world: "Since World War II, Canadians have been internationally perceived more as peacekeepers and, perhaps, even as being unreasonably polite." The paradox is that "the Canadian penchant to understand itself through hockey repeats masculinist formulas of identification that reflect poorly the lives of Canadians" (222). Yet one reason the Summit Series existed in the first place was to heal the image of Canada abroad, which had been damaged by violent play in earlier international hockey events. Talking about international tournament play in the 1960s, Macintosh and Greenhorn (1993, 100) claim that "the diminution of good will for Canada that stemmed from the 'brutish' and 'reprehensible' conduct of many Canadian hockey players ... [was] distressing to the Department of External Affairs." Further, "Canadian hockey players were often described by the [European] press as 'dangerous' and 'ruthless' and the Canadian team was frequently accused of 'hooliganism'" in the years before 1972 (99). The series would allow the country to recover its international reputation. Little did anyone know that it would have far more profound effects inside the country than outside of it. Commenting on 1972, Robidoux (2002, 221) says that "the series was filled with incidents of extreme violence" because the Canadian players responded to losing the early games by "resort[ing] to bullying and intimidation tactics and literally fought their way back into contention," suggesting the very attitude that the series had been designed to put in the past; however, he claims that what is remembered is not the violence but the heroism of the team as a symbol of Canadian identity. And here, of course, he is speaking about the effects within Canada rather than internationally.

Up until the series, Canadians had uncritically thought of their best hockey players as the definition of excellent, and of excellence in hockey as the definition of being Canadian. As Douglas Coupland (2002, 55) says in his recent *Souvenir of Canada*, "The thing about hockey in Canada as opposed to hockey in other countries is that the sport percolates far deeper into our national soil and thus affects everything that grows in it." The last thing anyone could have imagined is that Russian amateurs could beat the mighty Canadian professionals, so as Canadian representatives negotiated with the Soviet Union, the goal was to allow the Canadian players to show their talents. Most observers were comfortable with assuming that the Canadian team would win all eight games.

Jack Ludwig's *Hockey Night in Moscow*, first published in 1972, provides an important contemporary viewpoint. In the opening chapter, the journalist provides a glimpse of the Canadian mindset regarding hockey superiority: "One thing we believed they'd [United States, Europe] never grow – even with the help of our own seeding – was hockey players good enough to play in the NHL" (Ludwig 1974, 15). He then gives a brief account of the failures Canada had suffered in international play between the 1950s and the early 1970s; however, he ends with the comfortable assumption, which the country shared at the beginning of September 1972, that Team Canada, with players selected from the NHL rosters (but excluding a couple of key stars who had just "defected" to the newly formed World Hockey Association, a rival North American league), was "without a doubt 'the greatest hockey team ever assembled'" (17). It was assumed by the entire nation that the team "would put on a dazzle no Russian had ever witnessed before" (18). Though Ludwig speaks after the fact and somewhat ironically, the contrast between the perceived "us" and the other in his lines is so great as to render the latter irrelevant, and it did not take long for Canada to make this explicit.

When analyzing the Russian style of play (purely in order to create a rationale for Canadian superiority), the thinking went like this, as Ludwig (1974, 24) reports the pre-series scouting on the Russian team: "Their defencemen were slow, their pass patterns slower, their attack telegraphed and easily broken up by NHL players who, unlike athletes in an unfree society like the USSR, are taught to think for themselves, and always to think hockey." Ludwig himself admits that he saw the Russians practice, but he turned every one of their strengths into something that NHL players would capitalize on as weaknesses. And when, just after the series, he recounts the events, he is amazed at his own naiveté: "I ... assumed, as I think most Canadians did, that people who don't speak the Queen's English can hardly be expected to keep up with those who do" (26).

In fact, the Russians had been playing various sports at the international level, and winning, throughout the 1960s. But Canadian observers ignored the signs of USSR superiority because they were blinded by their belief that their own athletes had the superior worldview. When observing Russian Olympians, for example, who left "signs of Soviet mastery of fundamentals ... all over the TV screen," all the Canadian critic saw was rote, mechanical drill (Ludwig 1974, 27). The same thing happened when watching the Red Army hockey team perform the pre-game routine. Instead of the free-form Canadian style, where every player takes his best shot at the goalie, the Russians methodically shot at first the goaltender's left pad, then his right, then his glove, and so on. Canadian eyes took this as "merely technical and quite automatic" and assumed that it programmed the goalie to expect certain shots, something that would cause him to fail when faced with the superior and inventive Canadian shooters (27). Ludwig says that the Canadians, himself included, missed the obvious, which was that the exercise was scientifically designed to warm up the goalie for any possible eventuality. Canadians assumed "that drill without talent is a pointless operation" (28). This attitude made these further assumptions possible: "The brand of hockey played in the NHL was light-years ahead of anything Europe could come up with in this century" (Ludwig 28) and "any player good enough to make the NHL was obviously someone who didn't need further coaching ... He was NHL *stuff*, and that, like beauty being truth and truth being beauty, was all there was to know" (29, emphasis in original). Summarizing the Canadian view at this time is simple: Canada's ability to play the game was unequalled. This viewpoint was so complete that it existed without any external reference.

Canadian identity during the series

At the moment the USSR team deplaned in Montreal, the Canadian psyche had to account for the presence of the other, which was coded in a way strangely resonant of Leplanche's description of the formation of adult self-definition: as the child-like version of the mature self, troubling but ever-present (Frosh 2002, 397–98). In this context, the immature version of the adult self was the child learning to play a game that the adult had already mastered. To Canadians, the Russian players looked at first like "prep school students" (Hockey Canada 1978, 17). The Russians embraced this role both by continuing to maintain that they were in Canada to learn (Ludwig 1972, 73) and by practising, at least when the Canadians were around, as if their abilities were those of Canadian adolescents (Macskimming 1996, 25). However, the loss of the first game of the series forced Canadians to deal with the Russians in a new and more fully realized way. The other had become compelling and, in so doing, had turned from being childlike to being threatening.

When Frosh (2002, 399) discusses Melanie Butler's use of grief as a starting point for exploring "the intricate relationships between selves, communities, and otherness," he says that, in her thinking, "the experience of loss demonstrates just how much each of us is relationally engaged with others" and has the ability to "put us in contact with an area of unexpected dependence [on the other]" (400). So the series forced Canadians to struggle with the presence of the other in a couple of important ways. First of all, it brought the political and cultural other up close and gave him (in the person of the Russian hockey player) a human face, or, at least, an almost-human face.[7] But, more important, it caused Canadians to face the reality that they were not the only ones who could play hockey. Maybe they were not even the best. According to Frosh, "The 'ex-centric' location of psychic life (in and of the other) is what most challenges and draws the subject, enriching it and moving it on" (405). But this recognition is not always easy. He follows up by indicating that, "if the other is primary and one is torn apart by otherness within, then hatred for the other can become the over-whelming reality" (405). This is precisely what we see in the events that unfolded *during* the month of September 1972.

Ludwig (1972) recounts the shock with which the fans and press met the events of the first game. After going ahead 1-0 with less than a minute gone, and then 2-0 in the first seven minutes, Canada looked to have been right in its predictions of a sweep. But the first period ended tied at two, and Ludwig reports that, "in stunned amaze [sic] we sat, Canadians, Americans, NHL-advocates, and watched Team Canada try the usual catch-up NHL clubs were used to unleash" (40). He tells how, between the first and second periods, most of the press had nothing to say but that anything they did say simply recited the scouting reports, which rendered the Russian other invisible: "They operated not on what they saw but on what *the credo said*: Team Canada was the best collection of hockey players ever assembled together. Therefore Team USSR was unimportant" (41, emphasis in original); however, the scoreboard said differently. The Canadians lost 7-3, and, according to Ludwig, at first the reaction focused on the "bush league" behaviour of the Canadian players in the latter stages of the contest.[8] But he quickly dismisses this as a mere cover-up for the real reaction of the country to the game: "That loss was taken as a national castration" (47). And he indicates that newspapers portrayed it as a national disaster. His interpretation of the loss goes like this: "Our myth was shattered. Our one great dream was gone ... [W]hat were we going to be now that our one certainty was taken from us? Hockey! Our thing! Maybe our only thing. Without pre-eminence in hockey weren't we in danger of becoming a second-rate power (sic)?" (48). His use of the "sic" heightens the ironic tone of his question. He quotes the *Montreal Star*, whose editorial page had this to say on the Sunday following the loss: "Hockey is more than a game to Canadians, because it is – or so we fondly supposed until Saturday night – the one form of human endeavor in which we are the world's best. It is an important ingredient of our national pride, and an expression of our national character" (49), yet this feeling was going to be difficult to maintain in the face of a suddenly very real Red Army team.

The editorial takes an interesting turn when it skirts past the real cause of the defeat – the team's poor play and self-delusion, which allowed a complete underestimation of the strengths of the other side – and names the culprit as, surprisingly or not, Americans. The problem, the piece indicates, was that the players had been sold out to the newly Americanized NHL, and the game had been turned into show business for the American market, which, the theory went, preferred the stylish antics of stars to the solidity of team play (Ludwig 1972, 50). In terms of the present discussion, one might take this conclusion as suggesting that Canadians could ignore the other that had defeated them and continue to exult in their superior ability at the game because, even though they had lost to the Russians, the fault was not theirs and the credit not the Soviets'. In other words, the national self-definition was temporarily rebuilt with a crucial third term introduced into the now troubling binary of us-versus-them. The slippage was now us-as-we-would-have-been (were it not for the Americans) versus us-as-the-Americans-have-made-us, the Russians sliding neatly out of view. Of course, the us-as-we-would-have-been exists always and only on a plane of projection, and the series was not played between literary characters but between hockey players; thus, any attempt at recuperating the national self-respect had to be tested not in theory but on the ice.

Games two to four hardly provided a relief from the pain of the first loss, and, by the end of game four, fans were booing the team, something to which the players, in the person of Captain Phil Esposito, took offence. This led him to make a now-famous speech, in which he said that he and all the Team Canada players were playing for their country and were terribly disappointed in the fan reaction (*Canada's Team* 2002). As he spoke, he presumed a definition of patriotism, which was the very thing the country was trying to work out as it faced the compelling other of the powerful Soviet team.

Interestingly, Ludwig (1972, 80) says that the fans were not booing the players for their lack of commitment so much as the style of play they resorted to – a combination of the above-mentioned rough play and an attempt to please the crowd by a fancy yet completely ineffective "dipsy-doo and head fake" style. Read another way, Ludwig is reiterating the clash of the two worldviews cited earlier. The Canadian players were resorting on the ice to the Western way of thinking, which prized the efforts of the individual exercising his freedom, whereas the Soviets were dramatizing their collectivist mentality, the same one that drove their economy and politics. The irony was, of course, that in jeering the Canadian players for their use of this style, Canadian fans were inadvertently booing the players for acting as Canadians believed that Canadians should act. It simply was not considered possible that the Russian way of doing things could work, whether in a hockey arena, in business, or in government. So while booing their values, Canadians still held them firmly, and they could not bring themselves to admit that their identity might need to take into account this other that was so forcefully asserting itself. Thus, it is no wonder that, with the fourth game over and the series 2–1 for the Russians with one game having been a tie, "What had happened ... [was starting to] constitute a 'national identity crisis'" (88). And so the team, along with several thousand fans, packed its bags for Moscow, Esposito's promise of an apology to each and every Canadian if the Russian fans booed their team in Moscow ringing in everyone's ears.

Being in Moscow only reinforced for many Canadian fans the superiority of their way of life to that of the Russians, who experienced constant shortages and lineups. Even the Moscow arena in which the games were played was poorly equipped, a symbol of the country's lack of sophistication in the pursuit of consumer goods which Canadians took for granted. Thus, the question on many minds, as Ludwig (1972, 103) reports, was: "What was this [Russian] team doing challenging men of financial status and security? Team Canada ... couldn't see why a higher standard of inflation didn't carry with it a guarantee of victory." Once again, this shows that the Canadian idea of a national self, with all of its complexity (from economics to politics), was fully focused on the game.

As the final four games proceeded, Canadians, players and fans alike, became united through a common belief in the strength of the enemy, and they struggled to deal with the USSR's emergence as a compelling other. Again to cite Frosh (2002, 400) discussing Butler: "With every loss something dies inside, that something being the fantasy that we are what we are, independent and autonomous and different from the other to whom we are connected." The Canadians began to see that they were in the presence of an other who would come to be crucial in their self-definition, though the task of revising the latter was daunting and confusing.

By the eighth game, the series was tied, Canada having lost game five to go behind 3-1-1 but having won the next two to make the final game the deciding one, with the teams coming into it at 3-3-1. The outcome of the series, which saw Canada squeak a victory out in the last thirty-four seconds of the final game to win four games to three with one tie, should have placed alterity at the centre of Canadians' cultural self-definition. Instead, Canada briefly recognized the Soviets as other but then embarked upon a process of turning those eight hockey games into epic – a process that continues to this day. Paul Henderson's goal, which broke a 5-5 tie, was transformed into "the Goal," thus creating the possibility for the Canadian public to overwrite all other meanings that had been given to the series.

Canadian identity after the series

In *Why I Hate Canadians*, Canadian commentator Will Ferguson (1997, 76, emphasis in original) says, "For the first time [the day of game eight], I became aware of belonging to the group, this *thing* called Canada." The binary equation us-versus-them had been coded over the 1972 meeting of two hockey teams to provide a tool of identity creation. However, to be Canadian today is not to be "not-Russian." It is to be, if "not-anything," "not-American," as is evident in the spoof of the beer commercial. How, then, has the series maintained its currency as creating a defining sense of what it is to be Canadian now that the Russian other has faded from the imagination? It has been erased in its specificity but, simultaneously, has been recreated more generally as symbol.

Ludwig (1972, 30, emphasis in original), writing in the immediate aftermath of the series, says that his story "has to account for why a country could be brought so low by the loss of Game One and sail over the moon with joy and delight by the victory in Game Eight and the series. But much more important is the opportunity the series – and the experience in the Soviet Union – offers us to reconsider how we think about hockey and *ourselves*." But his pleas would be disregarded as the shock of the events, especially the early losses, receded; instead, the focus would come to be on Team Canada's ultimate victory.

What has happened in the years since, in other words, has been exactly what Ludwig (1972, 31) feared when he says, at the end of his second chapter, "We sank through the floor in Game One and told ourselves that the chance to chant 'We're Number One' after Game Eight wiped away all that happened on September 2 in Montreal [and all that had been learned about a new way to play the game]." He describes the post-game eight events as "a roaring loving celebration to signal the rebirth of something that almost died. Canadians felt that reports of a country's death and preparations for a nation's funeral were now exaggerations" (194). "This Canada had just escaped losing the one supremacy – or illusion of supremacy – left" (ibid.). Canadians were left with the thought, "*Oh, what a great night this was to be a Canadian*" (195, emphasis in original). But Ludwig's emphasis is not on the epic nature of the victory; rather, speaking in 1972, he says that "our last word has to be something more than: 'We won, didn't we?'" (200). He wants Canadians to pay attention to what the Russians had taught them about hockey, something he spends a good deal of his book discussing. But all these years later, the cries of victory are what most characterize discussions of the event.

The current discourse over the series is best represented by Roy Macskimming's 1996 *Cold War: The Amazing Canada-Soviet Hockey Series of 1972*, to which I have already made reference. What is interesting to note from the outset is the title, which, unlike Ludwig's *Hockey Night in Moscow*, puts the series more in the political realm than in the sporting realm. Macskimming, in fact, covers the same set of factual material found in Ludwig but with a much different emphasis. Whereas Ludwig portrays Canadian nationalism within an ironic frame, showing that, if the series taught Canadians anything, it taught them lessons about how the Soviets *played hockey*, Macskimming focuses on the patriotic self-definition that he sees as having emerged from the series. He takes it for granted that the series was about having a sense of being Canadian, losing it, and regaining it with the victory in game eight; however, he forgets the specifics of how this happened, particularly the presence of the other. As a result, in his retelling, Macskimming turns the series into epic by employing a process that sounds much like Légaré's (2002, EP6) description of the creation of Inuit cultural identity: "To be efficient, symbols must be exaggerated and dramatized by actors who create a reinterpretation of a group's past history and traditions in order to organize the social relevance of political or social claims."

Mikhail Bakhtin, in "Epic and the Novel," provides a clue as to how the lived reality of September 1972 was transformed into myth and how this created an identity for a cultural group. In the genre of epic literature, the existence of "absolute epic distance separates the epic world from contemporary reality" (Bakhtin 1981, 13). The epic puts its speaker and listener "in the same time and on the same evaluative (hierarchical) plane" but keeps the images represented, the "world of the heroes ... on an utterly different and inaccessible time-and-value plane" (14). What's interesting with regard to a consideration of the formation of identity is Bakhtin's claim that "the space between them is filled with national tradition" (14). In summary, Bakhtin says that "the epic as it has come down to us is an absolutely completed and finished generic form, whose constitutive feature is the transferral of the world it describes to an absolute past of national beginnings and peak times" (15).

In fact one might observe this process from the beginning of *Cold War*. In the Introduction, Macskimming (1996, 2–3) says that, in the series, "We witnessed the acting out of our national myth, put to the test at last." And he follows this with, "By sharing in the enactment of the myth, Canadians – temperamentally so fractious and resentful a people, then as now, on grounds of language or religion or ethnicity – joined together in a rare moment of unity" (3). Like Ludwig, he acknowledges that the series changed the Canadian way of playing, but he ends the chapter with these telling words: "And we can appreciate even better [in the retelling] one of the great mythic dramas in the history of sport" (ibid.). His first chapter details the various nationalistic points of view that preceded the series' opening game and, in this respect, mirrors what Ludwig had written years before; however, his second chapter is worthy of note. Rather than moving directly to the events of the first game, he tells the story of going, in the 1990s, to player Pat Stapleton's house in search of the puck that had been used to score the winning goal in game eight. The chapter unfolds as a quest, immediately casting the book's emphasis in the light of the series' decisive moment, the vindication of Canadian superiority in hockey. The fact that the puck is not produced only adds to the sense of mystery, or to what Bakhtin (1981, 17) describes as follows: "One can only accept the epic world with reverence; it is impossible to really touch it, for it is beyond the realm of human activity, the realm in which everything humans touch is altered and re-thought." As long as that puck exists as an idea, its significance can remain grand and untraceable. Once actually seen, however, the myth loses its lustre. MacSkimming leaves Stapleton's house disappointed. Oddly enough, he says that leaving without having touched the puck created some doubts not only as to its authenticity but also as to the authenticity of the victory it represents (MacSkimming 1996, 40). Ensuing chapters, however, do not do anything to take away from the mythological quality of the series (on the contrary, they enhance it), nor does the placement of this chapter at the beginning of the book before the puck, any puck, has been dropped.

In describing that game, MacSkimming begins with the conclusion, again framing the contest as something that reaches to the core of

Canadian self-definition, something Ludwig did only after describing
the actual events. Macskimming (1996, 42) says, "Sixty minutes of
hockey will have the shattering force of revelation ... In one evening,
a large piece of the cherished bedrock of Canadians' understanding
of ourselves is exploded." The use of the future "will have" creates
the sense of epic distance Bakhtin (1981, 17) refers to when he says
that "the epic world is constructed in the zone of an absolute distanced
image, beyond the sphere of possible contact with the developing,
incomplete and therefore re-thinking and re-evaluating present."

As he talks about the aftermath of the first game, Macskimming
claims, as did Ludwig, that war became the appropriate metaphor
for this "test of our national character." And he goes on to say that
"any war triggers a primitive human archetype, genetically imprinted
from time immemorial: Us vs Them" (MacSkimming 1996, 59).
However, as the book moves forward, it reverts to an emphasis on
the ultimate victory by the Canadian players, indicating (e.g., when
talking about the loss of game three) that, though things look bleak,
the team will figure out a way to prevail (92). When speaking of
game five, Macskimming again resorts to mythological language
when referring to the Russians: "Their perseverance is never more
indefatigable, their consistency never more daunting, the knack for
scoring in rapid-fire clusters never more awesome or demoralizing"
(153). As he starts his summing-up, which occurs, significantly
enough, before he even gets to the last three games (all won by
Canada), he puts the series into its later context: "The series did
more for national unity than a dozen royal commissions and any
number of constitutional conferences" (157). And he further claims
that the coaches "bore the ultimate responsibility for the success or
failure not merely of their hockey team but of their country" (180).

Thus Macskimming's book is subtly but tellingly different from
Ludwig's in that it emphasizes from the outset the valorization of
the (eventual) winning of the series and, in so doing, erases in large
measure both the lessons learned (which ended up changing Canadian/
NHL hockey) and the fact that the series was hardly an unqualified
success. It was, rather, an up-and-down trial wherein the other came
increasingly and inevitably into view. At the end of September 1972,
no Canadian could really have felt that his/her self-definition could

be exercised in the absence of an other (at least with regard to hockey), as had been the case in the time preceding the series. Yet, immediately following that night in Moscow, as the details of how Team Canada almost lost were transformed into the epic story of how it (and Canada as a whole) won, the process of erasing the other began. Who was defeated, and how, no longer mattered. What mattered was that Canadians' sense of who they were had been confirmed and then placed into the zone of an epic past, untouchable except as symbol.

Canadian identity and postcoloniality

The series gave Canadians a sense of who they were by giving them a moment when they became "us," and there are all sorts of reminders of 1972 in Canadian discourse, from history books to hockey game commentary. Proving that the series has been embedded in popular culture is not only the ways in which it has, over the past ten years, been mined for its value as seller of kitsch (from replica jerseys to bobble-head dolls) but also the attempt to recreate it during a reunion series in 1987 and a commemorative dinner held in Russia in 2002 – a dinner attended by the prime minister and several players, one of whom, Frank Mahovlich, is now a member of the Canadian Senate. This shows that the events of those eight games thirty-plus years ago live very much in the popular imagination. But for whom?

In 1972, Canada's population was 21.8 million (Earle 1995, 119), a large percentage of whom were descended from immigrants from Western Europe. In 2001, the population was 31.7 million, of whom 5.4 million were foreign-born, a little more than half from places other than Europe (www.statcan.ca). A multicultural Canada is exactly what was predicted in the 1970s by then-prime minister Trudeau, although his vision was of the celebration of the diversity of the country as it was rather than of a country that could sustain its population only through immigration. As such, Canadians who consider themselves inheritors of this newly self-confident nation post–1967 or 1972, might now see their sense of self-identity threatened and, thus, might evince nostalgia for the series in an entirely different way from what I have described thus far. For them, the series could be a touchstone to a past that is now inaccessible but that remains "pure" in their imaginations because it is "Canadian" in the sense that the "I am Canadian" campaign is Canadian – white, middle-class, presumably heterosexual. As Manning (2000 EP3) says, "'Being Canadian' is synonymous here with 'being nationalist,' but only if you can relate to the terms of the engagement," which are "exemplified by a white, male, beer-drinking, hockey-watching average Joe."9

Assuming that it is fair to say that immigrants would not find much resonance in a hockey series played over thirty years ago,10 one might read the nostalgia for the series as a sign of two things: (1) that the original moment is gone (and, along with it, any real political power that such a clear definition of the Canadian self might have yielded) and (2) that those who keep the series alive do so in wistful remembrance not just of a Canada that at that moment had a clear sense of who it was but also of a Canada that is no longer, culturally and ethnically, what it was. There is a pressure, in other words, which comes from Canadian postcoloniality, to forge a new definition of Canada – one that incorporates otherness in a way that challenges many of its residents because it asks that they accept that Canada is a place that has its others *within* its boundaries – the very boundaries that, as Légaré (2002, EP4) points out, were important in creating identity in the first place. Nostalgia for the series, in this context, might be read as a rejection of the Canada of today and an attempt to embrace a Canada that seems, from the perspective of distance, to have been a less complicated place.

With today's compelling other, the United States, right next door, the need for a self-definition that allows for political and cultural resistance seems urgent, especially since the threat of invasion is no longer military but political (e.g., through actions such as closing of the US border to Canadian beef after 2002's mad cow scare and the increasing takeover of Canadian airspace by American television programs and sports). Perhaps it just seems to some people that it would be easier to create cultural resistance to the American threat if life could be more like it was (or now seems to have been) in 1972, when "the team's triumph is ours, just as its defeat would have been ours" (Macskimming 1996, 235).

NOTES

1 Where articles were obtained electronically, "EP" refers to the Electronic Pagination as downloaded from the database *Project Muse*. Available at: http://muse.jhu.edu.

2 The campaign began with "I am" in 1993, a series of ads promoting Canada's virtues, including "bilingualism, diplomacy, and multiculturalism," according to Ira Wagman (2002, EP9). The series attracted popular attention as a cultural phenomenon with "The Rant," the 1999 version of the ad discussed here. For a history of the entire run of "I am," including the ways in which parodies of the ad have entered public discourse. See Wagman (2002).

3 I use this word a number of times, but for the sake of a cleaner read, will not continue to place it in scare quotes.

4 The Canadians did not realize at the time that, since the Soviet Union had no official professional league, their best players were called "amateurs" but were every bit career hockey players. In fact, unlike the NHL players of the day, they trained year-round and, thus, came into the series in far better condition than the Canadians, who had meandered through a summer training camp with the unchallenged assumption that the series would be an easy tune-up against soft opponents.

5 Witness the cover of *Maclean's* volume of contemporary history entitled *Canada's Century* (2001), which features a picture of Paul Henderson leaping in joy after scoring "the Goal" as the central image, displacing the more familiar Mountie in a canoe, which takes its place at the side. The series is also discussed in fiction, among other places, in David Adams Richards' *Nights Below Station Street* (1997, 77–80). Richards' narrator says, "For Adele who had always loved hockey, and especially the Montreal Canadiens, this 1972 series between the Canadians and the Russians, was the one spiritual happening she could think of" (80).

6 Jonathan Arac, discussing American cultural identity and the case of Ralph Ellison's canonization, indicates that the reference guide created to give readers an entry point into Laplanche's and J.-B. Pontalis's work does not contain an entry for identity but, rather, one for "identification," the definition of which is the "psychological process whereby the subject assimilates an aspect, property or attribute of the other and is

transformed, wholly or partially, after the model the other provides"
(Arac 2003, EP5).

7 "Almost" human because accounts of the series continually mention the
   Russians as robotic, with their similar square-cut hair and expressionless
   faces. See Macskimming (1996, 44).

8 The Canadian players resorted to violent tactics as the game wound
   down. In doing so, they were actually reverting to the very forms that
   had created Canadian identity through sport one hundred years before,
   as detailed by Michael A. Robidoux (2002, 213–14) and discussed in
   part earlier.

9 Compare, for instance, MacGregor (2003, EP5), especially where he
   indicates the opinion of several Canadian historians on "The Rant":
   "[Michael] Bliss believed that the advertisement was pathetic, depressing,
   and an embarrassment to Canada; it was nationalism without content."

10 But here one must note Richard Gwyn's (1996, 56–67) comment that
   "hockey remains the quintessential Canadian sport, the great assimilator
   of the children of immigrants."

PART TWO

FORGING IDENTITY THROUGH FICTION

Cover of Street & Smith's *Sport Story Magazine* 50, 1
(January 1936), featuring a Leslie McFarlane hockey
novelette. Street and Smith Archive Serials, Special
Collections Research Center, Syracuse University Library.

4

"Just part of the game"
Depictions of Violence in Hockey Prose

JASON F. BLAKE

Much academic writing on sports sets out to explode the myth of the sports world as a utopian play-realm. At its best, play and its realm is autotelic, unmotivated by material interest. As Bernard Suits (1978, 15) writes in *The Grasshopper: Games, Life, and Utopia*, "for 'play' we could substitute the expression 'doing things we value for their own sake.'" We do not often play shinny because we have to or because we want to gain something concrete or specific by giving ourselves over to play's frivolity. It is because of this freedom from external forces that Friedrich Schiller (1962, 619) believed human beings are most human when at play. It is also this concept of play that gives the term "professional player" the scent of oxymoron. If play is supposed to be without recompense, and therefore the opposite of work, how can anyone "play" for a living? Mihai Spariosu (1991, xii) finds that play "may well be of those phenomena that ultimately elude power" and therefore "seems to be on the order of Utopia." Indeed, Suits (1978, 176) goes further by claiming that game playing "is the essence, the 'without which not' of Utopia" and that "the games we play in our non-Utopian lives are intimations of things to come."

Games are a break from bread-winning routine life, a chance for us to take risks without risking anything serious, and a virtual parallel existence, outside of regular time and space. The leap of faith that convinces us that it is somehow important that a little black disk cross the goal line also offers a nice break from the rationality that governs our daily life. To summarize with an often cited (and often criticized) utopian definition: "play is a voluntary activity or occupation executed within certain fixed limits of time and place, according to rules freely accepted but absolutely binding, having its aim in itself and accompanied by a feeling of tension, joy and the consciousness that it is 'different' from 'ordinary' life" (Huizinga 1955, 28). The main problem with utopian visions of play and sport (one that the myth-exploders pounce on) is that sport is not always play. Even Johan Huizinga, the theoretician and definition-provider many lean on for support, was sceptical about equating sport with play. He saw the spectacle of modern sport leaving the "play-sphere proper" and becoming a "thing sui generis: neither play nor earnest" (197). In the years since Huizinga's death at the hands of the Nazis while under open arrest, this departure has become even clearer. There is nothing utopian about lunatic hockey parents, lock-outs and strikes in the National Hockey League, instances of sexual abuse among players and coaches, the tremendous opportunity costs of chasing a puck, and – the topic of this chapter – violence.

Though it is foolish to argue that sports are an absolute, timeless world apart – if for no other reason than that the clock of our lives continues to tick even as we play a game of shinny – the positive, *playful* aspects should not be overlooked. First there is the fact of impunity. We may play both shinny and the stock market, but only shinny lets us try things out without dire consequences. In some other hockey worlds, you can even bodycheck. Aggression that would be scorned off the ice, or even in other sporting arenas and cultures, is allowed, endorsed. Violence is also tolerated. One punch means a red card in soccer. In North American professional hockey fisticuffs means a five-minute penalty.

This chapter focuses on violence. More specifically, it focuses on violence and the idea of catharsis in hockey fiction. This usually means fights, which are included in almost every lengthy work of hockey fiction. The first part of the chapter looks generally and briefly at fighting and violence within the context of aggression and utopian play theories. The second presents a few textual examples from works such as Roy MacGregor's (2002) *The Last Season*, Hanford Woods's (1997) "The Drubbing of Nesterenko," Bill Gaston's

(1998) "Your First Time," Mark Anthony Jarman's (1997) *Salvage King, Ya!* and Frank Paci's (1999) *Icelands*. These passages are examined for the attitudes towards hockey violence, particularly fighting, that they portray. The texts were chosen because they portray violence from a variety of angles, from the enthusiastic enforcer to the traumatized fan, from the self-ironic journeyman to the up-and-coming skills player who abhors fighting. Is hockey represented as a culture of violence? If so, can violence and play co-exist? Is violence in hockey condemned in these texts? These are some of the questions I try to answer.

In his seminal work *On Aggression*, Austrian zoologist Konrad Lorenz (2002, ix) defines aggression as "the fighting instinct ... which is directed *against* members of the same species." He begins by looking at some feisty fish and works up the food chain to conclude that "sport indubitably contains aggressive motivation" (271). And this is good. We, like the fish, are full of "aggressive urge" and sport allows for its "cathartic discharge" (272). Among the various –ologists, this theory of innate aggression and its necessary release is widely disputed, as is the positive role sports play in this discharge. Although Eric Dunning and Norbert Elias believe that "mimetic leisure forms have replaced aggressive or violent forms" – that is, that modern sports have helped the "civilizing process" by supplanting earlier blood sports – others are less enthusiastic (Dunning and Elias 1986, 53). In the "other" view, aggression is a learned behaviour, by no means innate, and "aggressive environments serve to arouse aggressive responses, even among spectators" (Gruneau and Whitson, 177).[1] Laura Robinson's (1998, 10) *Crossing the Line: Violence and Sexual Assault in Canada's National Sport* is a book-length exposé of how the competitive hockey world apparently propagates violence and is a world in which "ethical behaviour is often not highly valued." Though fan violence in North America is rather limited, soccer hooligans across the ocean provide compelling circumstantial evidence against the belief that watching a game is a healthy way of blowing off steam. Be that as it may, among North American hockey fans catharsis theory is near gospel. We have all heard the argument that the odd fight is a relatively benign affair that is far less dangerous than a high stick. More formally: "The catharsis hypothesis suggests that fighting in sports provides controlled and symbolic outlets for aggression that might otherwise manifest itself in more serious forms" (Gruneau and Whitson 1998, 177). When one thinks back on the most famous incidences of on-ice violence, such as the Eddie Shore crippling of Ace Bailey, Gordie Howe's smashing of Lou Fontinato's face, or the stick attacks that landed NHLers such as Dino Ciccarelli and Marty McSorley in court, it is hard to imagine what the "more serious forms" of aggression could be.

Referring to the aggression and violence in hockey, Hugh MacLennan (1989, 10) has written, "to spectator and player alike, hockey gives the release that strong liquor gives to a repressed man." This is moving into the territory of Aristotle's *Poetics*, in which the philosopher wondered how it is that we can watch a bloody, tragic play and somehow feel good. His famous conclusion was that drama imitates "incidents arousing pity and fear" to accomplish the "catharsis [purification or purgation] of such emotions." We and our emotions are manipulated by actors playing out a script. The spectator identifies with the characters on stage, suffers by proxy, and then puts the fake tragedy behind him or her. MacLennan's language is the same: we anticipate and accept violence, watch it, experience a "release" and then go back to being model citizens.

Though MacLennan's language is in line with Aristotle's, there are some significant differences. First, sport is dramatic, but it is not theatre in the traditional sense. Hockey and opera performances each involve grace, beauty and skill; each is laden with symbolic value, and may indeed say much about the culture that spawned it; and, in certain sports, violence "elevates deep play to high drama" (Jennings, Zillmann, and Raney 1988, 260). But there's always a hiccup – namely, sport provides dramatic action without a script and is therefore more open in form if not in interpretation than any work of art. Allen Guttmann (1992, 157) points out that even "the most 'dramatic' ball game is very different from the experience that Aristotle analyses in the *Poetics*," and he is therefore doubtful of the "concept of catharsis as it relates to sports." Unlike literal and literary drama, in hockey even the actors do not know who will win. Hockey is real and is limited only by the rules, while an individual play is *art*-ificial and determined by the text. Even a tame hockey game can contain more actual violence and bloodshed than *Macbeth*.

MacLennan fuses "spectator and player," saying that a release is felt whether you are in box seats or in the penalty box. This sort of feeling of catharsis among spectators is difficult to prove. As Daniel Wann et al. (2001, 198) have said, "there is virtually no empirical evidence validating the existence of catharsis in sport." To muddy the waters further, sports fans steer between identifying and over-identifying. In other words, while a minimum of identification is required in order to achieve catharsis – we have to care about the protagonist – too much identification can lead to problems if the team loses. It is difficult to see any "cathartic discharge" of "aggressive urge" when a team's fans go on a violent rampage.

Of course, literature cares little about the empirical, and most hockey fiction (like most hockey fans) adheres to the idea that there is some sort of cleansing and a corresponding improvement to the person through hockey. But aside from physical fitness, there are few obvious benefits to playing hockey (in terms of health, the injuries one collects while playing hockey usually far outweigh the cardio-vascular or muscular benefits). Skills learned while playing hockey are difficult to transfer, and it is difficult to imagine another area of life in which a good slapshot can save the day. Brian Sutton-Smith (1997, 46) writes of "play's occasional but not regular extrinsic adaptive value." In other words, the benefits are not linear, and it is therefore difficult to find a cause-and-effect relationship between what we learn on the ice and what we can apply to the rest of our lives. This does not mean, of course, they there are no benefits. They are just difficult to spot. A.J. Liebling (2004, 6) jests about this quest for linearity in *The Sweet Science*, his collection of *New Yorker* articles on boxing: "If a novelist who lived exclusively on applecores won the Nobel Prize, vegetarians would chorus that the repulsive nutrient had invigorated his brain. But when the prize goes to Ernest Hemingway, who has been a not particularly evasive boxer for years, no one rises to point out that the percussion has apparently stimu-lated his intellection." Liebling whimsically implies that, for many a punch-drunk boxer, there is a mind sharpened by ring "percus-sion." The point, I believe, is that analysis of the benefits of sport, particularly violent sport, should be carried out on a case-by-case basis. And with that I cease treading sociological waters and move to literary examples.

Paul Quarrington's witty novel *King Leary* shows that the reforming value of sport comes from transferring energy and instilling values rather than from transferring skills. Two delinquent boys are sent to a reform school and are straightened out somewhat by the hockey-playing priests. The fathers' tautological motto? "To Keep A Boy Out Of Hot Water, Put Him On Ice" (Quarrington 1994, 34). A mischievous boy on the ice is not out breaking windows for kicks. In this case, the boys are not just redirecting energy, they are also learning discipline, the value of teamwork, and all the other traditional (and therefore often criticized) benefits of sport. But what about the hot water we get into on the ice, when aggression spins into pure violence while we are supposedly *playing*? The dividing line between aggression and violence is thin, but in few sports do the latter intrude as clearly and as often as they do in hockey. Any NBA basketball or Major League baseball fight will definitely make the highlight reels; a hockey fight *might* be shown. It is expected and therefore nothing out of the ordinary. In keeping with this "fact of hockey life," most hockey fiction casts at least a passing glance at the spectre of violence and fighting in the game.

In Lynn Coady's novel *Saints of Big Harbour*, the young hockey-playing Guy Boucher is jumped and pummelled by an older boy on the street for no apparent reason. He remarks, "I got the crap beaten out of me, worse than ever in my life" and then compares the incident with a hockey-related, albeit off-ice, attack the year before: "Even the guy from the dance last spring wasn't that bad. At least I knew what it was about ... It was about hockey, so it made sense" (Coady 2002, 151f). Guy's laconic and nonchalant "it made sense" must sound downright funny to the non-cognoscente because it so baldly states that violence and abuse in hockey is allowed, understandable, and therefore acceptable. It is another shade of the myth of hockey's being a world apart, a world in which violence can be both expected and forgiven. Furthermore, it is violence *controlled* by the referees and even by the unwritten codes (such as "not running the goalie" or "not attacking much smaller players") that govern the game's violence. Though beaten up in both cases, the later attack is more unsettling to Guy because it is random, unjustified.

Guy Boucher's nonchalance mirrors the common belief that in a rough game such as hockey emotions will boil over and that acts of aggression, even violence, are inevitable. Though not necessarily premeditated, violent actions will occur in between goals, offsides, and icings. Lawrence Scanlan's book *Grace under Fire: The State of our Sweet and Savage Game* contains a long letter from novelist Guy Vanderhaeghe, which takes up and articulates the limited viewpoint of *Big Harbour*'s Guy Boucher: "Outrage is frequently expressed by hockey people when violence which would never be condoned on the street is threatened with prosecution in the courts. Hockey is assumed to somehow be exempt from the rule of law. And hockey culture is unlikely to change because there is so little internal criticism" (Scanlan 2002, 148). After noting that violence could be eradicated from the game if tougher penalties were doled out, Vanderhaeghe ends his letter with a telling punch-line: "But that would make it a pansy game" (ibid.). His self-ironical twist after lamenting violence in hockey points out that many hockey fans merely pay lip service to eradicating fighting; that is, they protest it while assuming it is really just "part of the game" (ibid.).

Others go further than Vanderhaeghe, saying that violence is not a *part* but the very essence of the game. In *The Arena of Masculinity*, Brian Pronger (1990, 22) writes: "athletic competence is actually a secondary feature of hockey, especially in the NHL – the real appeal lies in its significance as a 'man's game.' The masculine aesthetic of hockey becomes almost sacramental through its violence and bloodshed." The rhetorical verve of this passage definitely makes the point, though it should not blind us to certain inconsistencies. Suggesting that "athletic competence" is "secondary" is both exaggerated and tautological. It is exaggerated because even the toughest cement-handed team will not win most of its games, which, despite spectacles of violence, remains the goal of the game. It is tautological because "athletic competence" aids the enforcer and the goal-scorer alike. However, even if we take Pronger to task for exaggerating to make a point, the association of violence with hockey remains, and not just among the uninformed. How many other sports' non-fiction includes titles such as *The Ultimate Bad Boys* (a ranking of NHL fighters) or *The Violent Game*? "Hockey has a level of physical confrontation beyond that of most other sports," write Gruneau and Whitson (1993, 175) in *Hockey Night in Canada*. While many would surely read "physical confrontation" as a euphemism for violence, hockey is hardly uniquely physical and confrontational. Football and rugby tackles can be just as devastating, and many combat sports (such as boxing) are exclusively about hitting people. What does make hockey unique, however, is the fact that fights are tacitly sanctioned by players, coaches, and spectators, even while being scorned by the rules.

An example from a boxing tale should illustrate this split between boxing on the ice and in the ring. Jack London's short story "A Piece of Steak" is not about a hockey fighter but about Tom King, an aging boxer who takes on a much younger opponent in the hope of earning a few dollars. The story contains descriptions of a fight and insights into a boxer's mentality. King "struck to hurt, struck to maim, struck to destroy; but there was no animus in it" (London 1953, 73). In a previous bout he had aimed for and rebroken an opponent's freshly healed jaw "not because he bore any ill-will ... It was the game, and both knew the game and played it" (74). The juxtapositions of "maim" and "game," "hurt" and "played" horrifies because it links the frivolous and the injurious. The fact that this pain is inflicted without a hint of malevolence suggests the purity of the animal kingdom, at the expense of civilization. It also evokes the myriad anecdotes of hockey players who box on the ice, then go for a beer afterwards without a hint of "ill-will" or "animus." However, the tempting analogy is not entirely valid because, while hitting and hurting your opponent is essential to the sweet science, clear violence in hockey is, at least according to the written rules of the game, always value-added.

The first successful hockey novel for adults, Roy MacGregor's *The Last Season*, centres on Felix Batterinski (the happy batterer). It is a *Bildungsroman* about a role player, or "goon," and is an indictment of goonery in hockey as it was played in the 1970s. MacGregor leads Batterinski from his days as a boy in Ontario to the zenith of his career as a Broadstreet Bully in Philadelphia to his "last season" as a suddenly bumbling player-coach in a fightless Finnish league. In the novel, fighting is already an admission of failure, a secondary, back-door route to the NHL meant for the less talented. It is only after a child Bobby Orr skates rings around Felix and he is then benched for much of the game that Batterinski looks to his fists as a path to the NHL. When he finally gets a shift in the third period, he wreaks havoc and trades the bench for the penalty box: "I could hear their coach screaming. He was up on the boards, balancing and calling for a major. Good – that meant blood ... As I stepped off the ice a stretcher came through – the ultimate proof that I'd won" (MacGregor 2002, 20). The thumb of the author comes down pretty heavily here and sends the message that, while fighting is bad enough, feeling glee at injuring another boy is far more macabre, especially when fighting is not integral to the sport but "value added." If I can attribute a thesis to the novel, it is this: hockey is being destroyed by violence. While fighting and players like Batterinski have no role in the game, the fault lies not solely with the "hero" but with the system as a whole. After all, somebody had to hire Batterinski to play.

Every fan of professional hockey knows that violence and fighting seem to have an active and a useful role in the game. Hanford Woods fictionally examines that role in a short story entitled "The Drubbing of Nesterenko." Despite the real names and events described, "The Drubbing" is a work of fiction – one that implies a one-sided fight is more likely to be labeled violence. As the title states, the focus of the story is a fight in which the Habs' John Ferguson attacks the narrator's hero, Eric Nesterenko, in a Stanley Cup series: "I can still hear the voice of Danny Gallivan ... *Ferguson pummels Nesterenko with a series of right hooks, Nesterenko is on his knees, he's not fighting back, he's cut, he's bleeding badly ... linesman Pavlitch is struggling to pull Ferguson off Nesterenko, they can't get him off*" (Woods 1997, 247). The narrator despises Ferguson for crossing the line of accepted violence, though he cedes that the "outcome of the series was determined by the fight" (248). This is something we have heard very often and that belies the claim that violence is value added and superfluous in hockey because it is secondary to the goal of the game. In the vast majority of cases, violence on the ice is instrumental, it "always serves a utilitarian function" by intimidating, creating space, or setting the tone of a game (Robidoux 2001, 75).

MacLennan wrote of "spectator and player alike." Woods's story is obviously from the fan's perspective. In order for a release of emotions to take place, some sort of identification is required. If we do not care about the sport or people involved our emotions are not stirred. The problem here is that the spectator/narrator identifies too much with both Nesterenko and (negatively) Ferguson. He admits that "Ferguson was always a great fighter" but adds that he was "a crude hockey player to whom it was most important not to lose a fight" (Woods 1997, 244). He is "crude" because he attacks for the sake of it "not in response to any real or imagined aggression" (247). In the narrator's eyes he is a pure corruption of the game – like Batterinski in *The Last Season*. However, the signals sent by the text are mixed. By saying "the series was determined by the fight," the narrator tacitly accepts that violence can produce victory (the ultimate goal of the game), even while claiming that Ferguson is not a real hockey player and hating him for the violence.

Being a fan means hoping your team will win, and, at least momentarily, I am sure, we have all been happy to "win ugly," even with violence. Woods's fan differs from most because, years later, he writes "the blows with which Ferguson hammered Nesterenko ... are not of the past," though they are "buried in the sacred soil that nourishes all repressed events" (Woods 1997, 247). This is the language of trauma, the antithesis of catharsis or healthy, redemptive release that Aristotle and MacLennan espouse. As a result, the narrator admits that "it would give me pleasure to see him [Ferguson] injured" (245). So much for keeping us out of hot water. The story shows how the narrator is caught up in a cycle of violence by: (1) admitting the useful role of violence in the game, despite Ferguson's meaningless attack (he even states that "people who find hockey brutal are unnecessarily squeamish"); (2) desiring more violence; and (3) over-identifying with the violence, being unable to get over it (246).

More interesting than the mind of the spectator is the focus on the psychology of the fighter, the one inflicting, or risking, damage. Woods's narrator over-identifies with Nesterenko and simply cannot see why Ferguson must fight, especially since Ferguson does not seem to follow even the unwritten rules governing hockey fights. However, even if a fan identifies with a player or team to the extent of delusion, equating his or her fan support with the goings-on on the ice, a fundamental split between player and spectator will remain. When it comes to violence, for fans it will simply remain "an extension of the game they pay to watch; it has no physical bearing on their lives" (Robidoux 2001, 75). Woods's narrator repeats the common, and partly true, dictum that, in hockey, "fights, even the worst of them, are burlesques. A player has to lose his head [as did Ferguson] before anything real takes place" (Woods 1997, 246). In an off-ice existence, we have to "lose our heads" before a fight takes place at all. It is partly because of these limits that someone who truly enjoys fighting tickles the imagination in a Frankenstein's monster sort of way – because he goes beyond acceptable limits even within a culture of violence. Those that simply enjoy fighting and violence, such as Felix Batterinski, are easy to discount as marginal, different from the rest of us.

These limits are often thought of as "part of the game" and practically intuitive. They are not. Bill Gaston's short story "Your First Time" contains the mildly humorous but highly illustrative character of Dil Carnback, a Swedish goal scorer who is as clumsy in North America as Batterinski is in Scandinavia. The European "misse[s] the point" because "he had no sense of appropriate force. Blind to the flow of a game, he'd absolutely cream a guy, a non-threatening nobody, face in the glass, for no reason, in the neutral zone, and he'd wonder not only why he got a penalty but also why he got no accolades back on the bench, where he'd look around for the praise a good smear could get you. Or during that brawl, everybody dropping their gloves and a few guys going at it but mostly just orderly shoving – Dilly speared the guy he'd partnered off with" (Gaston 1998, 56). Aside from offering a refreshing break from the "chicken Swede" stereotype, Dil offers a counterpoint to Guy Boucher's "it was about hockey, so it made sense" in Lynn Coady's novel. Gaston provides a logical reason for Dil's behaviour, one that reminds the reader that fighting and violence are far from natural and not the only way to play hockey: "Dil couldn't respect a fair fight because he was too freaked out to see one" (56). Coming from a non-fighting hockey environment, seeing a fight is highly estranging and bewildering for him. Thus, he would not be equipped to see anything "orderly" about the "shoving," to view hockey fights as "burlesques," or to deem that fights make "sense" on the ice.

Mark Anthony Jarman's splendid *Salvage King, Ya!* is about a mini-Ferguson, a journeyman, boozing minor-league player named Drinkwater, who is just one expansion shy of the NHL. Drinkwater is the opposite of the slightly confused Dil Carnback, who longs to fit in, even while lacking the understanding of the unwritten rules of hockey violence. Never a finesse player, Drinkwater is well aware of the codes and uses them to prolong his career as he slugs his way from team to team: "I was traded for losing a fight in front of our bench. No one cared how I came out, only that it was bad *psychologically* for the team. I was gone in hours. Another suitcase open, my cheekbone killing me, double-vision" (Jarman 1997, 130). As a role player, Drinkwater is expected to do more than just "show up" for a fight. Unfortunately for his career prospects and health, he is not a very good fighter. Elsewhere in the novel, coming back to clarity after losing yet another fight, Drinkwater is asked, "'Know where you are?' ... I look around. 'Yeah. The fucking minors'" (140). Hockey fans will read this as more than a trite wisecrack. It is a reminder that the minors can be tougher than the NHL because an extra aggressive, even violent, edge can literally make a million-dollar difference in salary. At the same time we have Drinkwater's own realization that he is no goal scorer and that a tough guy who loses fights is not going to the NHL. Cribbing from the Communist Manifesto, Drinkwater comments: "Grinders of the world unite, you have nothing to lose but your teeth" (68).

Jarman writes against the well-oiled grain of considering the grinder's role off the ice as Dr Jekyll to Mr Hyde. He tries out a new possibility, surprising the reader with what goes on in the player's mind as he dukes it out. Drinkwater mentions an attachment to music and – in a pun on "whaling" – says, "some steroid headcase will be wailing on me and I'm humming 'Children behave, that's what they say when we're together'" (Jarman 1997, 73). This sounds much less like instrumental violence than absent-minded violence, as though Drinkwater is just another "worker of the world" daydreaming on the job. In yet another fight, Drinkwater provides his own colour commentary: "The ref wouldn't let me at the other guy and I was so wound up I clocked the ref to get rid of him and then clobbered the other joker who thought he was scot free. Sweater down, punch up, punch up, punch up. This should make Don Cherry's video, I thought" (153). There are hints of frivolity here: "joker," "scot free," and "clocked" are euphemistically playful. It's just a game, after all, where the utopians say we are all free to be ourselves. Contradicting this is the mechanical, repetitive, "sweater down, punch up, punch up, punch up" that shows the athlete's body as a tool or machine that goes through the motions. But machines do not think; here, the abuse of the body is coupled with self-reflection.

Drinkwater's reference to Don Cherry's video is more than a yearning for his fifteen minutes of fame, it is a reminder that, as Michael Robidoux has written, "violence on the ice can be seen as a highly expressive text that may establish a player's identity" (Robidoux 2001, 75). It is violence on display, a thought-out performance in real time for an audience – which means that sport moves towards art because Drinkwater is fighting according to a script. This refutes the home truth that violence is something that boils over when reflection deserts us and passion clouds judgment. Drinkwater – a should-be poster boy for traditional masculinity (hard-loving, hard-drinking, hard-fighting, hard-body) – thinks too much. He maintains an ironic distance from his surroundings. Irony and beating (or getting beaten) up are strange bedfellows.

Drinkwater is a kibbitzer in the game of his own life, and has an ironic, Thomas Mannian take on his world. In response to a pre-game speech he wryly comments: "The ex-goon coach actually gives a stirring speech without mentioning beating them in the alley ... Such candor and metaphor. I see Pulitzers in his future" (Jarman 1997, 86). In this world, language clearly suffers as clichés and hackneyed phrases suffice to send the troops out to fight. The self-evident truth that crackles under Jarman's sarcasm is that these are men of action and that language is all but irrelevant to what they do. After explaining the cryptically metaphorical speech to a team-mate ("If I'm a gentleman and you're a gentleman, then who will milk the cow?"), he reflects, "we're all gung ho but I notice when fastening the strap on my helmet, head tilted and hand up to the side of my head, that it's exactly like a woman putting on an earring.

I try to do it in a different way but somehow I just don't feel quite as brutal" (86). Here Jarman shows the gap between the life lived by Drinkwater and the life displayed for the crowd. Drinkwater is aware that he lives in a clichéd, atavistically masculine world. He is also aware of performing. He may *feel* less brutal, but no spectator would see anything remotely feminine in his hulking figure. Here we see another reason why the gulf between "spectator and player" is unbridgeable.

Perhaps because failure makes for more compelling literature, many hockey novels follow players on the downside of their careers as professional players.[2] Frank Paci's *Icelands* follows a trio of young, gifted boys as they play their way towards the voting age, though not necessarily towards the NHL. Andrew, a skilled but clean player who detests violence, finds himself at a junior training camp, where he is challenged by a talentless hockey player. Andrew is no Batterinski, the marginal character who loves fighting, nor is he a Ferguson or a Drinkwater (characters who are aware they have to fight in order to keep their jobs); but he is also not one of those rare players like Bobby Hull or Wayne Gretzky, whose immense gifts allow them to keep the gloves on and still keep their job. After Andrew scores a fine goal, a huge player with an "orange helmet," "a scruffy three-days' beard and the vicious face of a moronic Neanderthal," calls Andrew "Bobby fucken Orr" and attacks him (Paci 1999, 195). "It felt like time had stopped. This was the wall his whole hockey career had been inching toward. That he had to do something. That he could no longer skate away. That if he wanted to go to a higher level in the game, there was no getting around this cold impenetrable wall of ice (196).

Andrew sees in the beckoning Goliath all that is wrong with hockey, including the "different set of rules on the ice" (Paci 1999, 196). The very freedom of sport, the stepping out of daily life that leads us to the shinny rink, becomes an entrance into a violent other world – regardless of whether or not we harbour an "aggressive urge." The potential for a glimpse of utopia is ruined because, returning to Huizinga, some of the play conditions are unfulfilled. The fight is barely "voluntary," the rules may be "absolutely binding," but they are hardly "freely accepted," and, finally, though he keenly feels that the hockey rink is not "ordinary life," there is no joy or freedom. Andrew "was just a piece of meat on the rack, whether he fought or didn't fight" (196). This is the anagnorisis, the Aristotelian transition from ignorance to knowledge. Andrew recognizes the potholes in the hockey road he has travelled. Fighting seems to position hockey as the antipodes of true play. We expect a turning-point; instead, we have, "So, what the fuck! He dropped his gloves and barrelled into the wall" (196). This is not a boiling-over but a reasoned process. Andrew gives himself over to the fight in the same way that we subjugate ourselves to the irrational rules of the game when we play hockey.

I conclude by linking Drinkwater and Andrew, two hockey players with diverging attitudes on fighting. Jarman offers a very similar take on the dog-eat-dog training camp world and its expected brutality. His hero, Drinkwater, expresses the same thought as Andrew but in a minor key: "I go to training camp and I agree to go primitive. The Powers That Be like to see us peons duke it out, a feeding frenzy, a big 'roid rage'" (Jarman 1997, 178). Drinkwater's typically sardonic tone should not obscure how similar his outlook is to Andrew's. The resignation in Drinkwater's "agree to go primitive" does not differ greatly from Andrew's realization that he is just "meat on the rack" and his subsequent dropping of the gloves. In both cases the players feel that they *have* to fight in order to secure their place on the team. The ironic hyperbole of the "Powers That Be" refers, of course, to management, who are almighty in so far as they control Drinkwater's destiny and even his style of play. The line evokes *King Lear*'s Gloucester, who gloomily professes: "As flies to wanton boys, are we to the gods. They kill us for their sport." When violence enters the play-sphere, Gloucester, Andrew, and Drinkwater's "sport" is often far removed from any utopian play.

NOTES

1 Gruneau and Whitson (1993, 175–96) provide a useful overview of the competing theories as they pertain to hockey in their chapter "Violence, Fighting, and Masculinity" in *Hockey Night in Canada*.

2 Aside from MacGregor's and Jarman's novels, Bill Gaston's *The Good Body*, Richard B. Wright's *The Age of Longing*, Paul Quarrington's *Logan in Overtime*, and Robert Sedlack's *The Horn of a Lamb* all focus on formerly top-notch players far from the limelight of the NHL.

5

Win Orr Lose

Searching for the Good Canadian Kid in Canadian Hockey Fiction[1]

JAMIE DOPP

One of the basic functions of literature is to allow writers and readers "to experiment with possible selves ... to learn to take our places in the real world, to play our parts there" (Miller 1990, 69). Stories of initiation, of growing up, of coming to a new understanding in middle age or at the moment of death – all these kinds of fictions are basically about offering models for what it means to live a good life. When these kinds of stories take place in a hockey setting, the question of what it means to be a good person (a good man, typically, since the stories generally focus on males) perhaps inevitably takes on a Canadian emphasis. Is it possible to succeed as a professional hockey player and also to live a good life? What are the dangers of the quest for success? How does the quest for hockey success relate to the virtues that have historically played such a role in the self-definition of Canada? Or, to put it in the terms of my title: Can you be (or aim to be) a hockey star and still remain, at heart, a good Canadian kid?

A number of recent Canadian novels have attempted to answer these kinds of questions. In this chapter, I focus on three of them. Paul Quarrington's *King Leary*, Bill Gaston's *The Good Body*, and Mark Anthony Jarman's *Salvage King, Ya! A Herky-Jerky Picaresque* all offer sustained fictional treatment of professional hockey players at key moments of crisis in their lives. *The Good Body* and *Salvage King, Ya!* both have at their centres a career minor-league defenceman at the end of his career. *King Leary* tells the story of Percival "King" Leary, one of the early stars of the National Hockey League, and his attempt in later life to redress some of the awful things he had done as part of his drive to become the King of the Ice. Though there are many important differences between these novels, they all reveal a similar underlying pattern: they all mix elements of hockey lore with elements of Canadian national myth-making as part of the treatment of their protagonists and, in so doing, offer fictional treatments of characters who are defined not only by and against certain traditional forms of masculinity but also by and against forms of masculinity that have traditionally been identified as Canadian.

Two Canadian national myths are of particular relevance to the novels and to this discussion. These are the myths of the small town and of the North. I would like to outline the basic features of these myths before I proceed to my treatment of the novels; but, before I do, I should offer a perhaps somewhat predictable caveat about Canadian identity. Which is to say that, when it comes to Canadian identity, there is no such thing. What we call "Canadian identity" has always been problematic, in part because the distinctiveness of Quebec has put paid to the idea of a homogeneous settler culture but also because there have always been other subordinated groups – First Nations, immigrants from places other than France or England, working-class people, and most women – who have been marginalized in the process of imagining Canada as a national community. For various reasons, then, Canadians sometimes identify themselves not with a particular set of national characteristics but, rather, with the peculiar obsessiveness with which we keep asking ourselves what it means to be Canadian. Interestingly, Richard Gruneau and David Whitson, two of the most astute writers about the meaning of hockey in Canada, have suggested that the grip hockey has had on the imaginations and collective memories of Canadians may itself be related to the lack of an all-embracing Canadian identity. As they put it in *Hockey Night in Canada*, the problematic nature of Canadian identity has given hockey "even greater symbolic currency" as one of those institutions, along with "our system of national government, our public health-care system, and the CBC," that Canadians cling to as "truly Canadian" (Gruneau and Whitson 1993, 277).

The meaning of hockey in the three novels is very much intertwined with the Canadian myths of the small town and the North. The small town as microcosm of Canada has been such a pervasive myth that it was already ripe for lampooning when, in 1912, Stephen Leacock (1994) wrote his famous *Sunshine Sketches of a Little Town*. What Leacock so brilliantly captures in the sketches is the combined quality of nostalgia and knowingly ironic suspension of disbelief that is at the heart of what the small town represents. Leacock's speaker makes clear that Mariposa never really existed as we remember it and that people who now live in the big city are fully aware of this. However, the town retains a powerful hold on our imaginations precisely because we associate it with a simpler, more innocent time, a time that involves a romanticized version of our own childhoods, and we want to believe that we came from that place. More serious literary interrogations of the small town can be found in a host of twentieth-century Canadian writers (Robertson Davies, Alice Munro, and Margaret Laurence come immediately to mind, as so more contemporary writers such as Lynn Coady and David Adams Richards). In these portrayals, the surface idyll of rural or semi-rural life is shown to hide a complex reality of class struggle, religious intolerance, violence, and loss.

Behind the lampooning and literary interrogations is a longstanding popular identification of Canadian values with the small town. Canadians, we are told (or have often told ourselves), are characteristically thrifty, morally conservative, humble, and nice – virtues that are characteristic of small-town folk and that are reflected in the Canadian Constitution, which, unlike the grand claims of its American counterpart to found "one nation, indivisible, under God," more humbly establishes the goals of the nation as "peace, order, and good government." These are clichés, of course, and they have been rightly challenged by various writers in the last thirty years or so, but the identification remains. One place where Canadian identification is still very strong is in the characterization of hockey players. A truism about hockey even today is that the best players tend to be hardy simple young fellows from small towns. In *Home Game*, Ken Dryden and Roy MacGregor (1989) reflect the persistence of this idea in the set of photographs (of "things eternal") that open the book, all of boys in rural settings playing hockey outdoors (except for the outdoor portrait of Dryden's own Pee Wee-aged team). The opening chapter, "The Common Passion," gives privilege of place to small-town Saskatchewan in defining the nature of the common game.

True to type, the protagonists in Quarrington, Gaston, and Jarman all have small-town roots. Leary persistently refers to his hometown as Bytown, the earlier small-town version of Ottawa. *Salvage King, Ya!*'s Drinkwater is from Edmonton, which he describes as "a fair-sized city but ... more like a small town" (Jarman 1997, 72). The background of *The Good Body's* Bonaduce is only hinted at, but clues are offered in the apparently autobiographical pieces he composes for his writing class. Many of these pieces are heavily ironic, but not this one about the origins of his love for hockey: "Because it is dark and smoky inside. Because Grandad drinks and after he wakes from his sour moanings his mood is prickly and his eyes follow you, looking for reasons to shout. Because outside it is bright and clean, and the pond gives you magical speed" (Gaston 2000, 183). "The Birth of Hockey" goes on to touch on all the key elements of the small-town character of the original game, from the "bright and clean" natural ice of the pond, to the way the game allows poor country boys to escape the closeness of their family houses and dream of great deeds, to the way the playing of the game instills codes of morality and honour: "Because outside the rules are clear, to the point that if McIlhargy busts your shins again with the club he calls a stick you will fight him ... Because outside you make sure your little sister played, and that the teams are even because it's more fun that way" (184).

The typical Canadian spin on the small town is related to another myth that has had a powerful role in the self-definition of the country. This is the myth of the North. Carl Berger, in his aptly titled article "The True North Strong and Free," has done a fine job of explaining the provenance and main features of this myth. According to Berger, assertions linking the northern climate of Canada to the characteristics of the nation date back to the time of the French explorers; however, these claims were particularly influential as part of an attempt to distinguish the identity of the new nation in the half-century after Confederation. Berger cites Robert Grant Haliburton of the Canada First Movement as making the first fully shaped claim about Canada's destiny as a northern nation. Here is Haliburton speaking to the Montreal Literary Club in 1869: "Our corn fields, rich though they are, cannot compare with the fertile prairies of the [American] West, and our long winters are a drain on the profits of business, but may not our snow and frost give us what is of more value than gold and silver, a healthy, hardy, virtuous, dominant race? (Haliburton in Berger 1997, 86).

From the time of Haliburton on, numerous Canadian writers, artists, and politicians have articulated variations on similar themes. Basically, the argument has been that Canada's northern climate is responsible for a national character that includes physical hardiness, self-reliance, and personal virtue. The cold, frosty air has been said to have a kind of Darwinian cleansing effect – not only did it discourage immigration from the weaker "southern" races, but of those who did immigrate only the strong and those able to manage the special demands of freedom in this climate were able to thrive and thus mould the character of the nation. Much of this rhetoric was designed to distinguish Canada from the United States, where the milder "southern" climate was said to lead to degeneration, decay, and effeminacy. Ultimately, the northern climate was said to produce that most Canadian of characteristics, "the inclination to be moderate" (Berger 1997, 98).[2]

Although the racism inherent in the myth of the North was discredited as the twentieth century unfolded (among other reasons, because the identification of Canadians with the "Aryan" races, which included Germany, was hard to sustain in the face of two world wars), there has remained in Canada a persistent strand of national self-identification that has had to do with climate – often in explicit contrast to the United States. In the hockey novels, the virtues attendant on playing hockey are very much connected to mythic conceptions of the North. *King Leary* has great fun with the education of Leary at the hands of the monks, which becomes an extended satire on the strain of muscular Christianity linked to hockey through figures like Father David Bauer, a key developer and coach of the Canadian national team. The motto of the monks nicely

plays off the idea that vigorous exercise in the cold northern air will
lead to physical hardiness and moral virtue: "TO KEEP A BOY OUT
OF HOT WATER, PUT HIM ON ICE" (Quarrington 1994, 34). Leary's
quest to redress the wrongs of his life is an attempt to recapture the
wholeness of life as represented by the round rink, the perfect outdoor ice, of the monks. This ice is "hard as marble" and "blue-silver"
(37) and is reminiscent of the ice of the Ottawa canals, upon which
Leary first learns to skate, ice that is also "hard as marble" but,
more important, "strong and true" (7).

The challenges faced by Leary, Bonaduce, and Drinkwater are
symbolized, in part, by the fact that, in order to achieve professional
success, they must all go *south*. South, the United States, is where
the main NHL action is. This is perhaps most explicit in *Salvage King,
Ya!* where Drinkwater's struggles are figured as part of a metaphorical as well as a geographical journey. Drinkwater is a journeyman
in more ways than one. He describes his life as a marginal professional hockey player, with its many trades and promotions and
demotions, as a going "up and down, sideways" and a going "back
and forth, north and south, city and country" (Jarman 1997, 74,
22). Drinkwater identifies strongly with the West (both American
and Canadian) as a space of yearning and possibility, a version of
the North (as, indeed, the Northwest has often been imagined as a
single large space in Canada); he fears the East, American or
Canadian, as a place of urban decay; and he sees value in the South
only as a place to "blow off steam and blow some money" (167).
Ultimately, Drinkwater's attempt to orient himself is equated with
an attempt to navigate by "true north," and it is a mark of the
modern complexity of the space in which he finds himself that, at
the end of the novel, his growth in insight is marked by his recognition that "there is no true north." For this reason, his final acceptance
of a new life with his Intended is a tentative victory at best, very
much a salvage operation: "There is no true north. Despite this
confusion I attempt to draw a line right now and say, THAT was my
old life ... I have my few acres of snow and I salvage what I can
from the auto parts I have (272).

Salvage King, Ya!'s treatment of "true north" is indicative of how
Jarman, Gaston, and Quarrington show awareness of the extent to

which hockey and the meaning of the country have been subject to idealization and romanticization. Each shows a critical perspective that is not unlike Leacock's view of the small town, an awareness of how much nostalgia and a knowingly ironic suspension of disbelief are part of both hockey lore and Canadian identity. Indeed, as the analyses I have offered so far suggest, the novels quite deliberately situate something like a "Golden Age" of hockey in the mythic spaces of the small town and the North. This Golden Age is, like all Golden Ages, lost before it ever existed – and yet it persists as an imaginative construct and continues to exert a powerful attraction on the characters. One way to understand the attraction is through creating an analogy with debates about the Golden Age of hockey more generally. When was the Golden Age of hockey? To anticipate the answer a hockey fan will give to this perennial question (a question almost as perennial as the question of Canadian identity), the basic rule of thumb is this: date back from the fan's age to when he or she was eleven-years-old – *that* will be his or her Golden Age.

More seriously, what underpins the attraction of the mythic Golden Age is what it promises about masculinity. The mix of national myths and hockey lore in Quarrington, Jarman, and Gaston all work to invoke (and, to varying degrees, send up) ideals of masculinity that, over the years, have had a strong resonance in Canada. Here the myths of the small town, the North, and hockey become very intertwined as the masculinity celebrated in each is very much a traditional masculinity based on physical strength, toughness, and an ability to succeed by force of will. Gruneau and Whitson (1993, 191) summarize the model of aggressive masculinity traditionally offered by hockey as follows: "At its best this model of masculinity defines the real man as a decent person of few words, but with a powerful sense of his own abilities and the toughness and physical competence to handle any difficulties that might arise; a man that people respect and look up to but don't dare cross; a man who generally respects the rules that govern social life, but knows how to work outside them if necessary." Gruneau and Whitson go on to say that the willingness to go outside the rules links hockey to the masculinity stereotypically expressed by the kinds of movie roles usually occupied by John Wayne, and this is a valid point. However, I think a stronger parallel would be with the masculinity that is thought to characterize Canadian soldiers in the two world wars. One of the most interesting things about Canadian national identity, and perhaps what amounts to a contradiction for some people, is that Canadians are stereotypically seen as "nice" and "moderate," and yet, at the same time, Canadian soldiers have a proud record of military service, serving with distinction in some of the most ferocious battles in both world wars. One of the most retold stories about Canada is the way the nation "came of age" because of the contribution of its soldiers in the First World War. Though the success of the Canadians has been traditionally attributed to a number of factors, including the toughness and self-reliance embodied in the myths of the North and the small town, one of the factors was that, as soldiers of a "new" nation, Canadians were thought to be less class bound and tradition bound than were the English and French, and so they were able to adapt to the rapidly changing circumstances of the modern battlefield – to go outside the traditional rules of combat. In important ways, I think, the game of hockey, with its emphasis not just on toughness but also on speed and the ability to react quickly to changing circumstances, is the game that most closely embodies the kind of aggressive but adaptive masculinity traditionally ascribed to Canadian soldiers.

Going outside the rules is a key to success for enforcer types like Bonaduce and Drinkwater. One of the most fascinating aspects of hockey, like other of the more violent team sports, is how the sport sanctions – even celebrates – a willingness to dominate and intimidate even if it means going outside the rules, while, at the same time, there are also popularly accepted limits to the extent of the rule breaking. Some rule breaking is acceptable and even honourable (fighting) and some is not (a sucker punch). In their roles as enforcers, Drinkwater and Bonaduce travel the fine line between sanctioned and unsanctioned rule breaking, between toughness and outright brutality – a line that has always been much disputed in hockey (and the construction of certain forms of masculinity more generally). The role of enforcer itself is understood by Bonaduce and Drinkwater to be an honourable one, as long as it is performed within certain moral codes – codes that hearken back to the ethics of the outdoor ponds of Bonaduce's childhood. So Drinkwater understands that it was his role to be "an animal"; however, he didn't want to be an animal "all the time" (Jarman 1997, 130). Bonaduce is disturbed by the way fighting has changed during his career from something done to settle disputes, within a certain code of honour, to something done for the sheer spectacle: "Fighting was more calculated now, a career tool, a spectacle, no real honour left in it. And steroids" (Gaston 2000, 176). Like Canadian soldiers on the battlefields of Europe, old-time enforcers like Bonaduce and Drinkwater see themselves as ferocious warriors who nevertheless maintain a sense of honour, who are willing to break rules but only within certain limits.

Though *King Leary* does not have the literary density of *Salvage King, Ya!* and *The Good Body*, it does offer a similar complexity in its treatment of the national myths intertwined with hockey lore. The complexity emerges in part because Leary is an unreliable narrator, prone to "the blarney" as well as to the mental contortions of one engaged in an exercise of self-justification; thus, any time Leary waxes poetic about his own background or the meaning of the game the reader is well-advised to look for irony. In fact, a lot of the fun of the novel comes from how Leary's self-justifying bluster often unintentionally reveals something like a truth. For example, when Leary is traded by his best friend Clay Bors Clinton to the New York Americans, he arrives in New York to scenes of wild debauchery among his fellow players. To explain this, he points to the small-town backgrounds of the players: "One thing you got to understand is that back then hockey players were young Canucks from small towns, if they happened to be from towns at all. Many of the lads came from farmhouses so isolated that the cows had to ask directions home. [They came from places like] Swastika, Ontario ... East Braintree, Manitoba ... and St Louis-de-Ha! Ha! ... in Quebec" (Quarrington 1994, 154–55). On one level, the implication of this passage is that the players are simpletons unequipped to deal with the temptations of big city life; however, dig below the surface and you find ironies that, like Stephen Leacock's famous horseman, seem to ride off in all directions. The names of the towns ("Swastika" especially) hint that small towns already have a dark underbelly that has nothing to do with being corrupted by the big city. The Quebec place name, which is of a real town, hints at a connection to myths about "crazy Frenchmen" (another set of myths related to Canadian nationality) while also blurring the distinction between "blarney" and "reality" in the novel (if St Louis-de-Ha!-Ha! is a real name, how do you tell what is real and what is not?). The irony in the passage deepens when Leary, now the coach of the Ottawa Patriots, agrees with Clay to trade their life-long friend Manny Ozikean to the New York Americans, knowing full well that if anyone is likely to be destroyed by the wildness of the big city it is Manny. If Clay and Leary had ever inherited any small-town values, these values are completely compromised by the conversation in which they agree to trade Manny, each for his own venal reasons: Clay to steal Manny's girl Janey, Leary to protect his claim to the title of the greatest player of all time (189).

The mix of hockey lore and Canadian national myth-making in *King Leary* comes together in a hilarious and profound way in the subplot regarding Leary's nickname. Leary's tragic-comic assertions about his own status as "King of the Ice" are bolstered by the fact that he has this "Indian" nickname, "loof-weeda," bestowed upon him by a shaman-like old relative of Manny's called Poppa Rivers. Leary takes the name to be a reference to the near mystical quality of his skating. His lack of self-awareness makes him blind to the actually duplicitous quality of the name:

> "What is this *loof-weeda* business?" [Leary asks].
> "It is what I have decided to call you," [replies Poppa Rivers].
> "An Indian name, huh?"
> "Right."
> "What does it mean?"
> "Oh, a literal translation would be something like 'windmusic' or 'windsong.'"
> "Because of the way I skate?"
> "For sure ... The way you fucking skate."
> "*Loof-weeda.*"
> Then there was a hint of that smell again. (Quarrington 1994, 138).

The smell is described earlier as "like someone had made a stew with potatoes, death, and cow dung" (136).

The joke on Leary suggests how credulous he has been in his quest for the kind of "immortality" that such mythic-style names seem to offer. It also hints at all he has repressed or elided in his quest to maintain his "immortal" status.[3] Like his Shakespearean namesake, Leary's hubris has made him cling destructively to his crown, blind to those who truly love him. As a result, his personal life pretty much stinks. He betrays his wife and fails to recognize his son Rance as his true heir on the ice for, although Rance can perform the St Louis Whirligig, Leary's patented move, he also "skates like a girl" (Quarrington 1994, 48). And, of course, he betrays Manny by trading him to New York, where Manny drinks himself to death. Given the interweaving of elements of the myth of the North and hockey lore in the novel, it is important that Leary's nickname is an "Indian" nickname and that Manny, even with his red hair, is "mostly ... an Indian" (75). Leary's betrayal of Manny replays the racism explicit in the myth of the North, particularly its indigenizing claims for certain European settlers; the "healthy, hardy, virtuous, dominant race" envisioned by Haliburton as native to Canada had nothing to do with actual Natives. Leary owes much to Manny, including his life (which Manny saved when they were boys), and his response could be said to be much like that of the European settlers to the First Nations: the settlers avoided their debt to the First Nations and, instead, usurped the latter's claims to being the natural heirs to the land. All of this adds another dimension to Leary's belated recognition, when he finally gets to the Hockey Hall of Fame, that fully three-quarters of the players in the Hall were, like himself, "sons of bitches" (228).

The "loof-weeda" subplot points to an important distinction between the protagonists of the novels: Leary is a star player, a member of the Hockey Hall of Fame, whereas Bonaduce and Drinkwater are both career minor leaguers who only manage brief stints in the NHL. This distinction gives a different character to the crises they face. For Leary, the events that catch up to him have been the result of his ruthless drive to be the greatest player of all time.

King Leary suggests that it is this drive that allows Leary to take his natural talent, combine it with the coaching he receives from the monks, and turn it into the success that he enjoys. To a certain extent the novel portrays Leary's drive as a positive thing; like the historical King Clancy, he makes up for his lack of size with sheer exuberance for the game. "They kept knocking me down," he says about his first training camp. "I kept getting up" (Quarrington 1994, 64).[4] Leary's determination to succeed marks him as a hard-working Canadian kid, and, in fact, the way Leary compensates for his lack of size with a surplus of heart is iconic for how Canadians sometimes view the best of their national identity; however, Leary lacks the moderation in this drive that would make him a truly good Canadian kid. Leary's lack of moderation is figured by a wonderful, humorous inversion. Unlike the other hockey players, or sports writers like Blue Hermann, Leary does not engage in the kind of alcoholic debauchery so evident in the hotel where the New York Americans stay. Instead, he drinks only ginger ale. The irony is that he drinks ginger ale because "it makes me *pissed*!" (3 and 207). Ginger ale is linked in the novel to belching and farting and other (typically male?) methods of tooting your own horn. The fact that Leary's favourite drink is so apparently benign (a detail transplanted from the real life of King Clancy) only makes more starkly apparent how much he has indulged himself. The wreckage of his life is a direct result of his addiction to creating those "burps of glory" (207).

Interestingly, most Canadian hockey novels take as their protagonists not star players but marginal players like Bonaduce and Drinkwater. In the social order of hockey, star players are aristocrats (hence *King* Leary) but marginal players are working-class joes. Gruneau and Whitson see this class element as an enduring aspect of, especially, the rougher versions of hockey in Canada. "Rough hockey celebrates a hard man's approach to life," they write, "which has a long tradition in the history of Western popular cultures and is particularly understood and appreciated by working-class fans" (Gruneau and Whitson 1993, 189).

Gaston and Jarman play with and against the class associations tied to their career minor-league protagonists. As athletes, Bonaduce and Drinkwater are decidedly working class, not only in that they never achieve the kind of otherworldly wealth they see in some of the stars around them but also in that, on the ice, they play the quintessentially gritty roles of stay-at-home defenceman and enforcer. They are also throwbacks, on and off the ice, walking (or limping) embodiments of that more traditional version of masculinity emphasizing toughness and physical competence. But Drinkwater and Bonaduce are also more complicated. They each have an artistic side; the language each uses is seamed with literary allusions; each is also a lover – an aficionado – of music. Bonaduce, though he has faked his way into graduate school, also already has a legitimate university degree. Most important, they are each self-aware, in a way that perhaps only those who have had to struggle around the edges of success tend to become. This quality of self-awareness makes them both sometimes astute critics of the world around them – including, but not limited to, the world of hockey. Bonaduce, for example, is aware of the stereotype of the "stupid rough hayseed hockey players," but he (as well as his creator) also knows about the savvy of the players, the wit, the fact that there are different kinds of intelligence (Gaston 2000, 41). He also understands that macho posturing takes place in all kinds of different parts of society, including academia – as his hilarious comment on Phil "presenting" during the graduate seminar demonstrates (40).

That Drinkwater and Bonaduce are so self-aware adds poignancy to how *The Good Body* and *Salvage King, Ya!* portray the risks involved in the quest for hockey success. The costs of the quest turn out to be considerable. In addition to their lack of material security, Bonaduce and Drinkwater are faced with the breakdown of their bodies. The scars they have accumulated, though honourable within the code of aggressive masculinity within which they operate, also mark the gradual transformations of their bodies from young to not-young. Bonaduce also has to face the onset of multiple sclerosis, a disease that seems to represent the ultimate accelerated aging of his body and that contains a particular horror and fascination for him as a self-styled "body-person" (Gaston 2000, 41). Though the onset of the disease cannot realistically be linked to the battering his body has taken during his time as a hockey player, the symptoms of multiple sclerosis do work metaphorically to indicate the realities of aging and bodily weakness that Bonaduce has to face after hockey, realities with which the aggressively masculine culture of hockey has not prepared him to deal.

The biggest consequence of their quest for hockey success, however, has been its effect on their personal lives. Drinkwater and Bonaduce have both led the stereotypically itinerate and promiscuous lives of pro athletes. In the case of Drinkwater, this has led to a previously failed marriage and a real inability to commit to a meaningful relationship. Most of *Salvage King, Ya!* is devoted to Drinkwater's screwed-up relationships. When Drinkwater finally does commit to a monogamous relationship with the Intended, the commitment is made at a carnival among games of chance, and the tenuousness of the commitment is consistent with the ironic echo of *Heart of Darkness* in the name he uses for his fiancée. Like the lie Marlow tells Kurtz's Intended at the end of Conrad's novel, the commitment Drinkwater makes to his fiancée emerges out of a complex set of compromises and a morality that is anything but simple. He is right to imagine his ex-wife and several other women sneering *Ha!* (Jarman 1997, 282).

In *The Good Body*, Bonaduce returns to Fredericton at the beginning of the novel with the avowed aim of doing an MA in creative writing, but his real aim is to try to repair some of the damage to his personal life that has been caused by his pursuit of the hockey dream. First and foremost, he wants to reconnect with his son Jason, who is now a university student himself and a member of the University of New Brunswick hockey team. Some of the most powerful scenes in the novel have to do with his fumbling attempts to reconnect. What he hopes is that the camaraderie of being on a team together will be the catalyst for this reconnection. As he puts it: "Set a guy up, no matter how much he hates you he has to come and whack you on the ass" (Gaston 2000, 167). Perhaps the saddest moment in the novel occurs when Bonaduce finally realizes that he will never be the father he now wants to be to Jason. This occurs one day in the dressing room, when it dawns on him that the indifference his son projects towards him is not an act: "because the catchphrase he'd for two hours been breathing to himself, 'We're both pretending I'm no one special,' now transmuted to the thought *He's not pretending*" (201).

The roles of father and husband (or boyfriend before marriage) are fundamental to the traditional masculine identity that is so wrapped up in hockey as well as in the myths of the small town and the North. There is, then, a profound irony in the fact that the pursuit of hockey success turns Bonaduce and Drinkwater – like Leary – into lousy husbands and fathers. This leads to a final important question about the novels: Is the risk not worth the candle? Do the novels finally suggest that seeking after hockey success inevitably involves too great a betrayal of those values associated with being a good Canadian kid?

Certainly there is a strong cautionary element in all three novels. *King Leary* puts a Canadian spin on the dangers of excessive pride and ambition so identified with Shakespeare's "King Lear." *Salvage King, Ya!* portrays a world in which violence against women is at epidemic proportions, and the sexism and macho self-indulgence of the hockey world is shown to be deeply implicated in this. Even if men like Bonaduce and Drinkwater could resist the temptations of the professional hockey world (which come their way even with their limited success), there is still the basic problem of the demands of the lifestyle. As Ken Dryden (1983, 113) puts it in *The Game*, the problem with hockey from the point of view of a family man is that, no matter how hard you try to be a good husband and father, the demands of the season mean that, fundamentally, "your family learns to cope … without you."

And yet the novels are not just cautionary. What they reveal, I think, is a deep-seated ambivalence – literally, a pull in two directions – that reflects how professional sport in general, and hockey in particular, exists in uneasy relationship with the values of thrift, moderation, and, especially, fatherhood that are implicit in being a good Canadian kid. Alongside the cautionary elements there remains in the novels a strong attachment, self-consciously nostalgic perhaps, to the more traditional ideals of masculinity embodied in the characters. The characters are all written with a good deal of affection; it is hard, if you are a lover of hockey, not to feel some attraction to them or not to empathize (if you are a man) with the ideals of camaraderie and honourable heroic action that are promised by the quest. The adolescent Leary and Clinton books in *King Leary* work

to spoof the *Boys' Own* idealism with which hockey and other such
male sporting activity have been wrapped over the decades, but the
fact that the books continue to be popular, in all their strange modern
variations ("*Leary & Clinton Fight the Dogstar People*" [11]) is,
among other things, a sly comment on the part of Quarrington
regarding the continuing attraction of the ideals. Yes, Drinkwater,
Bonaduce, and Leary are all as much dinosaurs as is the sculpture
that overlooks the "Salvage King, Ya!" scrap yard, and there is a
strong sense in the novels that not only are times changing but also
that the changing of the times is not all bad. However, there also
remains something of value in the quest. As Drinkwater puts it, no
matter what has happened during his hockey career, at least he did
not "toil for the Canadian Imperial Bank of Commerce" (Jarman
1997, 40).

The most developed argument for the value of the quest is in *The
Good Body*. Though it is impossible to do justice to the complexities
implied by Bonaduce's story in a single paragraph, an important clue
is found in this passage in which Bonaduce compares the readers of
novels with the fans of hockey: "When you read a book you are
nothing but a fan. And fans of books have nothing – nothing – over
fans of hockey. That a puck is an utterly meaningless thing to chase
is exactly the point. They might never think of it this way, but hockey
fans are drawn to the spectacle of men who are the best in the land
at using their bodies to fulfil *pure desire*" (Gaston 2000, 136). At
the end of *The Good Body*, Bonaduce finds himself in the hospital,
completely incapacitated, having crashed his car and, just as violently,
crashed in his attempts to reconnect with Jason. And yet he still
manages to slur out a joke and to comfort his friend Marg, who
huddles tearfully beside him. What *The Good Body* ultimately
emphasizes is that the key value of the quest for hockey success is
that of life itself: we are creatures of desire, and our desires (to do
things, to accomplish things, to acquire things) can make us mean
and can make us suffer, but they can also lead us, through our very
meanness and suffering, towards enlightenment. Bonaduce learns a
great deal about what really matters when he is trapped in his crashed
car, and what matters is each and every moment – an awareness that
allows him to see "this light streaming glory through the orange

curtain" in his hospital room (269). Bonaduce has his own unreliable tendencies, like Leary, and Drinkwater, and anyone else, but when he implies in the novel's last line that the tears running down his face are not of sorrow but of laughter, we are inclined, at least in part, to believe him.

NOTES

1 Thanks to Doug Beardsley, my colleague and fellow hockey fan, for this title and for the encouragement to write this paper. May the Leafs have a fabulous season and only lose to the Bruins in the conference finals.

2 It was Canadian governor general Vincent Massey (1952–59) who wrote: "Climate plays a great part in giving us our special character, different from that of our southern neighbours. Quite apart from the huge annual bill winter imposes on us … it influences our mentality, produces a sober temperament. Our racial composition [is also mainly] from the British Isles or Northern France … from Scandinavia and Germany, and it is in northwestern Europe that one finds the elements of human stability highly developed. Nothing is more characteristic of Canadians than the inclination to be moderate" (quoted in Berger 1997, 98).

3 For a deeper analysis of what Leary has repressed as part of his quest see my own "Getting off a Good One" (Dopp 1999, 53ff).

4 According to Stan Fischler (1984, 73) in Hockey's 100, when the historical Clancy showed up to try out for the Ottawa Senators in 1921 he weighed in at 125 pounds – as a defenceman!

6

The Mystery of a Canadian Father of Hockey Stories
Leslie McFarlane's Break Away from the Hardy Boys

KAREN E.H. SKINAZI

Leslie McFarlane, born in 1902 in Carleton Place, Ontario, was deeply invested in his Canadianness. His many careers reflect his passion: in his 1940s work for the *Canadian Theatre of the Air* (writing scripts for the radio) and his job with Canada's Department of Munitions and Supply (writing speeches for the public relations department), McFarlane spent a great deal of time turning the culture of his country into a language for the people. He also turned that culture into accessible images; working for the National Film Board of Canada, he travelled the country making films about nationally acclaimed personages and landmarks, including *The Quest*, a film about the Canadian discoverers of insulin, Frederick Banting and Charles Best; and *Herring Hunt*, a movie about BC fishing that was an Oscar nominee in 1953 (Greenwald 2004, 211). He later joined the Canadian Broadcasting Corporation (CBC) television, where he became a network story editor. In 1960, *Liberty* magazine named McFarlane Canada's best television playwright of the year, and one of the shows he worked on, *The Unforeseen*, was named the best dramatic show on Canadian television (230).

McFarlane spent much of his life creating and promoting Canadian traditions, but at present, people who study him (be it through academic scholarship or nostalgic interest)[1] do so because they are determined to uncover the mystery behind "Franklin W. Dixon," writer of the popular American series, the Hardy Boys. Franklin W. Dixon never existed, but McFarlane was the first to adopt the pen name, and he used it for longer than any other ghostwriter of the Hardy Boys. For almost twenty years, McFarlane, as Dixon, described the escapades of two teenage sleuths who, in every new book, solved a new mystery.

The Hardy Boys, the children's detective series created by Edward Stratemeyer in 1926,[2] and written by a number of ghostwriters, has been popular among boys for almost a century. Its books have been reprinted and occasionally updated, and its spin-offs include a book series called "Casefiles," running from the 1980s to the 1990s; another called "The All New Hardy Boys, Undercover Brothers," which also has a graphic novel version, "The Hardy Boys, Undercover Brothers, Graphic Novels," both of which started in 2005 and are currently in full-swing; several television series, running in the 1950s, 1960s, 1970s, and 1990s; and PC games, which debuted in 2008. Along with its sister series, Nancy Drew (which was updated in a 2007 film), the Hardy Boys series has sold over 200 million books.

McFarlane wrote more Hardy Boys books than any of the series' other ghostwriters, and his late-life and postmortem fame rests on this work. This connection is unfortunate, however, not only because McFarlane took no pride in the series but also because, in the Hardy Boys, Canada seems as much a nonentity as was the series' "author," Franklin W. Dixon. In this chapter, I illuminate the body of McFarlane's works that have been overshadowed by the Hardy Boys. McFarlane was a man who saw Canada as a country that lacked a mythology, and he set out to transform a favourite sport into the language of nationhood. One of Canada's most prolific writers, McFarlane was writing hockey stories as early as the 1930s, and he continued to add to the literature throughout his life. McFarlane shared his passion with his son, Brian, who grew up to be the honourary president of the Society for International Hockey Research and a Hockey Hall of Fame inductee. Brian McFarlane is known to many Canadian hockey fans as a former Toronto Maple Leafs' telecaster, and he is known to even more fans as the sportscaster for *Hockey Night in Canada* who, for twenty-five years, shared his colourful commentary on the game. Brian McFarlane also writes children's stories, and they are of the same genre as his father's. Through his tireless writing, his belief in the nation, and his love of hockey, Leslie McFarlane helped to set the stage for his son, Brian, as well as to inspire scores of other Canadian children's writers to narrate the nation through hockey tales.

THE HARDY BOYS

I made no mention of the fact that my father could justly be called Canada's most productive contemporary writer ... Nor did I comment on the number of Hardy Boys books that he wrote under the nom de plume Franklin W. Dixon, books which sold in the millions, making him, I am proud to say, Canada's best selling author of all time. (Brian McFarlane, Introduction to Leslie McFarlane [1996])

Brian McFarlane gives more than a passing nod to his father's hockey stories. After all, long before Brian McFarlane tied his first skate, announced his first game, or tuned his first typewriter, his father lit up the arena on the page with the fervour of the patriot and hockey-lover. But even Brian is proud of his father because he was Canada's "best selling author of all time" – because of the Hardy Boys. Those who study McFarlane are generally set on writing exposés of the "secrets" of the multi-million-dollar Stratemeyer Syndicate for which McFarlane wrote the Hardy Boys. Following in the tradition of McFarlane's own 1976 autobiography, *Ghost of the Hardy Boys*, are Carol Billman's 1986 *The Secret of the Stratemeyer Syndicate: Nancy Drew, the Hardy Boys, and the Million Dollar Fiction Factory*; Deidre Johnson's 1993 *Edward Stratemeyer and the Stratemeyer Syndicate*; and Marilyn Greenwald's 2004 biography of McFarlane, *The Secret of the Hardy Boys: Leslie McFarlane and the Stratemeyer Syndicate*.

But the Syndicate did not define McFarlane, even if it has recently come to define McFarlane scholarship. Before he became a writer of the Hardy Boys, McFarlane had plans that were quite different. "I had my standards and these were the standards of Henry Louis Mencken," he reminisces in his autobiography (McFarlane 1976b, 136). As he sent his early fiction off to magazines, he pictured the reviews: "'A new voice in adventure fiction' ... 'brings the Canadian Northland alive'" (144). McFarlane imagined himself to be the next Great Canadian writer; that destiny, however, was not to be. McFarlane's books became incredibly famous, but McFarlane never became a Great Canadian writer. Despite – or perhaps because of – the author's "success," his dream failed miserably. Greenwald's recent biography of McFarlane might help some fans begin to rethink the fate of the author; one critic of the biography writes that he was touched by McFarlane's life story – "the melancholy story of a writer who dreamed of writing the great Canadian novel but created the Hardy Boys instead" (Ott 2004, 1503). Greenwald shows that, throughout his life, McFarlane worked on this "Great Canadian Novel," a novel "of the development of northern Ontario and all the romance and adventure that went with it," but he never had the time to finish it – a problem she attributes to his being so busy with the Stratemeyer Syndicate (Greenwald 2004, xiii–xiv).

Yet Greenwald misses a crucial point. While McFarlane never changed the face of Canadian fiction through his intended vehicle, the "Great Canadian Novel," he did help create the traditions of Canadian children's literature through a vehicle more suited to his style, temperament, and taste: hockey stories. Between vapid Hardy Boy mysteries, in which two perfect all-American boys contained all signs of subversiveness in their wholly contrived world, McFarlane wrote about hockey players who came from working-class families, boys whose fathers were struggling miners or dead, not famous American detectives. His hockey stories combined sharp Canadian reality with the smooth frills of fiction, allowing his readers to be exposed, through his writing, to the grittiness of life but leaving them with a solid feeling of satisfaction at the end of each book – a sentiment he felt Canadians deserved. When he moved away from Canada in 1926, he described the country that he left behind as one inhabited by a "dour lot, full of deprecation and mistrust, overly cautious, resistant to change and much given to religion, which meant that most of them were glum and disposed to frown on any kind of pleasure," a country with a miserable climate and a primitive culture (McFarlane 1976b, 39–40). This national image would become the very image that he would both channel and change in his hockey writing.

McFarlane did not realize this desire to change the face of Canada before his stint in the United States as a ghostwriter for the Stratemeyer Syndicate, a company built by a man who was every bit the patriot that McFarlane was. Unlike McFarlane, however, Edward Stratemeyer was an American patriot. Stratemeyer expressed his patriotism through the children's literature he produced, in which: "The travel adventures and those historical fiction titles set in foreign lands compare Americans favorably with other countries and people. The historical fiction taking place in the past eulogizes America's heritage and the progress of civilization. The outdoor stories illustrate the richness of America's forests and wildlife – America the bountiful" (Johnson 1993, 77). Ironically, Bayport, the town in which the Hardy Boys reside, can easily be read as an American twist on the Canadian city of Haileybury, Ontario, where McFarlane grew up. The landscape sounds remarkably like that of McFarlane's hometown; its borders are sheer cliffs rising above the water, covered in scars and old mining caves and tunnels. But the Hardy Boys, we are told, are "healthy American boys of high school age"; they are sons of a celebrated *American* detective, and they live under Prohibition, in an unnamed "State" (McFarlane 1927a, 20; McFarlane 1927b, 83).

Writing for the series, McFarlane strangely omits all mention of Canada except as a snow-bound dead zone. And even in the snow, there is no play, no hockey. Why did he keep his passions out of the writing for which he (or at least his pseudonym) achieved such fame? Perhaps the answer lies in the very popularity of the series; many a Canadian writer has rapidly found that Canadian local colour wins over few readers. In *When Words Deny the World*, Canadian writer Stephen Henighan recounts a story about one of his publishing failures. He is told that his book, lauded as a "great story" with "smart writing" that is "beautifully plotted," cannot sell, and the reason for this is simple: "'It's too Canadian!'" (Henighan 2002, 95).

But perhaps McFarlane simply wanted to keep his "real" writing out of his American cash cow. McFarlane swiftly grew to despise the Hardy Boys, calling Frank and Joe "the obnoxious Hardy brats"; yet, he wrote for the series from 1927 to 1946 (Greenwald 2004, 142). Despite many attempts to free himself from the Stratemeyer Syndicate's yoke, he found that the financial security that accompanied the Hardy Boys was simply absent when it came to his "Canadian" writing.

In 1945, in the twenty-fourth book of the series, *The Short-wave Mystery*, and near the end of McFarlane's tenure as the Hardy Boys ghostwriter, he finally takes his Boys on a Canadian adventure for the first time.[3] The representation of Canada is stark; it hearkens of the cold, daunting wilderness that is threaded throughout Canadian "adult" fiction. Pursuing a crook, Frank and Joe set off across the border.[4] As their plane descends onto a frozen lake, Canada is described as a blank, cold slate. In his brief sketch of the land, in a wholly unromantic and unglorified vision, the narrator will not allow a thing – anything, it seems – to make the landscape distinct and identifiable. "No monuments or landmarks guide the stranger," McFarlane might have written, as Douglas LePan (1987) did in his well-known poem, "A Country without a Mythology." What is the place, what marks it? Only the desolate white of winter. What do the boys see? McFarlane writes: "Below them the land had grown white, for winter comes early to the Hudson Bay country. Snow lay on the frozen ground" (McFarlane 1945, 200).

The boys trudge onward, heading north, always north. The scene is narrated by its absence of features. McFarlane (1945, 2003) writes: "At the top of each hill they scanned the country ahead, hoping for some glimpse of river," but the boys glimpse nothing. Finally, "when they reached the summit of a long snow-swept ridge," they see water, but even this vision of something is narrated by lack for the narrator adds that "there was neither plane nor cabin in sight" (203). Later, we read that the boys "had seen nothing resembling a cabin, a plane, or any kind of shelter" (204). The narrative weaves between the missing monuments and the interminable cold. There is little refuge from the world of winter in this Canada. There is no culture and almost no life. The narrator, through his series of negations, creates a Canada that is not now, not here; it is a country torn from time. A reader might have a hard time imagining, if s/he witnessed only the austere image fashioned for *The Short-wave Mystery*, that McFarlane was a great promoter of Canada, its nature, its culture, its people, and what he considered its sport.

It is possible to see McFarlane's two images of Canada – the almost invisible, harsh place in the Hardy Boys, and the thriving, adventurous place of his non-Hardy Boys stories – as two sides of the same coin. The winterscape of Canada in the Hardy Boys resembles Archibald Lampman's poem, "In November," where the narrator stumbles upon a "bleak and sandy spot," a "silent sober place" with only dead mulleins for company – the place that Northrop Frye, Margaret Atwood, and others have seen in Canadian writing time and again. Frye (1971, 141) argues that "winter is only one symbol, though a very obvious one, of the central theme of Canadian poetry"; and Atwood (1972, 49), in her 1972 guidebook to Canadian literature, *Survival,* shows the trend of Canadian writers to indicate that "the true and only season here is winter: the others are either preludes to it or mirages concealing it." Likewise, literary critic Sherrill E. Grace (1991, 247), who compares the American mythology of the West with Canada's of the North, writes: "Canadians invented themselves as northerners, and they keep doing so despite their terror of ice, snow, and drowned or frozen corpses." Yet, describing the wondrous moments of enjoyment from the bobsled to the rink outside of the American series, McFarlane (1996, 44) declares in one of his autobiographical books, *A Kid in Haileybury,* "Winter is for kids." The barrenness of *The Short-wave Mystery* is covered by games and cavorting children in his Canadian-content writing. The winterscape of his hockey stories, furthermore, articulates the boyishness hidden in the Canadian spirit, in all its nostalgic sentiment. If frozen corpses beneath the ice make up the Canadian adult literary topography, the hockey players above it skate on the Canadian children's literary landscape. Hockey allows for the sense of *play* in Canadian stories of frozen terrain – and, as such, hockey is the appropriate sport and subject for Canadian children's literature.[5]

NARRATING THE HOCKEY NATION

If there's a goal that everyone remembers, it was back in old '72
We all squeezed the stick and we all pulled the trigger,
And all I remember is sitting beside you.
You said you didn't give a fuck about hockey

And I never saw someone say that before
You held my hand and we walked home the long way
You were loosening my grip on Bobby Orr. (Downie 1998)

In the towns of the Canadian north country, hockey is more than a game; it
is almost a religion. (McFarlane 1933b)

Turn on the radio anywhere in Canada, and you might hear the way that Canadians embed hockey into the national imagination: the eponymous hero of Moxy Früvous's (1994b) "King of Spain" is called by the Toronto Maple Leafs to drive the Zamboni; Jane Siberry's song "Hockey" (1989) waxes nostalgic about Sunday afternoons on the frozen river; the Tragically Hip's "Fifty Mission Cap" (Downie 1992) tells a ghost story about Bill Barilko, whose goal won the 1951 Stanley Cup;[6] Tom Cochrane (1988) announces his son would be "up at five / Take shots till eight, make the thing drive / Out after school, back on ice / That was his life," because he was going to play in "The Big League"; and Stompin' Tom Connors' classic "The Hockey Song" (Connors, 1973) invites listeners into the revelry of the "good ol' hockey game." There is nothing "natural" about hockey's role in the Canadian consciousness; cultural critics recognize the problem of viewing hockey "as if it represents an organic connection with the Canadian landscape or national psyche – an essence that exists outside of the influences of social structure and history" (Gruneau and Whitson 1993, 25). Yet the tradition of reiterating hockey's importance in Canada is long-standing.

Part of the Canadian rhetoric of the public world of politics, the private world of family, and even the interior life of the spirit, hockey imagery is everywhere. In "Fireworks," the song excerpted in the first epigraph of this section, the initial image has multiple layers of meaning that reveal hockey's national rhetorical significance (Downie 1998). The description of the Summit Series collapses the distinction between game and war, turning a physical arena into a political one, where cold warriors can at least meet face to face, stick to stick, and fight for victory. Team Canada becomes a representative team of Canadians as it plays the Soviet Union in an epic battle of West against East. The broadcast from the Luzhniki Arena in the Lenin

Sports Complex becomes the figurative space where Canadian listeners and watchers can form a community. The goal is one that "everyone" remembers. Playing to a Canadian audience, the band need not explain that the goal is Paul Henderson's and that it won, for Canada, the 1972 Summit Series between Canada and the Soviet Union. The band's assumptions are clear: because "everyone remembers," their inclusiveness demands a national solidarity for those invested in hockey as well as those not so invested, those who watched the Summit Series, and even those not yet born. And yet, another, and equally important, way of looking at this image is on a much smaller scale than the political: hockey is necessarily a part of familial relationships, "Fireworks" insists. We know that the interlocutor, who is also the spouse, can "loosen" the singer's relationships to hockey and nation, but it seems that she cannot quite dissolve them. In fact, the way that the singer follows the image of the hockey game, with the explanation of "We hung out together nearly every single moment / 'Cause that's what we thought married people do," turns the game itself into a kind of wedding, almost echoing another Canadian band, Moxy Früvous, whose troika of life's stages has playing hockey coming first: "We'd like to play hockey, have kids and grow old" (Moxy Früvous, 1994a). Finally, in the Tragically Hip song, the grip that the narrator claims hockey has on him, the sheer belief in its power, functions as religious conviction. In this light, it is hard not to read Don Cherry's collars as marking him as the Priest of Hockey since hockey in Canada, in McFarlane's words, is "almost a religion" (McFarlane 1933b, 79).

For Canadians throughout the twentieth century and into the twenty-first, hockey has proven a binding force in narrative. The Tragically Hip's singer/songwriter Gordon Downie is, like Brian McFarlane, an "heir" to the love of hockey; his godfather, Harry Sinden, was the coach of Team Canada during the 1972 Summit Series about which he sings. He is also only one of many Canadian storytellers who has striven to convey the relationship between Canadianness and hockey. The earliest description of hockey by a Canadian writer comes by way of Thomas Chandler Haliburton, who recounted, in his tale of a Nova Scotian childhood at the turn of the nineteenth century, games of "hurley" on the ice. Hockey (or hurley) writing was not popular at the time, but had Haliburton (1796–1865) lived long enough, he would have found he was succeeded by many Canadian hockey writers spinning tales of the sticks – fiction and non-fiction, geared towards adults and towards children. McFarlane, whose tales of hockey surely cooled the brows of many a sweaty child waiting for the hot Canadian summer nights to end and hockey season to begin anew, finds his place at the vanguard of this tradition.

Thanks to McFarlane and the writers that followed him into the literary rink, hockey stories are an integral part of Canadian children's literature. In 1997, the journal *Canadian Children's Literature* hosted two issues entitled "What's Canadian about Canadian Children's Literature?" Both issues featured pictures that prominently referred to hockey stories on their front covers. The first bore a cheering child in a Toronto Maple Leafs sweater, and the second a mother holding up a Toronto Maple Leafs sweater to a boy who has passed out next to his worn-out Canadiens sweater. Although the essays beneath those images of hockey discuss a myriad of topics prominent in Canadian children's literature, it is notable that the editors could only come up with one kind of picture, representing one kind of Canadian children's literature, to grace their journal covers.

Hockey might be said to occupy the Canadian imagination as baseball does the American one (see Patell 1993). If the "established sports of a society mirror the culture of that society," then baseball and hockey are natural national parallels (Voigt cited in Patell 1993, 403). Although football has become the United States' most popular sport, the American imagination has always favoured baseball, a fact played out in American literature. Historian Jacques Barzun (1954, 159) wrote, "Whoever wants to know the heart and mind of America had better learn baseball, the rules and realities of the game"; hockey functions the same way in Canada. Accounts of father-son bonding are popular in American baseball and Canadian hockey stories. Cooperstown, New York, and Windsor, Nova Scotia – the so-called birthplaces of baseball and hockey, respectively – became "twin towns" in 1996, a municipal decision that promotes the towns as national iconographic equivalents. Yet die-hard Canadian hockey fans will refute this logic; hockey, they will say, is far more meaningful to Canadians than is baseball to Americans. Perhaps this statement is true. For a country whose mythology consists of believing that it has no mythology, the few symbols it does have become grand in scope.

Hockey is, of course, not exclusively Canadian, just as it is not exclusively for children; however, it often functions as such in the Canadian imaginary. Write the authors of *Hockey Night in Canada: Sport, Identities and Cultural Politics,* in the spirit of Benedict Anderson's (1983) *Imagined Communities*:

> Like an old song whose melody keeps running through your head, hockey's influences are something we can't forget. Hockey was the one thing in our youth that virtually all boys seemed to have in common – the stuff of everyday conversation, the regularly shared experience of after-school and weekend play. Perhaps the strongest of all our feelings of commonality came when we watched *Hockey Night in Canada* on Saturday nights. Even at an early age the TV program made us feel like part of a national community. (Gruneau and Whitson 1993, 2)

For Gruneau and Whitson, as for the various people they quote – Ken Dryden, Roy MacGregor, Al Purdy, Scott Young, and Peter Gzowski among them – hockey is the defining image of Canada and is the culture within which they grew up. This culture, however, is not the culture within which McFarlane grew up; rather, it is the one he helped create.

WRITING THE WRIST SHOT

The Canadian boy grew up in a proper state of humility. His reading taught him that British boys were courageous, daring, ingenious and always in the right so that they always came out on top while incidentally, having more fun than anyone. At the same time his reading taught him that American boys were likewise courageous, daring and ingenious and, moreover, so devoted to honest toil that they always wound up rich. Canadian boys, who apparently had no history worth writing about and no forebears who ever made it as heroes of books, were clearly made of inferior stuff. (McFarlane 1976b)

It was a body-check and a clean one, but if Jerry Flynn deserved the "Dynamite" appellation it was on that stop.

Newton was stopped as if he had been shot. His skates flew out from under him, he staggered and went to the ice with a crash that left him sprawling. And while the Redshirt fans were yelling, Jerry had the puck and was streaking down the ice.

He was at center ice and going like mad. A wing came flying down the frozen surface in pursuit, but Jerry turned on an extra burst of speed, and the Greyhound wing's frantic stab at the puck missed. He saw the defense crouching, waiting for him; he hit straight for the center, let drive with a low, whistling, savage shot just as they closed in to nail him.

They nailed him, smashed him in a bone-crushing sandwich. But his shot was away, and it was one of those red-hot drives that will trick the best of goalies. Even as the defensemen smacked into Jerry, the goalie was frantically lunging to stop that blistering shot, only to have it whiz beneath his arm and into the twine. (McFarlane 1975a)

While McFarlane's hockey players inherited some of the adventure and intrigue of his Hardy Boys, these Canadian creations of McFarlane, unlike their American relatives, engage in less-than-savoury endeavours. They also take their hockey quite seriously. Exciting and attuned to a hockey-loving audience, McFarlane's stories vividly describe the sport without lapsing overly into play-by-plays and are didactic without being sentimental.

From his early days as a hockey commentator and editor, to his stories of the 1930s in the magazine *Sport Story*, to his 1953 documentary film about hockey in Canada ("Here's Hockey"), to the children's Checkmate Series he wrote for Methuen in the 1960s and 1970s, McFarlane spent much of his life thinking and writing about his favourite sport. He often revelled in a time "before the days of the big gates, before hockey became a multimillion dollar business, before Stanley Cup playdowns ran to dozens of games, before the big-league teams could claim youngsters in the draft" (McFarlane 1975a, 10). To McFarlane, this time was a simpler one and a better one – a time when Canada seemed to have no history, no culture, no power – and yet, hockey was a real sport. He imagined hockey to be big enough to fill Canada's holes; but hockey, like all cultural rituals, needed its interpreters.

Unlike Frank and Joe Hardy, the boys who inhabit McFarlane's hockey stories are healthy (Anglo) *Canadian* boys, generally from small towns, often developing their senses of self through the possibilities hockey offered – both internally, through the examinations of skill, perseverance, and integrity, and externally, through interactions with Americans and French Canadians and fame. In his early story, "Throwing Down McCloskie," published in 1933, several years into his writing of the Hardy Boys, McFarlane created a character named Chesty Kane who is a successful goaltender; in some ways, he's a one-man show. The announcer, perhaps cast in the mould of a young McFarlane, gleefully tells the crowd that, despite Cousineau's banishment to the penalty box and the opposing Greenshirt players' great skills, the Wolves have a fighting chance because of the goalie: "It's in! It's in – No – Kane gets his foot on it. He's down in the net – players are piling on top of him. Kane saved that one! The referee is calling them back. If the Wolves win this game, they can thank Kane, folks. He's a wonder!" (McFarlane 1933a, 23). Kane, winning the game for the Wolves, expects glory, but he is treated instead to aloofness. His teammate Cousineau has only unkind words for him, and the coach is not much friendlier. How has the star player gone wrong?

McFarlane wants to teach his character a sense of humility, but not too much. McFarlane is highly invested in creating just the right sort of hero for his hockey stories. Under the literary influences of the much-read British series the Boys' Own and the American series the Rover Boys, Canadian boys learned much humility; it was the British chaps and the American lads, after all, who were the heroes of all the stories. The Canadian boys, seeing no representation of Canadian heroism, concluded that they could never be heroes of any kind. McFarlane sadly reports: "This probably explains why the adult, male Canadian today is a docile, modest fellow who knows his place and is never given to throwing his weight around" (McFarlane 1976b, 153).[7]

McFarlane's American boy-heroes, the Hardy Boys, show no signs of Canadian docility. Yet McFarlane found the brashness associated with Americanness no more appealing. It is the middle ground he aims for in his hockey stories, where readers find a "purer" version of the sport; hockey is less about survival and more about polishing both skills and ethics. McFarlane has his character stoop low, by his standards; Kane consorts with Maxie Mandel, a shady character (with a Jewish name, to boot!) who tries to get him to throw his game to get back at McCloskie, the coach who would not support the star. When that plan fails, the scheming Mandel blackmails Kane. But in the end, integrity triumphs – because hockey is a game that is bigger than folly. Chesty Kane cannot help but do his best. After all, "That was goal-keeping. It was marvellous coordination of eye and muscle that had sent Chesty into the big-time hockey. He could no more have restrained himself from attempting those hair-raising stops in the heat of the battle than he could have restrained himself from breathing" (McFarlane 1933a, 28). In the end, he plays to win.

"Why, he couldn't throw the game if he tried," declares the narrator of the character who resembles a hockey-playing twin of Shoeless Joe Jackson – the version of Shoeless Joe that did *not* throw the 1919 World Series, that is. "Hockey! It was born in him. Hockey – the game! Bigger than himself" (McFarlane 1933a, 31). Kane wins the game, McCloskie is proud of him, the gangsters Mandel has promised would kill Kane had he won actually wanted him to win, and the "cheap skate … Mandel" has run off, leaving Kane without the devil's influence henceforth (32). A happy ending indeed.

The Canadian content is subtle in the first story that McFarlane placed with the American magazine *Sport Story*, probably because he figured that the magazine aimed for a larger audience. That assumption, however, was unfounded. In the same issue that contained "Throwing Down McCloskie" the reader would also find an article entitled "Hockey Brothers." There, he/she would learn that almost "every family with more than one son sends the brothers out into the world to become hockey players" (Hendy 1933, 85). What the reader might notice, however, is that it is not "every family" but something closer to "every Canadian family"! As the author, Jim

Hendy, reels off the "hockey brothers" – the Smiths, the Patricks, the Cooks, the Bouchers, the Carsons, the Cleghorns, and so on – he also locates these men. The Smiths are from Ottawa, Ontario; the Patricks are of Drummondville, Quebec; the Cooks are from Kingston, Ontario; the Bouchers are from Ottawa, Ontario; the Carsons are from Bracebridge, Ontario; the Cleghorns are from Montreal, Quebec. The list goes on.

In fact, it seems almost as though an American had to justify his relationship to hockey. In Eric Rober's (1933, 5) "Rink Jinx," another story in *Sport Story*, a character named Sonny Vanin needs to win over his teammates who were "curious to see just how much an American-born, college-trained hockey player could do." Rober explicitly contrasts this handsome, educated American with his peers. The presumably French-Canadian Desmains, we read, is "ugly" and "low-browed" (6). The narrator explains that the two "were opposites: Vanin, the educated, refined college product; Desmains, the ignorant, bluntspoken result of plenty of hard knocks, dirty deals, and a rough-and-ready game, hockey" (ibid.). The narrative reminds readers constantly, in a kind of refrain, that Vanin has to show everyone "what an American-born, college-bred hockey player could do" (7). Interestingly, invested as Vanin is in his "American" ideology – playing as though it were a "solo" game and basing his actions on the belief that "a man was what he rated himself" – Vanin fails to note that Desmains, or "Frenchy," as he is called, is a valuable friend (13).

Perhaps coming to recognize that Canadianness was more than acceptable in hockey writing, McFarlane (1933b), in "The Wrist Shot, his second publication in *Sport Story*, cast clearly Canadian characters in the Canadian north country. The hockey players in this story work at the Eldorado Mine. This choice of locale is not random; McFarlane first wrote about Gilbert Labine, co-founder of the Eldorado Gold Mine, in his *Maclean's* article, "A Canadian Eldorado," published in 1931, wherein he describes the sub-Arctic conditions faced by Labine (a fellow Haileyburian) and E.C. St Paul (his partner and co-veteran of the Cobalt rush). McFarlane's (1931, 12) article details the men's journey through one of the "most forsaken spots on the face of the globe where they hoped to find the end of the rainbow." McFarlane writes of these men with awe, claiming that the "LaBine find" in the "Canadian Eldorado" could "play a part of the greatest historical importance in the destiny of the Dominion" (13). Of course it did play a major role in Canada's history – and the world's. Little could McFarlane have realized that the uranium Labine discovered would become the source of the atomic bomb that killed tens of thousands of people in Hiroshima some fifteen years later.

Although McFarlane could not have known how prescient his comments about Labine's uranium would be, what he did know was that this was a great find and that it was made by a Canadian. And what was at stake for McFarlane, throughout his career, was elevating Canadian culture. So it is no surprise that he wove the miners of Eldorado into a story for an American magazine.

In "The Wrist Shot," we learn how contagious the passion for hockey is in the north country. "Hockey in the two rival gold camps was more than a game; it was a fever," explains the narrator (McFarlane 1933b, 79). The boss in the story reminds his workers, who are also his players, of the gravity of hockey: "'You men know,' Cardigan said in his clipped, metallic voice, 'that we take our hockey seriously in the mining camps'" (77). How seriously? The men soon find out: if they lose the game, they lose their jobs. The time is the Great Depression; the question on everyone's lips is, "where can a man get another job in these times?" (78). How seriously? We read of bribery, kidnapping, threats of murder – all over a game of hockey.

In the end, the heroes prevail. The Eldorado player who is almost killed discovers that "the wrist shot had again proved its worth" – not only does it win the team the game but it also saves the protagonist's life when he shoots the puck into the gun-wielding villain's face. As in *The Dynamite Flynns* (McFarlane 1975a), in which one of the Flynns is forced into a gambling racket, almost killed in a car crash, and wrongly imprisoned by competitors determined to break up the incredible dynamism of the hockey-playing Flynns, in "The Wrist Shot" hockey is both great fun and a game of life and death.

The Dynamite Flynns tells the story of two cousins raised in a hockey household. Their uncle, Iron Mick, teaches the boys the sport for fun; he does not want them to pursue it as a career. Mick's sudden stroke means the Flynns have no money for college – or anything else. The boys are soon off to the Redshirt Camp, and, after making the team, they reach Toronto, the Mecca of hockey. The narrator, conflating place and sport in one image, exclaims with zeal: "Toronto! Maple Leaf Gardens! Yonge Street. Opening night of the hockey season." The place is necessarily a Canadian one for, although the Flynns travel to Chicago and Detroit and other hockey-playing cities, no place exemplifies the essence of hockey for McFarlane and his characters as does Canada.

In addition to the nationalistic engine driving McFarlane is a moralistic one, and *The Dynamite Flynns* is, as is typical of McFarlane's yarns for youngsters, a cautionary tale. On arrival in the big city, the narrator tells readers that "the tempo of Toronto is enough to knock any rookie off-balance, at first" (McFarlane 1975a, 42). Although he adds, "hockey fans are hockey fans in any rink," the big city lure outweighs the comfort of routine (ibid.). One of the Flynns allows himself to be seduced by fame and glory, and he is almost destroyed by his ego. He forgets that hockey is about love of the game – and he suffers the consequences. McFarlane needs readers to recognize the sheer thrill of a good, clean game. The Flynns' victory on the ice is a victory over vice. When the Flynns learn that their competitor Newton has aided in Dan Flynn's downfall, Jerry Flynn had "only one burning desire – to defeat Newton where the defeat would sting the worst. On the ice" (115).

Though it is exciting to follow the intrigues that are raised and solved over games of hockey in McFarlane's writing, there is something to be said as well about how exciting it is to follow the games themselves. In *Squeeze Play*, we can see how he exalts in his description of how Furlong, uncovered, *steams* to the goal mouth. He writes: "The pass came across to him and he let fly. Eaton took it on his chest, grabbed vainly for the puck, and then fell forward to smother it. But the puck rolled under his arm, and then Furlong was in like a flash. He scooped it up, flipped it over Eaton into the net" (McFarlane 1975b, 69). You can almost hear McFarlane's words being announced in a 1920s movie theatre to an audience of anxious fans. In his stories, McFarlane seems to recapture what he believed was hockey's heyday – the 1920s, when, as he writes in his autobiography:

> Stick-handling, all but a lost art these days, was highly esteemed because a forward pass was not permissible. To see Shorty Green or Bill Cook thread their way through a barricade of swinging sticks, to see Charlie Langlois or Babe Donnelly wind up behind the net and go zigzagging all the way down the ice to draw out the goalie and slam the puck into the net was to see hockey at its thrilling best ... With only two substitutes the regulars had to be iron men to go at top speed for sixty minutes. No such nonsense as a minute of ice time and a three-minute rest. (McFarlane 1976b, 113–4)

McFarlane raves about the goalies, the referee, the goal umpire, the natural ice, and, most of all, the fans, who gave themselves up to mass lunacy. He found inspiration in the sport that drew all kinds of ordinary Canadians from stern, religious Canadian life onto the ice or into the stands, sharing a passion. *This* Canada was what made him passionate not only about stick-handling and shutouts but also about nationhood.

CANADIAN CHILDREN'S HOCKEY STORIES

McFarlane carved the way for later hockey writers. He did not begin as a writer of hockey fiction – or of fiction at all. As a young man in the 1920s, McFarlane was the sports editor for the *Star Weekly* in Sudbury, Ontario, and this is where he learned to narrate hockey. He went to all the hockey games, and, as he describes it:

> The telegraph people invited me to dictate the play-by-play accounts to their man. When a game was played in Sudbury I would take up position beside the operator, start talking, and keys would start clicking. Two hundred and fifty miles away, in Sault Ste Marie, a man at a typewriter would translate the clicks into words and hammer out pages of script, in duplicate. These pages would be rushed to the local movie theatres, the lounges

of the curling clubs and the hockey clubs, to all the places
where the Sault Ste Marie fans could gather. (McFarlane
1976b, 116)

The same process was repeated in other cities as he followed the
Sudbury Wolves around the province. "So even before radio arrived,"
McFarlane writes, "I became one of hockey's first broadcasters with
the power to interrupt pool games, curling matches or the screen
adventures of Colleen Moore and Richard Dix while hundreds of fans
hung on my words and read from the long takes of copy" (ibid.).

Only after he was already embroiled with the Stratemeyer Syndicate
did McFarlane begin penning hockey fiction. James Keeline (2000),
a McFarlane aficionado, has discovered a large number of hard-to-
find McFarlane titles. McFarlane wrote many, many stories, and
some of the titles Keeline lists make immediately clear McFarlane's
material: "The Wrist Shot," "Goal Getter," "Hockey Highway,"
"Dynamite Flynns," "Hockey Comes First," "The Two Pucketeers,"
"Trouble on Skates," "Rink Buddies," "Goalie Garrison's Goal,"
"Skating Fool," "Don't Bet on Hockey," and "Stanley Cup Jitters"
were all published in the magazine *Sport Story* in the 1930s.
McFarlane's (2005, 2006) hockey stories have recently been collected
and republished as two collections called *Leslie McFarlane's Hockey
Stories,* edited by his son Brian (and with the covers bearing the
qualification: "Best-selling author of the Hardy Boys"!).

McFarlane might be little-remembered now, but we can only
imagine the number of people who were inspired by his pucketeers
skating down hockey highways. He could hardly have known that
he would help spawn a country of hockey writers. Between the time
that McFarlane began writing his hockey stories and the time that
his literary career – and life – ended, the only truly prominent hockey
fiction was Scott Young's trilogy, *Scrubs on Skates* (1952), *Boy on
Defense* (1953), and *A Boy at the Leafs Camp* (1963).

McFarlane wrote the majority of his hockey stories in the 1930s,
but before he died, he made a comeback – in much the same way
as does Duke Blake in McFarlane's story, "Nobody Plays Forever."
Duke Blake (perhaps an allusion to Canadiens' coach Toe Blake) is
an older hockey player about whom a sports columnist writes,

"Everyone in hockey seems to realize that Duke is all washed up except Duke Blake himself" (McFarlane 1975b, 85). Duke Blake has his last chance. During his last game, Duke was "checking, blocking, stick-handling like a wizard"; soon he had "batted the disk into the open net," and "as the light flashed, and the Mohawk crowd groaned with disappointment, and the Flyers flung their sticks in the air," the game ends (108, 110). We read that "the siren sounded. Duke heard it with a smile. It was the end of his hockey career. Now he could hang up his skates with honor" (110). McFarlane was no different. Despite spending most of his time on an American series in which he had not much interest, he was able to return to the literary ice and end his career the way he began it.

As a result, the 1960s and 1970s had McFarlane publishing hockey stories again, mostly revisions of pieces he had written for *Sport Story* in the 1930s: *McGonigle Scores* (McFarlane 1966), *Squeeze Play* (McFarlane 1975b), *The Dynamite Flynns* (McFarlane 1975a), and *Breakaway* (McFarlane 1976a). Canadian hockey stories, in particular those classified under juvenile fiction, began to proliferate at this point, as can be seen in table 1. The writers steep themselves in the Canadian tradition of hockey fiction, even as they challenge and revise it. When Etienne takes his cousin to play ice hockey for the first time in David Bouchard and Dean Griffiths's *That's Hockey*, for example, he explains that everyone has to wear a number nine Canadiens hockey sweater – "You know, like the Rocket" – words practically taken from the narrator of Carrier's "The Hockey Sweater"(Bouchard and Griffiths 2004, 4). While Carrier's characters extend their loyalty to Maurice Richard much further, copying the way he styled his hair, laced his skates, and taped his stick, Bouchard's boys take a less fanatic approach. Roy MacGregor, who began his hockey writing career with *The Last Season*, says he owes his inspiration to Scott Young – although he feels *Scrubs on Skates* is not quite relevant anymore. In 1995, MacGregor created a series called the Screech Owls about a Canadian hockey team. The books came at the request of the publishers, McClelland and Stewart, who, in turn, had been asked by librarians to create books suitable for boys reluctant to read (which is to say, those aged nine to thirteen) (Jenkinson 1998). Although the publishers imagined a series focused primarily on hockey, MacGregor had a better idea: "Why don't we use the best methods for getting kids to read books, and that, to me, is mystery or adventure. I think I can invent a team, and we'll have them travel around so we've got different locales and we'll always try to have a mystery in there" (n.p.). The result is a series that finds its true forefather not in Scott Young but in McFarlane.

In fact, McFarlane might be said to have fathered another series that combines mystery and hockey, a series written by his own son, Brian McFarlane. The Mitchell Brothers series, starring Max and Marty Mitchell, two teenaged boys from Haileybury, Ontario, who are wooed by hockey scouts, like to read the Hardy Boys books, and find themselves involved in the town's many adventures, owes much to the writer's dad. The backstory of their first episode, *Fire in the North*, stems from an article of the same name written by Leslie McFarlane (republished as the book *Fire in the North* [McFarlane 1972]) and that of *The Softy at Center (Season of Surprises)* stems from a story entitled "Softy at Center Ice," which McFarlane (1936) wrote for a pulp magazine. While McFarlane's influence is most palpable in his son's series, it can be seen widely. McFarlane's desire to create a unique culture, to interlace hockey and nationhood in a literature for his people, has truly been realized.

Not everyone recognizes this fact. "It astonishes me, and I've tried to understand why it is, that, first of all, hockey, as a theme in literature, is not taken seriously ... I've tried to figure out so many times why it is that hockey doesn't seem to register on the CanLit scale," wonders Roy MacGregor (Jenkinson 1998, n.p.). For a country that seems so invested in parading itself as a "hockey nation," and now has an abundance of children's hockey stories (as table 1 illustrates), it does indeed seem strange that hockey literature is *not* taken more seriously, that Canadian hockey writers of the past are *not* dug up and given their due. They should be – and McFarlane seems a good place to start.

CONCLUSION: LIKE FATHER, LIKE SON

Brian McFarlane is not best known as Leslie McFarlane's son, but he is well established as a true man of hockey. Hockey junkies will have read *Brian McFarlane's World of Hockey*; *Brian McFarlane's History of Hockey*; *Proud Past, Bright Future: One Hundred Years of Canadian Women's Hockey*; *Still More It Happened in Hockey: Still More Weird and Wonderful Stories from Canada's Greatest Game*; his series Brian McFarlane's Original Six; or others of his dozens of books on hockey. These books have made him one of the most comprehensive hockey historians alive. Brian McFarlane is a patriotic scholar, and his research repeatedly brings Canada's involvement in hockey history onto the page. He points out, for example, that the early hockey scholar, British journalist Ian Gordon, traced the sport to Windsor Castle, circa 1853, even though hockey was written about in Windsor, Nova Scotia, prior to 1810. Many other Canadian "origins" of hockey can be found in *The Puck Starts Here: The Origin of Canada's Great Winter Game, Ice Hockey*, and other of his books in which he attempts to establish the sport once and for all as a Canadian one.

Where did this love of the game come from? Mordecai Richler gives one the sense in which the importance of hockey is passed down in Canadian families as he describes the way he imagines his son, far off in the future after his death, will tell his own son what the boy's grandfather was like in "Cheap Skates": "There were hockey games on TV, and if I dared to tiptoe into the living room to inform him, say, I've just won a scholarship to Harvard, or I'm getting married tomorrow, or, 'Hey, congratulations! My wife just gave birth – you're a grandfather,' he would glare at me and say, 'Not now you fool. We can discuss such trivialities between periods'" (Richler 2002, 141). Indeed, writing the foreword to *Dispatches from the Sporting Life*, Noah Richler recalls his father's preferred place on Saturday nights from September to May: "on the living room couch, watching *Hockey Night in Canada*" (ix). He remembers watching with his father the Canadians play the Russians in 1972, going with his father to the Montreal Forum to see the Canadiens for the first time, listening to his father calling the Canadiens "Nos Glorieux" (xi). Noah Richler knows that hockey was a part of his father and, more important, a part of his relationship with his father.

Brian McFarlane sets his Mitchell Brothers series in the 1930s – significantly, the time when his father was writing his hockey stories.

He actually wants to expand that time span, however, for the simple reason that he wants to weave more of Canadian history into his hockey tales:

> This gives me the freedom to take them back to [NHL Hall of Famer] One-Eyed McGee's day. Let them learn all about hockey at the turn of the century, how they played with very limited equipment and short sticks, and the game is just as rough and rugged as it is today ... I can take them back to the Riel Rebellion. I have them going back to Niagara Falls to 1860 for the great high-wire walkers of that era. And Max even gets out there on the highwire to help rescue the Great Farini. That's in a forthcoming book. He was a marvelous Canadian and had a wonderful story to tell. As a lot of Canadians do. (N.a., "A Second Generation")

Brian McFarlane concludes by saying, "I guess we're such a laid back or modest nation, that we don't really acclaim our heroes like the Americans do." His father, of course, tried to create Canadian heroes, and a Canadian heritage, in his many occupations, writer of hockey stories included.

Leslie McFarlane, in the end, probably found the greatest satisfaction not in the millions of Hardy Boys books sold but, rather, in the fruitfulness of his offspring. Although McFarlane's contributions to hockey literature seem all but forgotten today, his son's are too plentiful to be ignored. "Old Man, look at my life. I'm a lot like you were," sang Neil Young (1972) to his father, hockey writer, Scott Young. So, too, could Brian McFarlane have written to his father, and so, too, could the many hockey writers of Canada write to their literary predecessor Leslie McFarlane.

Table 1
A selection of hockey fiction in Canada (1950–2007)[a]

Year	Title	Author
1952	Scrubs on Skates	Scott Young
1953	Boy on Defence	Scott Young
1963	A Boy at the Leaf's Camp	Scott Young
1966	McGonigle Scores	Leslie McFarlane
1967	Hockey Wingman	Andy O'Brien
1973	Hockey Fever in Gogan Falls	R.J. Childerhose
1975	Squeeze Play	Leslie McFarlane
1975	The Dynamite Flynns	Leslie McFarlane
1975	She Shoots, She Scores	Heather Kellerhals-Stewart
1976	Breakaway	Leslie McFarlane
1979	The Hockey Sweater (Le chandail de hockey)	Roch Carrier
1983	My Mother Made Me	Sharon Brian
1983	The Last Season	Roy MacGregor
1987	King Leary	Paul Quarrington
1987	Logan in Overtime	Paul Quarrington
1989	Bad Boy	Diana Wieler
1990	The Divine Ryans	Wayne Johnston
1991	The Magic Hockey Skates	Allen Morgan
1991	Yuletide Blues	R.P. MacIntyre
1994	Two Minutes for Roughing	Joseph Romain
1994	Shabash!	Ann Walsh
1995	Hockey Night in Transcona	John Danakas
1995–1997	Lightning on Ice series	Sigmund Brouwer
1995–2004	The Screech Owls series	Roy MacGregor
1996	Face Off	Chris Forsyth
1997	Hat Trick	Jacqueline Guest
1998	Salvage King, Ya!	Mark Anthony Jarman
1998	Shoot to Score	Sandra Richmond
1998	The Youngest Goalie	Brian McFarlane
1998–2007	Hockey Heroes series	Mike Leonetti
1998	Hockey Heroes	John Danakas
1998	Hockey Heat Wave	C.A. Forsyth
1999–2000	Slapshots series	Gordon Korman
1999	Alex and the Team Sweater (Jersey in the US)	Giles Tibo
1999	Alex, numéro 2	Giles Tibo
2000	Alex and the New Equipment	Giles Tibo
2000	Our Game: An All-Star Collection of Hockey Fiction (updated/revised version of The Rocket, the Flower, the Hammer, and Me [1988])	Ed. Doug Beardsley (incl. Hugh MacLennan, Morley Callaghan, Clark Blaise, and W. P. Kinsella)
2000	"The Scout's Lament" in 19 Knives	Mark Anthony Jarman
2000	Rookie Season	Jacqueline Guest
2000	Brothers on Ice	John Danakas
2001	Offside	Cathy Beveridge

Table 1 (continued)

Year	Title	Author
2001	*Power Play*	Michele Martin Bossley
2001	*The Kid Line*	Teddy Jam
2001	*In the Clear*	Anne Laurel Carter
2001	*Finnie Walsh*	Steven Galloway
2001	*50 Mission Cap*	Adrian Brijbassi
2001	*Rink Rivals*	Jacqueline Guest
2002	*A Goal in Sight*	Jacqueline Guest
2002	*Danger Zone*	Michele Martin Bossley
2002	*Red-line Blues*	C. Reghelini Rivers
2003	*On the Hockey Highway*	Brian McFarlane
2004	*Grouille-Toi Nicolas*	Giles Tibo
2004	*That's Hockey*	David Bouchard
2004	*The Stanley Cup Dream*	Brian McFarlane
2005	*Alex and the Game of the Century*	Giles Tibo
2005	*Alex and Toolie*	Giles Tibo
2005	*Where's My Hockey Sweater?*	Giles Tibo
2005	*The Softy at Center*	Brian McFarlane
2005	*Coaching the River Rats*	Brian McFarlane
2005	*Leslie McFarlane's Hockey Stories*	Leslie McFarlane
2006	*Leslie McFarlane's Hockey Stories 2*	Leslie McFarlane
2007	*Blind Date*	David A. Poulsen

[a] Some titles are taken from Cordukes's compendium of Canadian hockey writing and from the Library and Archives Canada website, "Backcheck: Hockey for Kids."
*http://www.collectionscanada.gc.ca/hockey/kids/index-e.html (viewed 11 March 2009).

NOTES

1 Popular websites about McFarlane include: "The Mysteries of Canada: The Man who was Leslie McFarlane," by Bruce Ricketts, which begins, "Do you remember the day that Fenton Hardy and his two sons, Joe and Frank, were walking with Aunt Gertrude and Chet Morton down the side walk in downtown Haileybury, Ontario?" (http://www.mysteriesofcanada. com/Ontario/man_who_was_leslie_mcfarlane.htm [viewed 9 October 2007]); the Wikipedia entry that begins, "Born Charles Leslie McFarlane in Carleton Place, Ontario, he is most famous for ghostwriting many of the early books in the very successful *Hardy Boys* series using the pseudonym Franklin W. Dixon" (http://en.wikipedia.org/wiki/Leslie_ McFarlane [viewed 9 October 2007]); and "The Writings of Leslie Charles McFarlane (1902–1977)" compiled by James D. Keeline, which

begins, "If most people know Leslie McFarlane today, it is because of his contract work with the Stratemeyer Syndicate on the early volumes of the Hardy Boys series" (http://www.keeline.com/McFarlane/ [viewed 9 October 2007]). Even his obituary recognizes him by virtue of his work on the Hardy Boys and other Stratemeyer Syndicate series: "To young detectives worldwide, he was known under the pseudonyms Carolyn Keene, Roy Rockwood and most famously Franklin W. Dixon author of *The Hardy Boys* series" (http://archives.cbc.ca/IDC-1-68-292-1543-11/ on_this_day/arts_entertainment/leslie_mcfarlane_obit [viewed 9 October 2007]).

2   Stratemeyer began as the ghostwriter for the books of established authors Horatio Alger, Jr and Oliver Optic. He wrote romances, dime novels, and boys' serials. He employed many pseudonyms, and he ultimately used his formula fiction experience to form a fiction factory, wherein he hired writers to write under his names, following his scripts. Stratemeyer's fiction factory produced almost all of the popular juvenile series at the turn of the twentieth century. See Billman (1986), Johnson (1993), and Prager (1971).

3   While McFarlane was taking a break from the Hardy Boys to develop himself as a writer, the interim ghostwriter, John Button, had Frank and Joe travel to Canada in *The Twisted Claw*. Not terribly familiar with Canadian geography, Button has the boys visit "St. John, Newfoundland" (Dixon 1939).

4   The boys ingeniously deduce that, because the felon calls himself "Hudson," he must be hiding out in Hudson Bay. For McFarlane, this association might have been obvious; for Bayporters, presumably living not too far from the Hudson *River*, and very far from Northern Ontario, the deduction is almost unbelievable.

5   In Canadian children's literature, hockey allows for a great sense of possibility. If ice in Canada's harsh nature is essentially unconquerable, in the arena, it becomes a safe and fun space for experimentation. Hockey functions as relief from the potential dangers (loss does not equate to loss of life, and the game can be played repeatedly). The literature reflects this shift. Johan Huizinga (1970, 9, 13), one of the earliest scholars of play theory, known best for observing, "All play means something," sees play as having a cultural function (satisfying communal ideals) as well as having a representative function. In hockey, the event that is acted out is

the group struggle to achieve victory on/over the ice. The play version "interpolates itself as a temporary activity satisfying in itself and ending there" (9). Like Freud's interpretation of dreams, Huizinga's interpretation of play involves a displacement of desire onto a fantasy world in which victory is always possible.

6 Barilko disappeared that summer, and only once his remains were found, eleven years later, did the Maple Leafs win the Cup again. As haunting as the curse of the Bambino was to Boston Red Sox fans, the legend of Bill Barilko enacted a relationship between the ghosts of hockey past and future – or so the Tragically Hip would have listeners believe.

7 His conclusion resonates in the ears of many Canadians, who are more than familiar with "tall-poppy syndrome," an Australian phrase Calvin Trillin applies to Canada in a *New Yorker* article that recounts the trials and hardships of newspaper mogul Conrad Black, a Canadian who dared to be successful. Trillin (2001, 62) relates the story the late novelist Robertson Davies liked to tell about the Canadian reception of the news that prime minister-to-be Lester B. Pearson had won the Nobel Peace Prize: "'Well!' somebody said. 'Who does he think he is!'" The nickname for Jean Chrétien, the former prime minister of Canada – *le petit gars de Shawinigan* (the little guy from Shawinigan) – reproduces this psychology of humility.

PART THREE

BUYING AND SELLING IDENTITIES
Hockey as Commodity

"A Hockey Crowd with Real Class." Toronto Maple Leafs playing the New York Rangers at Maple Leaf Gardens (November 1941), Archives of Ontario.

to affluent new audiences, women, and children" (Kidd 1996, 199). These new audiences played an important role in reinforcing the culture of respectability: "It was only natural that women, who previously hated to dress for stodgy old arenas of yesteryear, were glad to wear their best to see the Maple Leafs in their new arena. And just as surely as the apparel of the lady fans stepped up in quality, that of the young men followed suit" (Selke 1962, 94).

How readily, however, should we accept popular representations of hockey spectator experiences? Were there more women among the hockey crowds in New York and Toronto after the opening of new arenas? Did they all dress in evening clothes? Did spectators observe the presumed norms of "civility and decorum"? Were these commonly understood, and did their observation enhance or inhibit the experience of spectators? How do we reconcile traditional notions of staid, well-behaved spectators with the Stanley Cup-celebrating fans in Montreal in 1935, who as "a mob of fans occasionally surged and heaved against the [dressing room] door" (Jenish 1992, 118)? What evidence is there to support these modern-day accounts, especially as they assert common behaviours and shared experiences? Were there differences between the red seats, as Dryden notes, and other sections in the arena?

SITES OF SPECTATORSHIP AND CONSUMPTION

As the scholarship on commercial hockey makes clear, sports spectatorship was an important cultural practice in urban Canadian society in the early twentieth century. In her study of arts institutions in Canada, Maria Tippett (1990, 10) cites a commentator on the concert scene in Montreal who, in 1907, observed that "there was 'seldom any excitement manifested over concert tickets' while it was 'not unusual to see a line of men two blocks in length waiting patiently for the opening of the box office where tickets for a hockey match are on sale.'"

Yet it is not enough to assert that spectatorship was important because of sport's significance as a cultural practice. It remains to establish where spectatorship was taking place – both specific venues and the larger historical context – and with what meanings the practice was imbued. In the 1920s and 1930s, there were plenty of places to consume sports besides hockey arenas. Stadiums were being built in the 1920s for sports other than hockey in order to attract paying customers and house/host the spectator experience. In 1923, for example, London's Wembley Stadium was built primarily as a soccer venue, though it also hosted the 1948 Olympic Games (Hill 2003; Hill and Varrasi 1997).[1] In North America, prior to the development of professional hockey, baseball emerged as a commercial spectacle with specially designed facilities, especially in the United States. In the years leading up to the United States' involvement in the First World War, franchises in the professional major leagues – there were three in 1914–15 – built new facilities in Detroit, Chicago, and Boston, among other places (see White 1996). Of more specific interest, new professional ballparks were built in both New York and Toronto during the 1920s. Yankee Stadium (opened in 1923) and Maple Leaf Stadium (1926) offer interesting points of comparison for the development of sports spectatorship in these two cities (see Sullivan 2001; Cauz 1977; Field 1993). It has been argued elsewhere that the construction of Maple Leaf Gardens in 1931 needs to be viewed within the wider context of a changing urban landscape and an emerging entertainment economy (Field 2002). Accordingly, the building of Maple Leaf Gardens is best understood not solely in terms of developments in professional hockey and the NHL, but alongside the construction of Sunnyside Bathing Pavilion, Maple Leaf Stadium, Eaton's College Street store, and renovations to the Royal Ontario Museum in the preceding decade. Similarly, the construction of Madison Square Garden needs to be considered in the context of the building of Yankee Stadium, Radio City Music Hall, the Roxy, and countless other theatres in the years before and after 1925. The same argument can be made that the lived experience of the hockey spectator (indeed any spectator) did not occur within a vacuum but, rather, among an increasing array of consumption possibilities in the 1920s and 1930s.

RECREATION, CONSUMPTION, AND SPECTATORSHIP

In point of fact, Canada has taken such a stride forward in her theatrical life during the past five years ... its people, through necessity – and without much balking – have merged their amusement interests with those of the United States until today New York is as much the source of supply for Toronto and Montreal as for Pittsburgh and Buffalo ... this is the day of a *theatrically new Canada*. Optimism is rampant. Towns and cities have almost gone delirious upon suddenly found wealth from land speculation. Thousands of eager spenders have been created, as it were, overnight. (Black 1913, 18, emphasis in original)

Allen (1990, 258) is more prosaic than this 1913 drama critic, but no less direct, when he notes of the late 1920s, "with money so plentiful, New Yorkers were not hesitant to enjoy themselves." The emergence of an entertainment economy in the early twentieth century offered consumers a plethora of consumption and spectatorship opportunities. Much has been written about the transformation of leisure into consumption and the emergence of an urban North American consumer society in the early twentieth century (see Bush 1993; Cohen 1990). However, as one critic has noted, these studies, in general, have not "satisfactorily explored the specific role that consumers have played in the development of that consumer culture" (Cohen 1990, 553). Taylor (1988) argues that the commercial culture that emerged in New York City in the late nineteenth and early twentieth centuries was a "pastiche," defined not only by what was produced but also by how and by whom it was consumed. As he argues of this culture – vaudeville, amusements parks, and the "penny press" – "the significance of commercial culture lies in the complex circumstances surrounding its creation, in how New York's diverse population was orchestrated to fabricate and consume it, and in how it helped consumers from across the social spectrum to decode the city" (129).

Within this considerable literature on the emerging culture of consumption, some scholars have argued that sports spectatorship needs to be understood as one of the many commodities available to urban consumers in the late nineteenth and early twentieth centuries. Chief among these is Stephen Hardy, whose reviews establish commercial sports as a significant commodity in the urban setting (Hardy 1981; Hardy 1997; see also Barth 1980; Nasaw 2002). This is not to suggest that sports spectatorship was the only, or even the most predominant, emerging urban spectatorship and consumption opportunity that residents of New York and Toronto could attend outside the home. But, to take gender relations as a case in point, these new practices had the potential to substantially affect social relations. Erenberg (1984, xiv-xv) argues that, "unlike the entertainments of the Victorian era, various forms of popular culture in the twentieth century sought to bring men and women together." The early twentieth-century development of one segment of these entertainments in New York and Toronto – the theatre and cinema – is revealing when trying to place sports spectatorship in its larger context because, as Jancovich, Faire, and Stubbings (2003, 42) note in a cultural geography of film consumption, "a whole series of new spaces and public activities emerged which were not only acceptable for women, but actively courted them: exhibitions, amusement parks, galleries, libraries, restaurants, tea rooms, department stores and, of course, picture houses."

LEGITIMATE THEATRES, VAUDEVILLE HOUSES, AND CINEMAS

The scholarly literature on the theatre pays far greater attention to the producer than to the consumer. Much research has focused on architecture and architects, impresarios and performers, but little attention has been paid to the people and experiences these theatres were intended to house. A two-volume edited scholarly collection on theatre in Ontario in the nineteenth and twentieth centuries makes virtually no reference to audience (Saddlemyer 1990; Saddlemyer and Plant 1997). Robert Fairfield argues that architecture history and theatre history need to be considered in tandem, "since the design of theatre buildings was, in varying degrees, influenced by what was to happen in them." Yet, he offers no discussion of just who was "in them" and the nature of their experiences (Fairfield in Saddlemyer 1990, 214).[2]

While, in the late nineteenth century, the focus of legitimate and vaudeville theatre in Manhattan remained located on Broadway between Union Square and Madison Square, concert audiences were drawn to a new venue on West 57th Street, just south of Central

Park. Carnegie Hall opened in 1891 to a capacity audience of 2,800. But it was in and around Times Square that New York theatre was to build a substantial base in the early twentieth century. While the district's boundaries shifted – most narrowly defined as 43rd to 50th streets between 6th and 8th avenues – this area was home to "the largest, most complex, most concentrated and most diversified theatrical center in the history of the city" (Henderson 1973, 192). There were eighty theatres built in the Times Square district in the first three decades of the twentieth century, with the Shubert brothers being the best-known and most powerful of New York's theatre impresarios. The offerings of these theatres ranged from legitimate theatre to vaudeville to burlesque, but, as Mary Henderson (1973, 188) has noted of this substantial investment in infrastructure, "the development of the area around Long Acre Square [renamed Times Square] into the new theatrical district exactly coincided with the flurry of construction that was affecting all of New York." However, it was in the 1920s that New York theatre boomed. At a time when it cost approximately $1 million to build a theatre, twelve new theatres opened in 1924 alone (Stern, Gilmartin, and Mellins 1987, 229). In the 1927–28 season, New Yorkers could take in 257 different productions in seventy-one theatres, even though the cost of a top-priced ticket had more than tripled that year (Henderson 1973, 193).

Not surprisingly, New York's major movie houses took up residence in the same area, and, until the fading of vaudeville theatre in the late 1920s, many of these venues doubled as theatres and cinemas. The first great movie palace was the Capitol, built in 1919 with seating for 5,300. It was "the world's largest theatre and the ultimate movie palace" (Lindsay 1983, 80). Seven years later, Samuel "Roxy" Rothafel, who had been a producer at the Capitol, opened his eponymous Roxy Theatre at the northeast corner of 7th Avenue and 50th Street. Costing $12 million, and seating 6,200 moviegoers, the Roxy was now New York's largest and most expensive movie house (Allen 1990, 260–1). The New York theatre scene was completed in December 1932, with the opening of Radio City Music Hall within the new Rockefeller Center. Seating 6,200, it was the last of the great American movie palaces (Lindsay 1983, 97). With the new Madison

Square Garden opening a block to the west in 1925, the Times Square district was home to a vast array of public entertainments: "It was in the late 1920s that Times Square reached the peak of its development, with hotels, office buildings, restaurants, dancing halls, and movie palaces clustering along Broadway and Seventh Avenue, and the low-scale legitimate theaters crowding the side streets" (Stern, Gilmartin, and Mellins 1987, 229).

Much like Carnegie Hall, the Toronto music scene was dominated by a large concert hall built in the 1890s under the aegis of a capitalist benefactor. Massey Hall opened in 1894, with a seating capacity of 3,500, which made it Toronto's largest indoor venue (see Kilbourn 1993). The Royal Alexandra became one of Toronto's primary destinations for touring productions of legitimate theatre when it opened in 1907 with a capacity of 1,525. The Royal Alex was among the earliest spectator venues in Toronto to take the needs of the audience into consideration in its design. It was the first theatre in North America to have air conditioning and the first to use cantilevered balconies, ensuring that support pillars did not obstruct audience views (Lindsay 1986, 6). Soon afterwards, "other fine theatres, such as the Winter Garden on Yonge Street (1914), sprang up to meet the growing demand for live entertainment in the heyday of vaudeville and for the new motion pictures" (Dendy and Kilbourn 1986, 155).

At the start of the First World War, Toronto had two legitimate theatres – the Princess and the Royal Alexandra – that hosted touring productions (Lindsay 1986).[3] The Grand Opera House and the Majestic "offered run-of-the-mill melodramas, comedies and musicals in touring shows to mostly middle- and working-class audiences" (Russell 1989, 20). But it was in the vaudeville market that competition was most intense. Shea's operated two large theatres in Toronto: the Victoria (built in 1910 and seating 2,000) and the Hippodrome (built in 1914 and seating 3,200). A second US entrepreneur, Marcus Loew (who was financed by New York's Shubert brothers), opened Loew's Yonge Street in 1913 (seating 2,194) and its upstairs companion, the Winter Garden (capacity 1,422) a year later. In 1920, N.L. Nathanson opened the 3,626-seat Pantages Theatre, which, at a cost of between $600,000 and $1 million, was Toronto's costliest theatre. All of these theatres were built in and around what was becoming known as the "theatre block" in Toronto, with the Royal Alexandra being the furthest removed from this concentration (Olsheski 1989, 42; see also Dilse 1986). Also in 1920, Loew's signalled the northward shift of Toronto's public amusements by adding the 3,000-seat Uptown Theatre on Yonge Street, south of Bloor Street.

EXPLORING HOCKEY ARENAS WITHIN THE CULTURE OF CONSUMPTION

Ultimately, studying the construction and subsequent experience of hockey arenas within the context of a consumer culture makes sense. Some sports scholars explicitly consider the array of entertainment choices available to consumers in the early twentieth century as alternatives to sports spectatorship. Within the literature on soccer, scholars agree that the "size of football crowds thus seems to have been broadly determined by the ability of working-class people to pay for fairly cheap entertainments, and implicitly by the lack of alternatives to football available to them" (Fishwick 1989, 55). Johnes' (2002, 117) analysis of female spectators, while somewhat paternalistic, makes a direct comparison to the movie house as a viable alternative to soccer spectatorship: "Compared with the comforts of the increasingly popular cinema, soccer, with its standing in uncomfortable conditions for long periods, probably held little appeal for many working-class women anyway." And Fishwick's (1989, 51) look at soccer in Sheffield in the interwar years catalogues the many possibilities open to a predominantly working-class audience:

League matches between the wars cost 1s to see, no mean sum for 90 minutes' entertainment. There were cheaper luxuries available to the working class that competed with football in times of hardship. There were, for example, at least 49 picture palaces in Sheffield in 1932, charging only 6d for a matinée in drier, warmer and more comfortable conditions than generally prevailed at Hillsborough or Bramall Lane. Nationally the number of cinemas rose during the 1930s from 3,300 in 1929

to 4,967 in 1938. There was also competition from the local
greyhound track, which charged 6d in Sheffield, and perennially
from cigarettes (1s a packet in the 1930s) and beer (8d a pint).

Hockey spectatorship was only one alternative within the panoply
of public amusements. There are other more compelling reasons to
consider hockey spectatorship within this universe of consumption
choices. From a straightforward, chronological standpoint, the construction of Madison Square Garden and Maple Leaf Gardens was
concurrent with other developments that influenced the consumer
economy, from the construction of new movie houses to the emergence of radio as an important medium. Furthermore, the "geography of consumption" reveals the important ways in which hockey
arenas were part of the changing landscape. In New York, the Times
Square theatre district was bounded on the north by "Roxy"
Rothafel's mammoth theatres, the Roxy and the Capitol. A block
away, at 50th Street and 8th Avenue, Tex Rickard built his new
Madison Square Garden. Hockey fans could have had no doubt of
the other spectator opportunities available to them. Meanwhile, in
Toronto, hockey arenas had long been found near other spectator
venues. The Maple Leafs' original arena on Mutual Street was just
north of Toronto's "theatre block," while Maple Leaf Gardens
opened a block east of, and a year after, Eaton's new College Street
department store.

The architectural elements of the new arenas alluded to other
elements of the new consumer culture. As Howard Shubert (2002,
60) notes: "Several of the new arenas featured the kind of marquees
with flashing lights more typically associated with theatres and cinemas." This was no accident, as Shubert goes on to observe: "Two
of the arenas, at New York and Detroit, were even designed by noted
'theatre' architects – Thomas W. Lamb and Charles Howard Crane
respectively" (ibid.). Crane was in such demand in Detroit that "he
designed over fifty theatres in the city, including all the major houses
in two successive theatre districts" (Morrison 1974, 1). In 1927, he
inaugurated his first NHL arena, Detroit's Olympia. But the most
prolific North American theatre architect of the early twentieth
century was Lamb. He was responsible for some of the most

important theatre and movie house construction across the continent. In New York, his designs included the Capitol and the Strand, while in Toronto he was the primary architect on Loew's Yonge Street and Winter Garden, the Pantages, and the Regent. Olsheski (1989, 34) notes: "In 1920, of the five vaudeville houses in Toronto, three had been designed by him." Five years later, he designed the seminal sports arena of the period, Madison Square Garden.

This link between hockey arenas and movie houses – through the architect of record – is less remarkable when one considers the connections at the entrepreneurial level between these public entertainments. When Marcus Loew's Theatres Limited was incorporated in February 1913, Lawrence Solman was listed as a member of the board of directors. At the time, he was a partner in and manager of the Royal Alexandra Theatre. Solman would be involved in a wide array of public amusements over the next twenty years. The Shubert brothers, New York's pre-eminent theatre impresarios, employed him as the manager of their Canadian operations. Solman also operated the Toronto Island Ferries and Sunnyside Amusement Park, owned the city's professional baseball team and its stadium on Toronto Island, and was also involved in Mutual Street Arena (Russell 1989, 27; Field 1993, 6–7).

Loew's northern competitor on the Yonge Street theatre block, N.L. Nathanson's Pantages, was financed in part by J.P. Bickell (Russell 1989, 27). Bickell was the president of McIntyre Porcupine Mines, but he was also a primary investor in professional hockey in Toronto. It was by convincing Bickell to remain invested in the St Patricks in 1927 that Conn Smythe was able to purchase the franchise. Bickell, in turn, would become president of Maple Leaf Gardens. Nathanson, while primarily interested in the theatre, was also invested in the local hockey team. Before Smythe purchased the club, team owners received entreaties from American interests, and, as Kidd (1996, 205) notes:

The owners of the Toronto St Pats – J.P. Bickell, Paul Ciceri, N.L. Nathanson, and Charlie Querrie – almost sold their franchise to a Philadelphia partnership. Selling to the Americans was nothing new to Nathanson. His 1920 sale of his string of

theatres to the US chain Paramount Pictures enabled it to form
a Canadian subsidiary, Famous Players, of which Nathanson
became the first president.

But what perhaps united the sports entrepreneurs with other
amusement capitalists was their aspirations. Vaudeville, theatre, and
movie house owners all sought to infuse their entertainments with
the scent of respectability. NHL owners, as we have seen, fit this
mould. Conn Smythe, for one, explicitly believed that building a
new, modern arena would lend respectability to his enterprise.
Smythe's oft-cited remark – "We need a place where people can go
in evening clothes ... a place that people can be proud to take their
wives or girlfriends to" – is taken as evidence of this ideology (Smythe
1981, 103). And, to this end, Frank Selke argued that Smythe was
correct because "the completion of Maple Leaf Gardens must surely
be listed as the most important single factor in giving the game its
new status" (Selke 1962, 94). But Smythe also made a direct connection between respectability and the regard in which theatre-going
was held at the time. The spectator experience he offered before
building Maple Leaf Gardens failed, in his words, to "compete with
the comfort of the theatres and other places where people can spend
their money" (Smythe 1981, 102–3). Indeed, as one popular account
has observed, Smythe "pitched the grand new edifice as a kind of
sporting Carnegie Hall, a place that would lift hockey forever out
of the realm of cigar-chomping hustlers and back-alley knockabouts"
(Wilkins 1999, 46). To be clear, these aspirations were not just about
making an entertainment facility respectable in form; they were also
about making the experience of consuming or spectating within it
respectable in practice.

THE HOCKEY SPECTATOR EXPERIENCE

The experiences of hockey spectators in New York and Toronto in
the 1920s and 1930s need to be considered alongside the ways in
which scholarship has considered the historical experience of spectating. The preponderance of historical scholarship of sports spectators,
at least in the English language, has been developed within the

scholarly study of British football (soccer). These accounts have proceeded from a relatively straightforward premise. British football historians have tended to characterize football spectators as "decent, ordinary folk" (Walton 2003, 11). In stepping beyond soccer scholarship, the most comprehensive historical study of spectatorship, perhaps the only one, is Allen Guttmann's (1986) *Sport Spectators*.

However, the way in which spectator behaviour, specifically acts deemed "violent," dominates both Guttmann's and the British soccer scholars' analyses is one of two broad critiques that can be levelled at the literature on spectatorship. Before moving on to issues of spectator behaviour, I first look at the ways in which scholarship has characterized the composition of spectators.

The British soccer literature presumes a fairly homogeneous historical "crowd," one that is white, male, and working class. While there is likely a significant degree of truth in this supposition, it is not one grounded in an in-depth historical analysis of spectators. Moreover, many of the analyses that operationalize the notion of male, working-class soccer spectators also suggest a more heterogeneous appeal of spectatorship. Johnes, for one, notes how photographs of crowd scenes at pre-Second World War football matches can be used to ascertain the male, working-class nature of the crowd. But at the same time, he reveals other ways in which this evidence obscures demographic details: "Photographs of the area's popular banks show a sea of the flat caps that characterized working-class male dress and disguised differences of age and region" (Johnes 2002, 115). This spectator literature would benefit from a greater understanding of the many ways in which the identity of each sports spectator could be understood. One might, for example, at the most basic level, consider the questions that analytical categories such as social class, gender, and ethnicity raise for the study of sports spectators.

SOCIAL CLASS

Contemporary scholarship challenges the notion that sports fans are predominantly working class, offering instead a portrayal of a collection of spectators in which the middle class and wealthier elites are well represented (see White and Wilson 1999; Waddington, Malcolm, and Horak 1998). While these studies offer a perspective on ways to re-evaluate the contemporary spectator in terms of social standing, is it possible to historicize these notions? Guttmann (1986, 121) makes an interesting connection between social class, spectator violence, and the design of early modern sports venues: "Another means to the end was to construct stadiums and arenas to which access was strictly controlled and within which social classes tended to be separated by different ticket prices." Ignoring for the moment Guttmann's social control argument, his observations about stadium design point to the presence of spectators representative of a variety of economic and social circumstances. In arguing for the need to more thoroughly consider the composition of soccer crowds, Johnes (2002, 119) makes this point clear: "The existence of stands charging a 3s entrance fee suggests that affluent people must have attended in reasonable numbers, even if they were always a small minority ... soccer was clearly not the preserve of the working class alone."

GENDER

Historically, women have been sports spectators; their presence contours the experience of male spectators and requires that their experiences be incorporated into any analysis. Though not its focus, Guttmann's *Sports Spectators* offers some observations on women as spectators. His account of female spectators makes a clear, though implicit, connection between spectatorship and social class among women. In short, throughout the early twentieth century, working-class women were frequent spectators, though among the minority. Upper- and upper middle-class women were less likely to be found on the terraces at Wembley or in the balcony at Madison Square Garden. These women were more likely to be found accompanying men at country clubs, where the aristocratic atmosphere made their presence far "safer," in keeping with social mores of the day.

Guttmann's account of female spectators is not unproblematic.[4] Nevertheless, he demonstrates that, in the representations of the day – be they the popular press or lithographs – the prevailing sentiment was that women as spectators were adjuncts to men, who were the more knowledgeable, real fans. Women were companions, not interested observers.

In shifting the analysis to hockey, we know that women were playing organized versions of the game by the 1890s (McFarlane 1994, 6). But from the earliest games, they were also spectating. McKinley cites newspaper accounts of a number of organized nineteenth-century hockey games that make explicit reference to the presence of female spectators. For example, on the occasion of the first organized, indoor hockey game – 3 March 1875 – the Kingston *Whig-Standard* noted: "A disgraceful sight took place at Montreal at the Victoria Skating Rink after a game of hockey. Shins and heads were battered, benches smashed, and the lady spectators fled in confusion." Also, after an early Stanley Cup game in 1894, the Montreal *Gazette* noted: "Every lady almost in the rink wore the favours of their particular club" and "never did belted knight in joust or tourney fight harder than the hockey men" (cited in McKinley 2000, 10, 27).

These accounts (and others) of women as hockey spectators reaffirm many of the prevailing themes of women as sports spectators in the late nineteenth century: first, that women were frail and needed to be protected, if need be by making the game more respectable; second, that women's presence might improve the behaviour of largely male (and, though unstated) working- and middle-class crowds; and, finally, that women as spectators were largely adjuncts to men – men who were either their heroes on the ice or their companions in the stands. Not surprisingly, these attitudes also reflect contemporary concerns about women's participation in the "public sphere" more generally.

With the emergence of an urban entertainment economy and the construction of facilities such as Maple Leaf Gardens – whose fund-raising was explicitly linked to attracting female spectators – the question remains whether these characterizations had evolved by the 1920s. Scholars such as Kidd (1996, 95) and M. Ann Hall, among others, note that the 1920s have been labelled "the Golden Age of Women's Sport" (Hall 2002, 42). However contentious this moniker may be, we know that women were participating in organized sport at all levels, likely in unprecedented numbers. But, were they watching?

In 1931, while raising funds for his new arena project, Conn Smythe made it clear that women were among the audiences that he hoped to target upon the completion of Maple Leaf Gardens. A cartoon that appeared in a prospectus Smythe prepared to help raise money for his new arena from members of the public contains interesting messages about the female spectator. Within the cartoon, women discuss how a more comfortable arena will make them more likely to become spectators, pleased that the new Maple Leaf Gardens will offer a "ladies lounge" (see Field 2002). Throughout his life and in his memoirs, Smythe reiterated that his goal in building Maple Leaf Gardens was to create "a place where people can take their wives and girl friends." These "people" were obviously men, thus reinforcing older notions of women spectators as companions to "real" spectators. Also, the idea that a place was only of sufficient comfort and social standing when it appealed to the tastes of women hearkened back to notions of separate spheres. But the fact that Smythe was considering his building an evening "destination" placed it firmly within the constellation of restaurants, theatres, cinemas, opera houses, nickelodeons, cabarets, and vaudeville houses that had come to compete for disposable income in the 1920s. Moreover, the fact that Smythe targeted women – self-interestedly or not – was an acknowledgment that women had in some sense become public consumers of spectacle.

By the 1920s, traditional assumptions about the role that women played within the spaces of sports spectating had evolved. Nevertheless, these attitudes retained strong residual elements of late Victorian beliefs about women's "public" role as a purifying element. That these notions had undergone a subtle shift, and to reinforce the idea that sports spectating – in this case soccer spectating – was not the male bastion that has been assumed, it is worth quoting at length from Johnes (2002, 119) as he discusses the Welsh case in the decades prior to the Second World War:

> Thus, soccer may have been a predominantly male activity but women were getting more involved, especially in the years before marriage, just as they were in many traditionally male facets of life. Indeed, had the practical constraints that dogged

the lives of many women been removed, it is reasonable to suggest that they would have been there in even greater numbers. This recognition of the role of soccer in the lives of at least some women is an indication of the need to question conventional assumptions and narratives about gender roles. Working-class women's lives were not simply the stuff of motherhood, home and burden, and their involvement in soccer marked the game's incorporation into mainstream popular culture.

ETHNICITY

There is limited historical scholarship on the ethnocultural composition of spectatorship in North America. The narrative history of professional baseball in the United States is dominated by the view that, in large, urban centres in the northeast, supporting the local team was a vehicle of acculturation for the eastern and southern European immigrants of the late nineteenth and early twentieth centuries. In his study of sport and the Jewish immigrant experience in the early twentieth century, Peter Levine (1992, 17) asserts: "Aspiring immigrants eagerly embraced obvious and accessible avenues that permitted immediate identification as Americans." Steven Riess (1999, 47) on the other hand, argues that "new immigrants from eastern and southern Europe generally did not become baseball fans." However, he goes on to suggest that immigrant children who lived in inner cities were ardent fans (48). In reconciling these apparently contradictory notions, it is perhaps possible to suggest that scholars view baseball fandom and spectatorship in the early twentieth century as an instrument of acculturation primarily for second-generation Americans, the children of immigrants.

Little has been written on hockey spectatorship in either Canada or the United States in this regard. Gruneau and Whitson (1993, 101), however, make the following observation about the power of hockey as a unifying cultural force in Canadian society:

There was no other cultural form, no other popular practice, that brought the "two solitudes" [anglophone and francophone

Canada] into regular engagement with each other in quite the same way. Moreover, although millions of immigrants from other European countries had brought their own popular recreations with them when they moved to Canada, it wasn't long before their children and grandchildren were watching and playing hockey.

But what basis does this generalization have in lived historical reality? The cultural similarity that this argument bears to the rhetoric of immigrant children playing stickball in the street and sneaking into Brooklyn's Ebbets Field is unmistakable. But is it accurate? Do we know whether these same boys and girls were cheering on the Rangers and trying to sneak into Madison Square Garden in the winter? Or whether Toronto's early twentieth-century Eastern European Jewish population or post-Second World War Italian immigrant community sought out Maple Leaf Gardens as a place to "practise" being Canadian? The limited scholarship on sports spectators germane to each of these three analytical categories – social class, gender, and ethnicity (just three of many) – makes it clear that our assumptions about the composition of spectators need to be grounded in further historical research.

SPECTATOR BEHAVIOUR VERSUS THE SPECTATOR EXPERIENCE

While a greater understanding of the demographic composition of spectators is important to our understanding of the growth of commercial sport, as Fishwick (1989, 58) observes: "the composition of the crowds tells us more about the cast than the play." As suggested earlier, a prominent theme for the "playwrights" of spectator literature is a focus on spectator *behaviour*. This occurs at the expense of studying the *experience* of being a spectator and is no doubt a result of the influence of soccer literature on the study of spectatorship and the centrality of the study of hooliganism to soccer scholarship over the last twenty years.

Guttmann (1986) also focuses his history of spectators on their behaviours, his interest being primarily whether or not spectators engaged in "violence." He adopts a position consistent with the "civilizing process" of figurational sports sociologists such as Eric Dunning in order to evaluate the modernization of spectating. Yet, there are limits to the moral code, or civilizing process, whose operation, Guttmann asserts, resulted in decreased spectator violence in the nineteenth century. There is a difference between the articulation of moral order and its actual practise, between hegemony and resistance. Guttmann focuses extensively on the phenomenon of spectator violence, which he explicitly connects to social class. A useful addition to this discussion would be an assessment of the nature of the entire audience at the events at which violence occurs. If, by examining sports such as English soccer, where the crowd is predominantly made up of young, working-class males (regardless of whether or not violence occurs), scholars conclude that spectator violence is most prevalent among young, working-class males, then the argument becomes tautological.

Fishwick's (1989) history of English soccer is a useful starting point for refocusing the discussion onto spectator experience and away from behaviour, violence, and hooliganism. He rejects the idea that soccer crowds were "unruly mobs" and argues that emphasizing these kinds of behaviours obscures the predominant experiences of the vast majority of fans. To make this error is to miss the historical experience of spectating:

> The nature of the communities to which most spectators
> belonged, of the composition of crowds, meant that most
> spectators shared norms of behaviour according to which
> enthusiasm was not incompatible with restraint. It is a serious
> distortion, therefore, to study football spectators from the point
> of view of their occasional misbehaviour: it is simply not an
> adequate reflection of the relationship between the spectators,
> the game and society. (Fishwick 1989, 65)

Johnes (2002) notes that, for spectators at football matches – whether standing on the bank (and later the terraces) or sitting in the grandstand – the experience of spectating varied widely. It could include coping with the crush of an often over-crowded stadium. Furthermore, admission to a ground's embankment (the "bank") was the cheapest available ticket and came without the overhead cover found in the more expensive grandstand seats. In inclement weather, spectators would have to endure rain and mud. At some grounds, the banks were heaps of garbage covered in dirt, which could mean an olfactory battle with the "evil smell" from the underlying refuse (123). The experience of being a soccer spectator also usually involved alcohol, either through having imbibed oneself, through being among others who have imbibed, or both.

While Fishwick notes that fans engaged in cheering, taunting (barracking), and (infrequent) acts of violence, spectatorship allowed for other sensations. It had a symbolic value, and, especially in the industrial cities of England's northeast, being a supporter of the local team enhanced membership in the wider community. However, at a more elementary level, Fishwick (1989, 59) asserts that the *pleasure* offered by spectating must enter into any historical account of the experience: "No event could give such intense excitement and colour to so many working class people, combining passionate commitment in varying degrees with a sense of fun, as did a big football match."

The experience was also influenced by a spectator's location – where one sat or stood – within the ground, stadium, or arena. Locating oneself, both literally and figuratively, was part of the construction of the spectator identity. Spectator identities, however, were not rigid and immutable, and spectators could adopt any of a multiplicity of identities, depending on the circumstances. And, Johnes (2002) argues, safeguarding their identity was not always their overriding concern. Of a 1920 soccer match between Cardiff City and Swansea Town, he notes that "there was a rush from the queue for the grandstand to the popular bank after news spread that there were no seats left. Seeing this eagerly anticipated derby was more important than remaining separated from the 'bob bankers' [a nickname for the predominantly working-class crowd who paid a 'bob', or a shilling, for a ticket to stand on the embankment]" (133–4).

The experience at extraordinary games (e.g., FA Cup matches) was often quite different from that at mid-season league matches. High-profile contests might attract different people who "were turning out more for a social affair and an excursion than a game of soccer.

This was especially true of females of all classes whose numbers increased significantly at big matches" (Johnes 2002, 124). Yet, the more typical spectator experience was played out in the majority of matches without the hype of Cup match or derby. This leads to a final question about the spectator experience: should spectating be understood as an extraordinary event in the life of the early twentieth-century fan or was it a component of everyday life? Was it a special event or possibly routine and mundane? Could it have been both? Johnes suggests that, "for many supporters, soccer's attraction ran deeper than a fun day out, and the sport was an integral and routine part of their lives" (126).

CONCLUSION

It is on this issue – the role of spectating in the lives of spectators in the interwar years – that our understanding of North American ice hockey spectators falls short. The dominant characterization of spectators at the new facilities of the 1920s and 1930s comes from accounts of these buildings' opening nights. When Madison Square Garden opened in December 1925, the *New York Times* wrote: "In the tiers of flag-draped boxes was a social registered representation which was something entirely new in New York's long history" (Cross 1925, 29). The president of the Garden, Colonel John Hammond, noted that "there's more people here tonight than at a first night of the Metropolitan [Opera]" (Rickard 1936, 315). Similarly, the *Toronto Evening Telegram* called the 1931 inauguration of Toronto's Maple Leaf Gardens evening "a great step forward for hockey and hockey crowds" ("Toronto Citizens Must Measure Up to Hockey," 13 November 1931).

Descriptions such as these of the patrons who attended the opening nights at Madison Square Garden and Maple Leaf Gardens were not unlike those for the patrons of opening nights at other public buildings; in fact, Hammond made this allusion directly. On 15 December 1913, for example, Toronto's newest vaudeville theatre, Loew's Yonge Street, opened to "an audience dotted with posh people" as "politicians and millionaires turned out in force" (Russell 1989, 13). It is newspaper accounts of the openings of such buildings that give us some of the best insight into the nature of the spectators. But do "opening nights" provide the most representative audiences?

Beyond the gala occasions of opening nights, the study of spectatorship requires a greater consideration of "subsequent" nights. The meaning of the experience to spectators is important because sports entrepreneurs such as Conn Smythe were selling their attractions as a respectable alternative to a night at the theatre. In these terms, how should we think about spectatorship at Madison Square Garden and Maple Leaf Gardens? Was it everyday or extraordinary? Johnes (2002) may argue that, for many Welsh soccer spectators, watching a match was an important part of the routine of their lives; however, is the attempt to shift spectatorship from the everyday to the extraordinary what distinguished attempts in North America to create new spectator spaces?

NOTES

1 It is worth noting that, while North American sport venues in the 1920s were built with an eye towards enhancing the "respectability" of spectatorship, English soccer was patronized predominantly by working-class males and that Hill's work can be used to argue that Wembley was less influenced by the culture of respectability and more by the desire to build a larger ground. However, as Hill (2003) notes, the media regularly commented on the behaviour of the crowd.

2 On Toronto, see for example, Olsheski (1989); Russell (1989); and Lindsay (1986). On New York, see for example, Botto (2002); Chach, Fletcher, Swartz, and Wang (2001); and Henderson (1997).

3 Lindsay writes, "The Royal Alexandra was a 'legitimate' theatre, but it often strayed away from 'legitimate' productions; it even went so far as to show some Warner Brothers movies" (Lindsay 1986, 14).

4 In describing the spectators on display in a 1787 print entitled *The Prize Fight*, Guttmann (1986, 71) remarks that "a few tubby females appear among the generally nondescript spectators." He also cautions that "nineteenth-century and early twentieth-century fights were no place for a lady" (116). The tenor of such observations raises some concerns about how seriously Guttmann considers women as spectators.

8

Between a Puck and a Showpiece

Spectator Sport and the Differing Responses to Hockey
(and Its Absence) in Canada and the United States –
A Canadian Poet Looks at the Fate of the Game

RICHARD HARRISON

In the early 1950s, sociologist Leon Festinger infiltrated a doomsday cult. The resulting book, *When Prophecy Fails*, examines the history of a faith from prophetic birth to earthly disappointment and beyond (Festinger 1964). It's not often that we get the chance to see the faithful gather at the origin of their creed, grow as their religion is revealed, react to the failure of its predictions, and finally dissolve – all within a lifetime. Festinger's cult gave us that chance. The NHL is offering another – except for "the world will end soon" read "hockey will become America's fourth major sport."

You would think that, when a religion's prediction about the world proves false, the religion would lose its credibility among its followers. *When Prophecy Fails* says the opposite: when people find that their religion has led them astray, their more likely response is to believe in it *harder than before* – as if a more energetic belief in a religion (accompanied by a need to proselytize) can make up for a crucial but failed article of faith within it.

The inability of the NHL to secure anything like its projected TV deal in the United States has made it impossible to "money over" the contradictory forces of feudalism, capitalism, and trade unionism that have long operated in the League. And, as stakeholders fell upon each other against their own interests in a conflict most similar to the First World War, the NHL has slouched and staggered to a halt. I know that not all Canadians are hockey fans. I know that many Americans are. But where the American reaction on a *national* scale has been that of a group of people denied an entertainment most of them don't care about, the pattern of the Canadian reaction can be seen to follow that of Festinger's cult.

First, among the followers, we see a separation of the failure from the faith. Canadian newspapers responded to the announcement of the cancellation of the 2004/05 NHL season using terms that echoed and built on the terms used to announce Canadian victory at the World Junior Championships the month before: "It's Our Game!" crowed the *Calgary Sun* (5 January 2005, 1) after the win. "Canada's Game Lives On" announced the *Globe and Mail* (17 February 2005, 1) after the collapse, thus affirming both *hockey* and our *connection* to it even more fiercely in the face of its extended absence at the professional level than in the fleeting moment of victory at the level below). Further, beneath its headline, the *Globe and Mail* ran a photo of the Canadian pastoral – an eight-year-old boy (from Saskatchewan, birthplace of Mr Hockey, Gordie Howe, no less) playing shinny on a frozen pond near Lake Louise, the sun just brushing the tips of the Rocky Mountains like a gleaming crown.

And beautiful as it is, the picture is only a variation on a theme repeated throughout Canadian iconography right down to the five-dollar bill on whose reverse is a scene of children – one of them sporting Maurice Richard's Number 9 jersey – playing hockey on a frozen river. Next to them is a quotation from Roch Carrier's 1979 classic, *The Hockey Sweater*: "The winters of my childhood were long, long seasons. We lived in three places – the school, the church, and the skating rink – but *our real life* was on the skating rink" (Carrier 1997, 15, emphasis mine). In coupling that idyllic image with the announcement of the NHL's self-inflicted defeat, the *Globe and Mail* was telling Canadians what they already knew: that, in the absence of one of the key defining expressions of the term "Canada's Game" – the fortunes of the NHL and its players – Canadians were taking the burden of game and country onto themselves.

The NHL was long considered (even during the years it refused to test that claim) the place where the world's best players played the world's best game at the game's highest level. And, while other nations have identified hockey as one of their sports (there is an opera in the Czech Republic celebrating their Olympic Gold Medal win in Nagano), if not the most important, this picture and its rallying cry, its complex of political, historical, and emotional charges, could only work in Canada because only Canadians have identified themselves as hockey's chosen people (P. LeBrun, "History Lesson," *Calgary Sun*, 10 September 2004, 1).

As I've argued in *Hero of the Play* (Harrison 2004), hockey can be said to be Canada's game not so much because Canadians invented hockey as because hockey invented Canada. Or, to put it another way, in the myth of the origin of hockey, Canada finds all the elements of its own creation: winter; team work; hard work; the passing of tradition from parent to child, sibling to sibling; the idyllic blending of European and Native cultures; and the timeless expanse of a frozen pond upon which a human order can be imposed and a game begun. Indeed, if, in the myth of the infinite boundary of the baseball diamond, Americans find the image of the endless geography that underpins the virtues of their frontier spirit, then in the image of water frozen forever, Canadians find the image and condition for the Canadian virtue of endurance.

Part of that endurance could be found in our willingness to do without the NHL, and – at least in terms of online surveys,[1] letters to the editor, and calls to phone-in radio programs – to spread the good word of that very willingness. As part of our renewal of faith in the game, we shunned what was once its great exponent. Filling the gap left by the stoppage in NHL play, Canadians turned their attention and praise to every other hockey league in the country and criticized even more loudly the NHL game that had moved farther and farther away from the greatness established in the days of Béliveau, Richard, Howe, Hull, and Orr. Even Gretzky and Lemieux, whose presence at the table was seen as the League's last hope during the failed "uncancellation" of the season (17–19 February 2005), are seen to represent a game long lost to its best.

However, while Canadians mourned, raged, hoped, mounted a campaign of aroused apathy, or rededicated themselves to the game as it ought to be played (and prepared a court challenge to take back the Stanley Cup to boot) (R. McGregor, "There May Be No Hockey, But There Is a Real Challenge for Stanley's Cup," *Globe and Mail*,

4 May 2005, A2), and the powers that be tried to resurrect the
League on the ice and on American TV, I propose that the project
of the NHL to become the fourth major sport in North America – to
spread the Canadian sense of time over the American sense of
space – is flawed.

Every faith that makes a prediction about the world – such as its
end – makes that prediction for everyone, not just its followers. The
NHL promise wasn't just that hockey fans would continue to love
the game but also that the rest of the continent would love it just as
much – once it got to know it. It didn't. And the resulting scarcity
provided, just as scarcity always provides, the cause for war.

But this scarcity exists not because of the way NHL hockey is now
played (though the obstruction-filled performances in the early 2000s
didn't help); rather, it lies with what I conclude are the poetics of
the game itself. Hockey isn't – and can't be – an *American* spectacle.
The short reason for this, and the one Canadians love to quote with
the kind of tone used to talk of novices and children, is that Americans
can't follow the puck. Americans could do so, of course, and they
could do so in the numbers necessary to make up a substantial
national TV audience: they could, but they don't see the point.

Of the many definitions of "game" found in the *Oxford English
Dictionary* (online edition, 13 July 2005), the one offered fourth
best suits the purposes of my discussion: "A diversion of the nature
of a contest, played according to rules and displaying in the result
the superiority either in skill, strength or good fortune ['or,' I'd add:
'all three'] of the winner or winners." Definition 6 points out that
the game, so defined, is "terminated" either "by the victory of one
side" or by the realization that, according to the rules of play, no
victory can be achieved. Note that the *value* of the victory is exhausted
by its role as the mark of the game's end. Yet we confer great social
value on those who achieve that end, even though, in itself, it is
otherwise socially useless. If there is a social value to victory in a
game, then, that value is symbolic.

Games become sports, I would argue, when the skills necessary
to play them are the skills necessary to soldiering, and the victory
in the arena is symbolic of the victory in the field – a victory whereby
the fate of the whole society might be determined. Sports become
(major) spectator sports when the skills and strengths and good

fortunes they put on display serve large and economically significant sectors of the population as metaphors for the societies in which they are played, when watching them becomes – to roughly combine Aristotle's analysis of theatre with Canetti's work on crowds – an event through which, when properly understood, audience members experience the power of their own raised and discharged emotions.[2] But not just their emotions alone. Each member of the audience realizes (is *there* to realize) that he or she is publicly sharing his or her private identification with the physical accomplishments of the select few at the heart of the spectacle. As a private experience for which public participation is necessary, each audience member's reactions to the events on view mingle and blend – reinforcing some, suppressing others – so that the emotional life of the crowd is fed by and feeds the emotional lives of those within it. And the select few, trained and dedicated to the purpose, risk injury, even death, for the sake of an agreed-upon mark of victory. The crowd, physically safe, allows itself to be emotionally vulnerable in order to feel part of the victories or losses of the few. And what we might call the structure of the play – the rules, the necessary skills and attributes (including age and gender), the playing surface – as well as the marks of victory or loss, are themselves reflections of values deeply held by the audience. To be a spectacle, then, is to be both larger-than-life and yet confined. Perhaps all sport is the struggle of giants in chains: the spectacle is always enclosed by the arena, the stadium, or a part of nature partitioned, groomed, and bound by the play.

But what has to happen in sport – as opposed to theatre – is that the spectacular narrative defined between beginning and end has to be apprehended by the audience at the same speed and in the same order that it occurs. In fair play, things that happen in the third period can't rewrite those that happen in the first. Mistakes in scoring are not unmade once the scoring is in the books. (Results affected by cheating, however, violate not the order of events in the game but the bargain between players and audience; thus, the *status* of the result is changed, even though the events are not undone and the game is not played over.)

All audiences must be able to follow the play. All the major sports in the United States meet this condition. A basketball is bright orange and the size of a human head. A football in the air is a beautiful thing or an obvious mistake; on the ground, with a few play-action exceptions, the stop-and-start movement of the players indicates the ball's location in a man's arms. You could argue, too, that in the celebration of the tackle and the sack, American football has made game-pieces of the players themselves. Similarly, while a baseball is small enough to hide in one hand, the structure of the play, focusing on the corridor between pitcher and catcher – and the batter's explosive intrusion – tells everyone where to focus their eyes to find the ball. And even though golf involves an even smaller projectile, the golf ball's normal movements are proscribed by the course, and, in the game's climactic, scoring moment – the putt – it is a dramatically slow-moving white dot against an island of green. On television it can fill the screen with the intimacy of a close-up – and often does.

In hockey, the puck is frequently invisible to the audience – indeed, the more skilled the players, the less obvious it is. The game is full of fakery; stick-tape and skates are usually black; and the players cradle the puck, crowd around it, back-pass it and so on in order to obscure it. Shot, it disappears from view. As one of my students, an immigrant from Hong Kong, said of her first experience watching the game on TV, "What are they *doing*? There's *nothing on the ice!*" The only thing consistently observable in hockey – in the same way that a pitch, a basket, a tackle, or a putt is observable – is a fight.

Hockey has long tried to overcome the problem of the hard-to-follow puck. In its first incarnation, as recounted on its own website, the World Hockey Association (WHA) experimented with "fire engine red" painted pucks followed by pucks made of blue rubber, and when neither of these kept their integrity under normal wear (much less Bobby Hull's slapshot), it tried pucks with microchips inside so that their position could be *broadcast*. Decades later, the FOX network tried the same thing with glowing colour-coded streaks across the screen (World Hockey Association, 1). (The quest continues: on 16 March 2005, the AHL's teams from Cleveland and Rochester played in the Sabres' rink in Buffalo, where the ice has been painted pale blue, the bluelines orange, and the centre line indigo in the latest experiment to make the game easier to see on TV.) The earlier attempts not only failed to draw new audiences, they offended the hockey viewership already in place. In my opinion, hockey fans and hockey players feel the same way about not knowing where the puck is. To not know what's going on from time to time, to react to an anticipated but unrealized puck position, well, to quote Howie Meeker, "That's hockey!" The complaint that people can't follow the puck might be the language in which they express the problem they have with the game – if so, it's a symptom – but it isn't the problem itself.

And besides, the "invisible puck" as the root of hockey's unpopularity in the United States disappears when we consider the American fate of the game most like hockey but with an exceptionally easy-to-follow game piece: soccer. It's the world's most popular sport, yet American audiences remain indifferent if not hostile towards it. It's a game that children play. It's popular in certain localities, and, from time to time, Americans compete at world levels – interestingly, more successfully with women's teams than with men's – but it will never be Big League.

Why, then, is hockey a Canadian spectacle and not an American one? The answer comes back, I believe, to the function of spectator sports in general and the character of hockey and its audiences in particular. Like poetry, and unlike film, there are elements in hockey that cannot be translated into another language (even when the other language is called by the same name) without considerable cultural adjustment on a wider level than simply being able to follow what's going on or to understand the words. (Even then, given the continuous debate about the hegemony of the American film industry – and American morals and values along with it – I may be wrong about one country's film fitting more easily than its poetry into another country's life.) So let me approach the game as a kind of poem that broadly appeals to the people of one nation and not to the people of another. This appeal occurs not because of the inherent goodness of the poem but because its character embodies, or fails to embody, in both content and form, what each culture means and chooses to see represented to itself in a flattering light.

Like soccer, a hockey game goes through considerable stretches in which "nothing happens." Not *nothing*, of course, but nothing of metaphorical value to the watcher unused to the game. While in life a lot of what we do goes nowhere, so, too, in American spectator sports there is a demonstrable and rapid relation between action and result, work and reward. Hockey has always been about frustration – even before the current trend towards traps – and making the other guy look like he's playing poorly: what's on show is often not how a player reaps the rewards of his actions but how he confronts the frustration that comes with the absence of reward. Hockey is a spectacle of patience.

In hockey, the team is greater than the individual. In Canadian life the subordination of the individual to the group is a constant theme – one often, Canadians will tell you, quite mercilessly enforced on a social level, where to be said to rise above your place is a criticism. Still, we have universal medical care. In the United States, the reverse is true; the hope for an individual destiny greater than that of the group to which one belongs or into which one is born is universally on offer.

Hockey both loves and hates its own violence. It's a violent game, possibly more violent than any other, and though American football is considered to cause more injuries, the violence of football is understood by all to be an integral part of the game itself (Bird, 1). Though a hockey fight is always spectacular to behold (and anyone in the crowd when one erupts will tell you that it consistently brings people out of their seats), the hockey world has never been unified on the fight, either as part of the sport (like the heavy hit in football) or as not a part of the sport (like a fight in baseball). For a spectacle's audience to achieve the proper emotional connection to the events on show and, thus, the proper emotional catharsis, it needs to understand that the events are celebrated as symbolic of their character as a people. The sport needs to be clear about how the events are to be *felt*. I can think of no guilty pleasures that are embedded within the audience of American spectacles in the same way that fighting in hockey is embedded in Canadian audiences, whether condemned or regarded grudgingly as a necessity by those who consider themselves equally fans of The Game. In the United States, people do not rally around spectacles of ambivalence; in Canada, having something to debate for years is almost as good as getting a result.

As an aside, I note that the WHA version of hockey, which was much less conflicted about "rough play" than was the NHL version, was known to outdraw the NHL game when the two played on the same night in the same American city (World Hockey Association 2005, 2). Yet, despite that popularity, when the WHA merged with the NHL in 1979, the achievements of its players (following the lead of the merger of the American Basketball Association and the National Basketball Association, and as opposed to the integration of the American Football League with the National Football League) (see Friedman 2001) – including superstars Gretzky, Howe, Hull, and Frank Mahovlich – were *not* taken into an officially combined record book because, at least publicly, as I recall, it was argued that accomplishments in the weaker, fighting-heavy league counted for less than the work of the players who stayed in the NHL. This despite the WHA's having the overall winning record (33–27–7) against NHL teams in exhibition inter-league play (World Hockey Association 2005, 2).

And last, and perhaps most obviously, even though hockey had to move indoors in order to *become* spectacle, though hockey can be removed from winter, winter cannot be removed from hockey (see McKinley 2000). As much as our sports spectacles connect us to the virtues we celebrate, as well as sometimes, uncomfortably, to the qualities we repress as a society – both civil and martial – they also connect us to our conception of ourselves in nature. It is winter that gives us ice and lets the skate enable us to travel fast and angled to the horizon like birds. But winter also steals the warmth from our bodies if we let it; the nature that gives us hockey would kill us if we were left unprotected. From Vespucci to the Pilgrims to perhaps too many Hollywood films, the United States has been portrayed and has represented itself to its present and future occupants as the newest Promised Land, God's reward for the virtue of those who travelled to its shores and their descendants. American spectator sport is played on lush, green, and forgiving grass, or the crafted and shining surface of the hardwood – or artificial turf, an ingenious human-made combination of the two. The hockey game is forever tied to the chill reminder that God does not always provide, that even as we glide with steel on our feet, we know, in that darkly humorous Canadian way, that we dance and battle on ice, and that it is in ice, the prophets poetically remind us, that the world might one day end.

NOTES

1 On Wednesday, 24 November 2004, the SLAM! Sports: Hockey website
  had asked its readers the following question "What is your mood as the
  NHL lockout is close to wiping out the whole season?" and provided
  several options. Admittedly, the results are based on a system in which
  someone can "vote" more than once (although not more than once
  during a single visit to the site). Still, the answers are revealing, considering that the respondents were hockey fans going *to* a website dedicated
  to their troubled sport. Of the 14,635 responses, 1 percent were
  "Optimistic," 2 percent were "Hopeful," 1 percent were "Anxious,"
  11 percent were "Saddened," 4 percent were "Depressed," 21 percent
  were "Bitter," and 3 percent were "Traumatized." But an overwhelming
  57 percent were "Indifferent" (SLAM! Sports: Hockey 2004).
2 Obviously, in no way can I pretend that my brief and selective summary
  of the immense and subtle works of Aristotle and Canetti does justice to
  each man. Each thinker examined the phenomenon of audience and
  crowd behaviour in far subtler and more wide-ranging ways than I am
  able to do here. I have combined them, though, for two reasons: one is
  that Aristotle seems to me to confine his enquiry to the relationship
  between the members of the audience and the action on stage. That is to
  say, he's talking about what goes on within *individuals* as members of an
  audience. Canetti, on the other hand, broadens the field to talk about
  how the experiences of members of a spectacle's audience are affected
  and effected not so much by the spectacle itself as by the fact that they
  are all members of a *group*. What's fascinating to me here – and why
  I believe such an analysis is appropriate to hint at here and perhaps to
  follow up more fully later – is that, where other nations place the dramas
  of the gods, or military conquests, or religious ceremonies at the centre
  of the spectacles that define what they *mean* as a people in the world,
  Canada plays a game.

9

Forever Proud?

The Montreal Canadiens' Transition from the Forum
to the Molson Centre

ROBERT H. DENNIS[1]

As a part of social history, sports such as football in Great Britain or cricket in the West Indies have long provided a lens to study expressions of a nation's ethos (see James 1963; Vamplew 1988). Given its popularity and pervasiveness, hockey offers a comparable window into Canadian society and culture. While studies of this variety are becoming increasingly prevalent in the academic literature, there have been few attempts to connect the buildings where this sport is played to wider cultural-historical investigations. These buildings often transcend their exclusive designation as athletic venues and operate as cultural ones: the Forum, once home to the Montreal Canadiens of the National Hockey League, is one prominent case.

The events held in any building with an illustrious history can be read as a series of interconnected texts suggestive of a transition to modern life (Walden 1989, 287). Despite its commercial purpose and usage, the Forum also evolved as a public space in Montreal, and this fostered a deep-seated connection to French Canadians. The events that it housed reflected Quebec society, and their changing nature ultimately mirrored the province's political development as a modern nation-state.[2] With the steady increase in commercial events, the Forum did not forsake its "cultural resonance." This term denotes how the events that the Forum hosted resonated as cultural indicators: as an articulation of societal values vis-à-vis the province's development as a nation-state. The method used here analyzes cultural forms as a literary text, much as how, for example, Roch Carrier's *The Hockey Sweater* analyzes life in rural Quebec before the Quiet Revolution. When Molson Breweries – formerly the owners of the Montreal Canadiens and the Forum – opted to move the team from this public space to the ultra-modern Molson Centre (now known as the Bell Centre), they attempted to endow the new building with its predecessor's cultural significance. During the Forum's commemorative events, the company invented the tradition of the Forum within the French-Canadian narrative of the Canadiens, attempting to transport it from one venue to the other.

PUBLIC SPACE: THE FORUM AND THE EVOLUTION OF THE MODERN NATION-STATE

Built in 1924 for the Montreal Maroons, the Forum first hosted the Montreal Canadiens when they played against the Toronto St Pats, winning 7-1 on 29 November 1929. The team had normally played its home games on natural ice at the Mount Royal arena, but it was a particularly warm November, so the team asked to play its first game at the Forum. After the Maroons suspended operations in 1938, the building, distinguished by its hockey-stick-shaped escalators, remained home to the Canadiens for a grand total of 3,029 games. Including sporting, artistic, religious, and political events, the edifice welcomed over 90 million visitors in its seventy-two-year history.

The Forum, however, had an identity as both a private and a public space. Its private use as a hockey facility is easily identifiable: by taking a rink, placing it indoors, and charging admission, it quickly became a capitalist, corporate venture. Since the Forum was mainly a hockey venue, it also remained primarily a private one. And yet, it was also adopted as an important public space in Montreal. Here, however, one finds greater complexity: how was a public identity conferred on this arena? To answer this question, one must look to how the building resonated within the culture in which it was embedded. While the Forum remained significant to English Canadians living in Quebec, the building's cultural proprietorship belonged to

French Canada. Events at the Forum both shaped and reflected a fundamental process of change in the values of Québécois society, which preceded and later paralleled physical transformations within the state.

While this argument focuses heavily on the internal activity of the Forum, its external socio-spatial arrangement (i.e., its societal role in the community based on its physical location in the broader fabric of the city) should not be overlooked. The building's physical location at a cultural intersection has recognizable importance to the city's anglophone community. The Forum marks Montreal's western commercial limits, and, thus, its place in the economic life of the city should not be understated. Beyond its site emanates an eclectic mix of stores and entertainment venues (Abley 1998, 64). The presence of the Forum encouraged several development projects, including Le Faubourg; accordingly, the central concern surrounding the prospect of the Canadiens' absence was the effect on businesses along Ste Catherine Street from Guy Street to Atwater Avenue (V. Todd, "The Forum: Habs Had No Option," *Montreal Gazette*, 25 August 1989, A3). The specific location of the Forum integrated it into the Montreal community, while the Molson Centre, its successor, is far more removed from active participation in the contemporary urban landscape.

The Forum's location is at a key cultural crossroads in the city. Standing at the intersection of Atwater Avenue and Ste Catherine Street, the building, historically, has divided the diverse and varied populace in the City of Montreal from the affluent and anglophone residents in the City of Westmount. At these crossroads, the tense and contentious question that "sovereignty" plays in the province is contested. The Quiet Revolution inflamed the aspiration for sovereignty in the minds and hearts of many Quebecers, yet many others did not see separation as integral to a modern, independent Quebec. This location became important to many anglophone Quebecers, and it also became the face of a modern province for French Canadians confident in a federal country. The Forum exists in opposition to the Paul Sauvé Arena, which was traditionally used as a locus for political activity devoted to the separation of Quebec from the rest of Canada. An interesting juxtaposition that illustrates this point comes from the 1980 referendum on sovereignty. During the referendum campaign, Lise Payette, a Parti Québécois cabinet member, called opposition leader Claude Ryan's wife Madelene, and all Quebec women who were supporting federalism, "Yvettes." The name refers to a servile character in the province's French-language schoolbooks. Women of Quebec, many of whom supported federalism, responded to the derogatory comment with a pilgrimage to the city's cultural Mecca, the Forum (N. Wyatt, "Sovereignists Make a Few Advances since 1980 Loss," *Canadian Free Press*, 18 May 2000). In turn, former premier René Lévesque addressed 85,000 people at the Paul Sauvé Arena following the referendum's defeat. With regard to the referenda on separation, the Forum's socio-spatial arrangement in Montreal was connected with a political orientation towards Canadian federalism. This cultural significance was particularly acute among the city's anglophone population and was based on demography and location (Riley 1980). The building's external arrangement, however, is only one dynamic that is in play; the structure's place in public memory, in contrast, based on the events that it housed, articulates an alternate and textured cultural resonance among the Québécois.

In the early years of the Forum, the building's cultural connection to French Canadians emerged not as part of a political rationale but as part of a religious one. These, however, are not unrelated phenomena: Premier Maurice Duplessis, the province's leader from the mid-1930s to the late-1950s, ceded great power to the Roman Catholic Church in Quebec. Public funds were made available for the Church to facilitate education, health care, and the provision of assistance to the underprivileged (Baum 1991, 18–19). In the first part of the twentieth century, the broad convergence between religion and politics created a unique cultural climate in the province. The Forum's cultural connection to French Canadians in Quebec, therefore, initially emerged through housing events conducted by the Roman Catholic Church. The Church has traditionally played a crucial role in the cultural life of French Canada – dating back to the Jesuits' arrival on the shores of the St Lawrence River – and it continued to do so until the end of the 1950s (see Falardeau 1964). The close connection between the Church, the state, and the polity helped establish the building's early identity as a public space.

This significance, however, must be couched in a broader discussion of the events hosted at the Forum from 1924 to 1996, which reveals how these values developed in connection with the renaissance of the Québécois nation-state. Between 1924 and 1960, the Forum hosted a myriad of events affiliated with the Roman Catholic Church: a passion play of Christ's death (1928 and 1931), a Roman Catholic high school carnival (1939–58), a festival celebrating St Arsène (1939 and 1941), a festival for Roman Catholics from Verdun (1942–44), a festival remembering St Jean de Brébeuf (1942), a festival for the college of Jesuits (1944–59), a carnival commemorating St Louis (1946–56), a meeting of Roman Catholic Scouts (1952), and Holy Mass at midnight on Christmas Eve (1950–53) (Goyens, Turowetz, and Duguay, 1996, 232–42). The frequency and breadth of these ecclesiastical events reflect the Church's eminent place in a culture deeply rooted in religion. Though the building may have been chosen to host these events because it was the largest indoor venue in the city, the Church's de facto control over a traditional Quebec state fostered an association between its place in the provincial culture and the Forum as public area.

Social and political currents percolated at the Forum as Quebecers began to question the tenets of ultramontanism. An important event that ought to be mentioned at this juncture is the Richard Riot of March 1955 (see Di Felice 1999). Though protests against Clarence Campbell's decision to suspend Maurice Richard for the remainder of the season clearly reveal public discontent, this civic action needs to be contextualized within the general transition that was taking place with regard to events being held at the Forum. The riot coincided with the end of ecclesiastical gatherings (such as midnight mass) and the onset of more secular ones (such as ethnic and linguistic celebrations). For French Canadians in Quebec, the insurrection was part of a larger shift away from the traditional values of Duplessis-style nationalism and towards modern values associated with the democratic nationalism of 1837 (Baum 1991, 38).

The Forum provided a public place for the demonstration, quite literally, of the province's changing values. And the popular expression of this sentiment assumed its symbolic cultural form through a protest against the perceived injustice to a national icon (Baum 1991, 38). Thus, the Forum did exactly what its name indicates: it provided a forum for identity and solidarity suggestive of the will to make foundational changes to the nation-state. While it may not have been the start of the Quiet Revolution, it does show the public dissatisfaction with an anglophone's interference in the internal affairs of the province. Even though the events of 1955 prefigured central transformations in the state by several years, they remain a key moment in the history of the Forum precisely because they demonstrate public unease with Quebec's power relations.

The Forum's cultural resonance transcended its ecclesiastical beginnings, and the building's role as a public space entered the political domain. With the election of a Liberal government on 22 June 1960, the province underwent a period of rapid modernization. The Forum's events immediately mirrored this transition, and several of them reflected a rejuvenation of French-Canadian nationalism and its concomitant secularization of values: a meeting of *La Société bon parler français* (1954–55), an evening for Quebec's French-speaking Scouts (1955), Montreal's winter carnival (1961), an international winter carnival (1964), and a gala to celebrate St Jean Baptiste Day (1960–64). The first two examples relate to cultural celebrations based on linguistic distinctiveness; the third and fourth examples illustrate the rise in frequency of secular events and the decline of religious ones; and, despite the Forum's being used in subsequent decades to rally federalists, the final example shows the emergence of celebrations focused on a call for Quebec sovereignty.[3] The events at the Forum reveal the culture of the time; more important, however, they show the significant shifts in this culture. The public use of the facility changed with the transformation in the ethos of French-Canadian culture, thus legitimating the Forum's place in Québécois mystique and identity.

The period from the 1970s to the 1990s saw yet another shift: the full inception of a secular society and the rise of a commercial culture. While the former was particular to the Province of Quebec, the latter was ubiquitous throughout Western society. In 1973, the Forum hosted twelve concerts; in 1983, it hosted twenty-nine; and, in 1993, it hosted thirty-five. Absent from the building's schedule were events of an overtly cultural persuasion; in their place was a full slate of concerts and an expanded NHL schedule. This phenomenon is indicative of Montreal's transition from an industrial to a postindustrial landscape. Sociologist Don Slater (1997, 202) writes: "Post-modern transformations of the city are generally associated with a shift from the industrial city to the city as a place of consumption, entertainment, and services." Despite always maintaining a commercial identity, at least in part, these functions took full primacy in this period; yet, the building still maintained its cultural resonance. The spectacles that it housed continued to mirror the society within which it resided. The importance of the Forum had long been ingrained in Québécois culture, and though the building ceased to hold events that were obviously Québécois-specific, it did not relinquish its ascribed status as a cultural landmark.

Historical representations in popular media affirm this interpretation by showing the building's meaning in public memory. *Le fantôme de Forum*, a 1996 meta-drama from La Société Radio-Canada (SRC), which aired to coincide with the closing of the Forum, is an interesting and unique project depicting the centrality of the building to Montreal's working class. The work was produced by the Quebec government, sponsored by Molson, and has a ghost recount the history of the building. It combines the fictional story of a ghost at the Forum with a documentary-style narrative of the building's events and history. While the documentary aspect of the program is not particularly revealing of the Forum's cultural connection to the nation-state (except for an interesting juxtaposition of former Canadiens' star Maurice Richard with past premier Maurice Duplessis), the fictional aspect, which focuses on how the narrator became a ghost, is far more telling.

The fictional part of the work is very political, demonizing anglophones while elevating the plight of francophones. A French factory worker earnestly seeks to venture into the Forum to see Maurice Richard's five hundredth goal, only to be stopped by an English taskmaster. Consider this exchange:

"So where do you think that you're going?" asks the English factory owner.
"*C'est deja sept heures et demi ... Le match va commencer!*" replies the French working-class employee.
"Too bad, I need that order first thing in the morning," the gruff bourgeois owner replies.

*"Non mais la ... C'est parce que vous ne comprenez pas ...
Maurice Richard va compter sont 500 but ce soir ... Je ne peux
pas manqué ca"* the employee begs uselessly. (Le fantôme 1996)

The worker finally leaves his industrial job and takes the bus (indicative
of his paltry socio-economic standing) to the Forum. Getting off the
bus, he is hit by a car but manages to stagger into the lobby of the
Forum. As he dies, he hears the public address announcer proclaim
that Maurice Richard had scored his five hundredth goal. The ghost
then roams the Forum to reminisce about its vast history.

The depiction is a stark social commentary. In an editorial published
in *Le Devoir*, entitled "Le Forum, c'est le Québec," columnist Paule
Des Rivières quotes the work's producer, Michel Tousignant, who
defends his work by saying that it depicts the climate of the time
(13 March 1996). While the film's representation of a heartless
English bourgeois is severe, and the depiction of the linguistic divides
between worker and boss are lacking in subtlety, it does make a
good point about the political meaning of Maurice Richard, the
Montreal Canadiens, and the Forum. The appeal of Richard in
Quebec culture is based on empathy, especially among the province's
working-class francophone community; through the Montreal
Canadiens, the Forum was the particular context or the public space
that shaped and gave coherence to Maurice "Rocket" Richard as a
cultural icon. *Le fantôme de Forum* suggests that the values com-
municated by the building are fraternity, solidarity, and escapism,
and that it provides a locus of cultural activity that allows for the
subversion of anglophone domination and Duplessis-style ultramontanism. This popular representation depicts the cultural transition
and conciliation being played out within and without the confines
of the Montreal Forum.

THE INVENTION OF TRADITION: COMMEMORATIVE EVENTS AND THE CLOSING OF THE FORUM

The concept of "invented tradition" has been overused – even
bordering on the cliché – since Eric Hobsbawm and Terence Ranger

used it more than twenty-five years ago. It did, however, generate thought within the New Cultural History and, to some degree, inaugurated the field itself. It paved the way for the language of "commemoration," "memory," "creation of heritage," and, perhaps one of the more dynamic concepts to emerge of late, "historical memory" (Coates and Morgan 2002, 4). Unlike the social construction of "Scottishness" in Nova Scotia or an ahistorical appeal to antiquity (e.g., the kilt in Scotland), a discussion of invented tradition and the Forum is not designed to explain how an identity becomes generally embedded within a cultural ethos (see McKay 1992; Trevor-Roper 1983). Movements of this nature are subtle, take time, and are not noticed by participants. Invention, in this sense, contrasts with my use of the term. A particular moment – the closing of the Forum in this case – is used to create a constructed narrative: the history of the building is situated within the French-Canadian framework of the Montreal Canadiens in order to confer the cultural importance of the old building on the new.

The purpose of this invented tradition is to challenge collective memory, imposing a single hegemonic interpretation of events rather than permitting a pastiche of competing recollections (Gordon 1997, 21). Here the concept regains some of its importance as one returns to the overlapping reasons that Hobsbawm (1983, 9) postulated for invention: (1) to establish or symbolize social cohesion and (2) to legitimize institutions, status, and relations of authority. In order to achieve this balance, some moments were systematically marginalized, while others were aggrandized, and all were sensitive to the explosive nature of Quebec's political climate on the heels of the failed 1995 sovereignty referendum. In order to transfer the Forum's cultural resonance to the Molson Centre, it was axiomatic that Molson had to play an active role in so doing (see Bélanger 2000).

The economic gain from successfully conferring this significance was the primary reason for the shift from the Forum to the Molson Centre. Despite a consistency with the broader trend in the NHL of moving teams to new facilities, the design of this transition was to further co-opt the commercial success of the Forum, particularly as it lay embedded in a deep cultural connection to the city, the province, and the people. If the Molson Centre, a corporate space, could be imbued with the same meaning as its predecessor, then the public would adopt the commercial as the cultural. Though a multi-purpose facility, the Molson Centre was not designed to host the same events as those that had conferred the Forum with its legacy. Although the Forum's deep-seated cultural connection to the nation-state was largely a function of its history and the changing nature of Québécois society, the main purpose of the new building was economic return (immediately evident from higher ticket prices for events).

In the process of inventing the tradition of the Forum, the dichotomy between history (inquiry into the past) and heritage (encapsulating of history for present purposes) is evident (Lowenthal 1989, 147). This split is perhaps best articulated by the theme "Forever Proud," which referred to the legacy of the building, but ostensibly also functioned as a theme for the Canadiens' 1995–96 season. Despite seminal events like the 1976 Olympics, which were housed by the complex, the theme was framed primarily within the heritage of the team: its design was to invoke the powerful imagery aroused by the team's official name, *Club de hockey Canadiens*, and its nickname, *Les Habitants*, both of which appeal to French-Canadian nationalism. According to theologian Gregory Baum, the name Les Canadiens was given to the Roman Catholic people of North America by Lionel Groulx in the early 1900s. By fostering a romanticized version of their religious history, the name articulates French-Canadian Roman Catholics as a chosen people. This historical appropriation was designed to provide a bulwark against Protestantism, materialism, and modernity (Baum 1991, 33). The nickname Les Habitants also has this objective, evoking images of the farmers living on the shores of the St Lawrence. Ironically, it was bestowed by Lester B. Patrick, the owner of the New York Rangers, and only later took on this historical significance within popular culture. Jimmy Gardner and Ambrose O'Brien, two anglophone businessmen, created the team in 1909, when it was intended to be the counterpart to the Maroons, Montreal's English hockey team.

Molson used this connection to Québécois heritage to create a nostalgic fervour in Montreal and throughout the province. The theme "Forever Proud" linked the team's history to the building's legacy, and Molson put it on hats, T-shirts, posters, banners, and a host of other commemorative accoutrements. Ticket stubs from the 1995–96 regular season games at the Forum featured a different player from the team's past, and their reverse sides attested to his contribution to the legacy of the team and the building. The space allotted to both the English and French write-ups were comparable, though their substance reinforced the French-Canadian legacy of the hockey team. The entire history that the tickets recounted, starting with the opening game's depiction of the Forum and concluding with the final game's portrayal of the Molson Centre, framed the history of the building within the heritage of the team.

This interpretation best expresses Molson's need to solicit and actively involve the great players from the team's past. On Sunday, 11 March 1996, the Forum hosted a legends game. An event of this type is commonplace in the NHL, but in this specific instance it provided a way to visually and substantively uphold the year's theme. Acceptance of the move was conferred by the figures who were animating the building's narrative. The game, a 6-6 tie between the Canadiens legends and other former NHL stars, was secondary to the message that it suggested and was indicative of the dichotomy central to Molson's campaign. The cultural resonance of the Forum, encapsulated by the heritage of the team, was placed in binary opposition to the rest of the League and, by extension, North American culture. This move pitted a French-Canadian "self" versus a Western "other" in a match to inform public memory. Through myth building, an invented tradition secures the Forum's heritage so that it may be imposed on the Molson Centre. The commercial aspect of this act commodifies the legacy of the Forum and sells the impending transition with the blessing of prominent players in the team's history.

The season's theme – "Forever Proud" – and activities were a build-up to the Canadiens' final game, a 4-1 victory over the Dallas Stars, on Monday, 12 March 1996. Following the game, the Forum's closing ceremonies poignantly illustrated how the building's history was framed within a French-Canadian narrative that featured the Canadiens. Although these ceremonies were seemingly indicative of a moment of finality, in fact the building was used for various functions after this date, including games with the Harlem Globetrotters

and concerts by Melissa Etheridge and AC/DC. The Forum's invented
tradition was again evident when the public address announcer bel-
lowed, "Last minute of play at the Montreal Forum."[4] A red carpet
was brought out, forming a rectangular shape, and Michel Garneau
and Dick Irvin were announced as masters of ceremony. "The
Montreal Forum may be brick, but it was built on pride. The pride
of the men and hall-of-famers, you'll meet tonight, and the teams
that made it one of the most famous buildings in the world of sport
from Moscow to Los Angeles," announced Irvin. Irvin's comments
are curious because, in fact, the Forum was designed by a Scotsman,
John S. Archibald, and was financed largely by capital from anglophone investors (Goyens, Turowetz, and Duguay 1996, 14–15).
Necessarily, the attempt to tie the Forum's history to the French-
Canadian heritage of the team resulted in important lacunae. Absent
from this story, for example, is the labour that went into construct-
ing the building. Not only does the narrative omit the individuals
who physically built the edifice but it also omits those like Leo Foster,
an employee since 1945, who worked there. Important moments in
the building's history are also selectively omitted, such as a rally in
the 1970s at which labour leader Michel Chartrand had a confrontation with a Maoist dissident and the violence following the team's
Stanley Cup victories in 1986 and 1993. All the people, events, and
history of the building are reduced to a narrative comprised of select
players from the past.

The commemorative event continued, with Irvin proclaiming: "It
is one of the most beautiful hockey temples in the world." Following
the introduction, recognition was offered to those members of the
team's Hall of Fame who could not be there that evening (e.g.,
Howie Morenz and Larry Robinson). The second group to be introduced consisted of the coaches and managers, like Scotty Bowman,
who guided the franchise to its place in history. Then the players
were introduced – Guy Lapointe, Steve Shutt, Bob Gainey, Guy
Lafleur, Jacques Laperierre, Serge Savard, Jacques Lemaire, Ken
Dryden, Frank Mahovlich, Yvan Cournoyer, Lorne "Gump" Worsley,
Henri Richard, Dickie Moore, Jean Beliveau, Tom Johnson, Ken
Reardon, Elmer Lach, Emile Bouchard, and, perhaps the greatest
"Hab" of all-time, Maurice "Rocket" Richard – each receiving a

deserved ovation, including a stunning seven-minute tribute to the Rocket. After this extended break in the ceremony, hall-of-fame broadcaster René Lecavalier argued that the Forum had not only been home to the Canadiens but also to important international hockey events. With the introduction of former Soviet Red Army goaltender Vladislav Tretiak, the Forum was celebrated as a cultural backdrop to the Cold War. "In the Canadiens dressing room, there is one phrase that sums up the entire history of the team: 'To you from failing hands we pass the torch, be yours to hold it high,'" professed Irvin.

These words, taken from John McCrae's poem "In Flanders Fields," occupy a curious place within the history of the Montreal Canadiens. There is some debate about how they were incorporated into the team's mystique. The most commonly held account, however, has former coach Dick Irvin Sr inscribing them in the team dressing room during the 1940s (Les Glorieux! "Habs' Greats Bid Adieux to Forum in Style, *Toronto Star*, 12 March 1996, E2). Irvin, an anglophone from Saskatchewan, may have been using words associated with an English-Canadian conception of heroism to motivate his players. A competing account suggests that former coach Toe Blake appropriated them in the 1950s. Regardless, these lines of poetry were not designed for mass appeal. It was only later that they were integrated into the team's mythology, and they are now used to reinforce the French-Canadian vigour of the Canadiens. The words have been translated: "Nos meutris vous tendent le flambeau à vous toujours de le porter bien haut." Both English and French versions remain in the team dressing room at the new arena, and the latter is displayed prominently outside the general manager's office. The words were detached from their original meaning within a patriotic imperialist poem written by McCrae during the First World War (a war whose legitimacy was contested in French Canada) and were reintroduced as part of the Canadiens' heritage and as something that could be used to help close the Forum.

The ceremony concluded when Emile Bouchard, the oldest living Canadien, emerged from the team dressing room proudly holding a torch symbolic of the team's legacy. It was passed from each of the team's captains until it made its way to Pierre Turgeon, the captain

in 1995–96. He led the then current team in one final lap around
the rink. And, with this symbolic gesture, the Forum was closed. The
scoreboard descended from the ceiling; a banner displaying the words
"La Fierté Pour Toujours – Forever Proud," emerged as the final
statement on the Forum's history. Irvin concluded: "It is you the fans
who have always inspired the players and management of this proud
organization to always, always, aim higher." And, while this appeared
to be the final word, Garneau added: "Nous nous rendez-vous au
Centre Molson Samedi soir," thus suggesting that the cultural resonance of this public space would re-emerge Saturday night at the
Molson Centre. It would seem that the tradition continues.

Even though the narrative emphasized the contribution of "Les
Glorieux," a name conferred upon the Canadiens by French
Canadians, the closing ceremonies did include some international
events participated in by Team Canada. This inclusion was not meant
to subvert the invented tradition but, rather, to show sensitivity to
the political climate. Molson needed to transfer the deep-seated connection between the Forum and French Canadians while being conscious of the backdrop to the commemorative events: the failed
October 1995 referendum on sovereignty. Regardless, the construction placed an established consumer product within a narrative
framework that renewed its cultural legitimacy (Zukin 1991, 230–
31). While the ceremony was sensible and tasteful – an apt conclusion
for a cultural icon – it nevertheless reduced the cultural significance
of the building to the French-Canadian heritage of the Montreal
Canadiens. The torch theme not only symbolized this connection
but also showed that it could be transported to the Molson Centre.

This balance was consistent with the broader tone of Quebec's
political culture. In *Le Devoir*, an article entitled "Montréal restera
Francophone" (P. O'Neill and J. Chartier, 12 March 1996) was
positioned next to one entitled "Souvenirs de la maison hantée"
(J. Dion, 12 March 1996). The subject of the first article is Premier
Lucien Bouchard's appeal to Montreal's affluent English-speaking
community during a speech at the Centaur Theatre, asking them to
live in harmony with the city's francophone populace. Separation,
he urges, is not about making Quebec homogeneous but, rather,
about embracing pluralism and diversity. However, it should not be

forgotten that Montreal is a francophone city (O'Neill and Chartier). In the second article, Dion writes, "C'est fini. L'argent a parlé." After these opening words, strangely reminiscent of former Quebec premier Jacques Parizeau's infamous statement on the night of the referendum, the article goes on to say that the Forum takes flight because it rides on the coat-tails of Quebec's history. And yet, when the retrospective and elevated language of the article seeks to highlight the great events the shrine was home to, it points to the first game of the famous 1972 hockey summit between Canada and the USSR. *Le Devoir* itself, it would appear, had to appeal to its readers without alienating them. Interestingly, the *Montreal Gazette* offers a comparable juxtaposition, running articles entitled "Forum's Finale Is End of an Era" (Johnston and Wilton, 12 March 1996, A1) and "We Are All Quebecers – Bouchard" (S. Scott, 12 March 1996, A1). The tone of both newspapers, evincing the political culture of that particular moment, is consistent with the few recollections not part of the French-Canadian framework that are allowed into the invented narrative.

A balance between the invented tradition and the political climate was evident during the entire campaign. Even within the commemorative literature produced on the Forum, certain elements were emphasized while others were systemically exorcized from its official history. This was done delicately in order to maintain the compromise that Molson had struck. According to Rudy J. Koshar (1994, 216): "Buildings 'have' pasts because human beings create narratives that tell readers when a building was erected, what historical events it endured, who lived in it, and how it has been used … This process consists of discursively using building-pasts to 'build' those collective pasts that give continuity, stability, and familiarity to particular social configurations in particular historical context." The official book dedicated to remembering the building, *Le Forum de Montréal: La fierté pour toujours, 1924–1996*, does not, for example, make any substantial reference to the "Yvette" rally in 1980. While other moments are thoroughly detailed, this event's place is limited to a brief mention in the chronology: "Les Québécois pour le non" (Goyens, Turowetz, and Duguay, 1996, 250). Although it does include other major athletic, entertainment, and cultural events, the book, in order to strike the necessary political balance, carefully omits very important moments in the life of the building.

The crux of *Le Forum de Montréal* is the move to the Molson Centre. Its historical background offers a lead-up to a full-page colour photograph that depicts the Molson Centre and shows an accepting Maurice Richard donning a Montreal Canadiens hard hat and examining the new building. Molson launched a commercial campaign inviting people to the new building. Using the legends of the game is not the same as hiring other spokespersons. Each of the great players, Richard being the most prominent, represented an iconic affiliation with cultural space. Molson attempted to confer this connection upon the Molson Centre with the "Big Move Parade" on Friday, 15 March 1996 (Bélanger, 392). The commemorative event was split into twenty-four sections, each representing one of the team's Stanley Cups, proceeding from one building to the other. The event – consistent with Jonathan Sperber's (1992, 22–3) analysis of festival processions during the German Revolution of 1848 – claimed this new space for the nation. The parade literally tried to move the cultural resonance of the Forum to the Molson Centre.

Opened on the afternoon of Saturday, 16 March 1996, the Molson Centre was commissioned by two bitter political rivals: the premier of Quebec, Lucien Bouchard; and the prime minister of Canada, Jean Chrétien. This opening ceremony is perhaps what best represents the broad convergence between Molson's conciliatory attempts to connect the new building with Québécois culture. The free open house, held on Sunday, 17 March 1996, offered a chance for the populace to tour the new facility and was an attempt to foster a sense of public ownership. If the public could empathize with the Molson Centre in the same way that they had done with the commercially successful Forum, the result would realize Molson's primary goal of boosting the beer/hockey synergy in Quebec (Bélanger, 382, 392).

Blurring the lines between culture and commerce during the reorganization of a public urban space was a carefully conducted endeavour. In order to endow the Molson Centre with the Forum's cultural resonance, the Centre's invented tradition, while sensitive to the political climate of 1996, was constructed within the framework of the Montreal Canadiens' French-Canadian heritage. Each action –

such as the exhibition on hockey history held at Montreal's McCord Museum from 12 March 1996 to 1 April 1997 – attempted to confer the Forum's connection to the nation upon the Molson Centre. Framing the history of the building within Québécois heritage encapsulated the cultural importance of the Forum in public memory. Aspects of the collective memory were only allowed to co-exist within the invented tradition insofar as they co-opted dissenting opinion in the province.

CONCLUSIONS

Although the Forum's socio-spatial arrangement affirmed it as a locus for federalist activity during Quebec's referenda on sovereignty, the events held there created a link to Quebec's development as a nation-state. By inventing tradition, Molson used the heritage of the Montreal Canadiens to narrate the history of the Forum and to sell the team's move from a public area to a private area. The company usurped a cultural space and reorganized a public urban area for commercial reasons. Given the attachment the city felt to this space, it was imperative that the Canadiens' move be a major occurrence (Bélanger, 391–97). The backdrop for this move was the province's failed referendum on sovereignty, and a regard for Quebec's political climate was a concern during the Forum's closing ceremonies. In order to confer the Forum's cultural resonance on its successor, a particular historical narrative, with the theme "Forever Proud," was constructed. This narrative made full use of the French-Canadian heritage of the Montreal Canadiens (which, given the important role played by anglophones Archibald, Blake, Irvin, and others, suggests that this was very much an invented tradition). Molson encapsulated the legacy of the Forum though a living legends game and hoped to usurp the Forum's cultural resonance through a parade from one building to the other. The company strategically showed that the Canadiens' "living legends" offered their approval and that, consequently, the Molson Centre should be imbued with the same meaning as was the Forum. The "history-accepts-progress" message was designed to invent a tradition, the point being to reorganize a public area as a private one.

Following the departure of the Montreal Canadiens from the Forum, there was a growing movement to protect this space. During the week of the move, the *Montreal Gazette* ran a story on what the loss of this building meant to the community. One person who tried to save the Forum from cultural decapitation was a unionist turned lawyer. According to Bill Brownstein, "[Jean-Luc] Deveaux has since traded his union placard for a lawyer's gown and has moved to Westmount. He is proposing the Forum be turned into a centre for teaching international law and labour rights, because the venue symbolizes to him a convergence of Anglo- and Franco-cultures" ("The Crumbling of a Community," *Montreal Gazette*, 10 March 1966, A4). This outcry to preserve the Forum as a cultural space reflected the broader decline in public space within the urban landscape. Ultimately, it fell on deaf ears as the Forum was turned into an entertainment complex featuring a movie theatre. While cities still contain parks and recreational areas, the areas for cultural expression continue to decline. The Forum in Montreal, during certain points of its history, functioned more as a town square than it did as an entertainment venue. It is this loss that the public laments. The reorganization of urban space caused the local distinctiveness of the Forum to dissipate into the generic homogeneity of the Molson Centre. Without marginalizing the need for modernity that the new building quite legitimately represents, the historian of these developments must ask: will the Montreal Canadiens departure from the Forum stand as something that is "forever proud?" At times, it is difficult to establish the boundary between "true" culture and "commercial" culture; however, if one laments the pervasiveness of the latter, particularly at the expense of a building so beloved, then this phrase does seem a curious one.

NOTES

1 The author would like to thank Ian McKay, Gregory S. Kealey, Jackson W. Armstrong, Katherine Eddy, Sean Mills, and Patrick Arruda for their help in the preparation of this work.

2 Breaking it down into its constitutive elements, "nation" refers to the presence and growth of Québécois nationalism. The events that the Forum housed show the polity's increasing self-awareness as a sovereign actor. "State" indicates the province's physical and philosophical transformation from a traditional to a secularized entity. The cultural resonance of the Forum more accurately resides in its interplay between nation and state and their mutual development.

3 In Quebec, St Jean Baptiste Day has developed into a call for Québécois independence. Perhaps the most notable example of this in recent memory is the celebration following the failure of the Meech Lake Accord (1990). The day's events transcended their religious roots and became a manifestation of French-Canadian identity. For a discussion of the historical development and meaning of the national holiday, see Gordon (1997, 282–5).

4 This statement and others associated with the final game and closing ceremonies are transcribed from The Sports Network's (TSN) broadcast on 12 March 1996.

10

Manufacturing Players and Controlling Sports
An Interpretation of the Political Economy of Hockey and the 2004 NHL Lockout

JULIAN AMMIRANTE

INTRODUCTION: THE FRAGILE EMPIRE OF THE NHL

That hockey is a commodity is obvious. Yet there is also a prevalent notion that there is something unique about certain sport commodities and sporting events and that this enables them to be set apart from ordinary commodities like automobiles or cell phones.[1] While the boundary between these two types of commodities is quite permeable, there has been a certain stubbornness in maintaining an analytical separation. Perhaps this is because we cannot equate athletes and the display of their special talents with workers engaging in mass production for mass consumption.

Nonetheless, despite our propensity, as sports fans, to be nostalgic, we must recall that sports such as professional hockey have been businesses for a considerable amount of time and that, ultimately, they have become extensive industries. What is more, these businesses most often exist in the world's most commercialized societies. This is a fact; yet, so many are troubled when commerce dominates this area and hockey players (considerable salaries and endorsements notwithstanding) are considered as employees. Consider the antipathy that hockey fans exhibited towards the players during the 2004–05 National Hockey League lockout.[2] This seems to mirror the general indignation that sports fans harbour towards professional athletes. Yet the average irate fan continuously suppresses the important fact that, although professional hockey players have market power, they do not control the enterprises responsible for the commercialization that has overwhelmed hockey in Canada.

It may be that as hockey fans – or sporting fans – we selectively distinguish the way we react to commercialization, criticizing players while turning a blind eye towards those who control the industry. Despite this discord,[3] one cannot deny that ultimate control in the professional hockey industry rests in the hands of those who employ the athlete: the NHL and owners and managers of franchises, leagues, and media outlets. It appears that a yearning for a time when the "game" was played simply because athletes loved to participate – "the good old days" – continues to get in the way of prudent thought. Nonetheless, after we remove all the nostalgic underpinnings (repeatedly reinforced by hegemonic ideologies and discourses), we are still left with the feeling that there is something unique about the products designated as sports, leisure, and entertainment. The question then remains: how can we reconcile the unique character of these events and phenomena with their commodity status (Harvey 2002)?

The answer rests in understanding management-labour tensions in the hockey industry. In particular, we need to understand how the forms of competition and monopoly reflect the underlying exploitative nature of production, which means the production of sports labour. In this case, we are talking about professional hockey players, the supply of which can now be considered global. Thus, in this situation, I first attempt to understand how the main actors on the owner/management side of the equation have organized themselves in order to direct the production of sports labour in the form of the hockey player.[4] Having discussed the hockey player/athlete's demand for increases in salaries from the standpoint of labour supply and demand and investment in human capital, I argue that the NHL and its franchises increasingly moved into a precarious position vis-à-vis their individual and collective power bases as well as their legitimacy.

For instance, never have the NHL and its franchises been more powerful. From 1988 until the 1997–98 season, the League expanded from twenty-one teams to thirty teams, securing huge dividends. It made itself competitive in the US national market, which seemed to have been the plan since the arrival of Gretzky in Los Angeles. In 1990, the NHL was in eleven US markets, which were perceived to be regional; now it is in twenty-two US markets. This was unprecedented exposure, and it generated unprecedented revenues far beyond the proportions imagined by the owners of the Original Six. However, despite the League's capacity, it became increasingly obvious that the entity known as the NHL had moved into an incredibly precarious position. The manner in which the League expanded (and is now perhaps contracting, or at least rearranging its position in relation to the supply of hockey players) seems to have subjected it to a serious crisis. To be more precise, the greater its concentration into a larger-scale unit, the greater the possibility for the coalescence of the NHL Players' Association (NHLPA) – or workers. With this development, we have seen the potential and consequences of unionization in the form of the disruption of the production of the sporting event. At the same time, as the NHL and its franchises increased in size, we have seen a greater interdependence among hockey players/workers as producers and consumers on national, continental, and perhaps global scales and, consequently, the widening of the sphere of their common interests in decreasing the rate of surplus value generated by their labour and, in general, democratically restructuring production and consumption.

THE UTILITY OF ALL SPORTS: ATHLETES AS ECONOMIC AGENTS

The ubiquity of commercial sports has meant that their values have become the values of sports in general. For instance, the cynical use of performance-enhancing drugs by Major League Baseball (MLB) players is imitated by countless unquestioning high school, college, and amateur athletes who are trying to bolster their attempts to "make it," while athletes as young as six and seven years old are treated like commodities. At a deeper level, sports tend to transmit and reinforce the dominant class relations of the political economy as a whole. For instance, most fans of any sport have come to unwittingly accept if not celebrate a marketing relationship that symbolizes the economic and cultural colonization of the country. Every year thousands of young males of the former USSR, Africa, and/or Latin America effectively become migrant workers in a foreign country, while sports in their own communities remain underdeveloped.

It should be stressed that none of these situations is static as entrepreneurs continually adjust their behaviour in light of the general economic conditions and profit expectations, while athletes attempt to bargain for a larger share of the profits and better working conditions, and non-professional athletes and fans try to persuade governments to make changes. In fact, since the 1970s, militant players' unions, the women's movement, and growing numbers of other reform-minded movements have all, with varying degrees of success, attempted to make progressive changes.[5] Most professional leagues now have adequate grievance procedures, and, perhaps more significantly, a number of practices once the sole prerogative of management are now subject to collective bargaining. At the community level, the ideological hold of commercial sports has been challenged by national programs, such as coaching development schemes, which stress a much more public and civic philosophy. However, as long as capitalist relations of production continue to exist in sports, problems will always be present.

In this regard, let us point to what is perhaps the most misunderstood aspect of sports: the supply of professional athletes available in the international sports labour market. This has conventionally been viewed in either one or two ways, or a combination of both. The first view fundamentally embraces neoclassical theory, the dominant paradigm in economics today. In this view, the quantity of labour supplied in any industry is based on the decisions individuals make regarding how they will allocate their time between working and not working; that is, between income and leisure. The relevant price in this decision is the wage that workers expect to receive in the labour market. That wage is a payment to workers for the labour services they provide employers – services based on worker (and employer) expenditures on education and training, migration, and job search (Ehrenberg and Smith 1988, 292). Workers have a stock of skills acquired through investments that they and their employers have made in human capital, and they will consider seriously those jobs paying them a return equal to or greater than what they think they could earn in their next best alternative position. Non-pecuniary rewards and sources of monetary income, in addition to what their employers pay (particularly for professional athletes), play roles in this decision (Scoville 1974, 187–8; Hamermesh and Rees 1984, 280–3). It is also the case that workers consider expected lifetime earnings (Kaufman 1989, 343), and there is also the phenomenon known as compensating differentials – different rates of pay for jobs that may be more or less attractive. This is their reservation wage.

Nonetheless, most athletes, especially professional athletes, are paid far more than what their investment in their particular skills would bring them if they were earning their reservation wage working in their next best alternative occupation rather than in their given sport.[6] Hence, the monetary compensation the NHL and its franchises pay hockey players for playing hockey consists not only of their wage (a yield on investments made in their human capital) but also a premium over and above that wage. That premium is called economic rent, which is the cornerstone of free-wage labour.

A second view, also informed by neoclassical principles, concerns sports as entertainment and the provision of the event. In this view, professional athletes are performers employed by a sector of the entertainment industry. Sports figures who sign multi-million-dollar contracts differ very little from Céline Dion (who was paid an astronomical fee to perform in Las Vegas over a couple of years) or Jerry Seinfeld (whose annual earnings in 1998, as estimated by *Forbes Celebrity 100*, were $267 million). It can even be argued that professional athletes, as entertainers, have much in common with network news anchors and sports announcers and writers, individuals who are paid hefty sums to read teleprompters and to describe athletic events. When classified by economic functions – whether singer, actor, television personality, or athlete – an entertainer is an entertainer. In a market economy, the monetary compensation such individuals receive is based on two very familiar considerations: demand and supply.

Furthermore some athletes (like some entertainers) are endowed with unique talents or natural abilities/characteristics, and they work in industries in which such phenomena are a major input in the final service provided to consumers. No amount of practice or training can reproduce those qualities/attributes, certainly not in the short run and perhaps not even in the long run. Tiger Woods, Céline Dion, and Andrea Bocelli are individuals whose talents – or should I say cachet – cannot be replicated regardless of how long one practices or how much one spends on training and instruction. Moreover, as capitalism has grown in complexity, politics and culture, no less than economics, have experienced a renovation involving the conversion of old structures into new uses and the advance of commodification into new areas. This "new" condition assigns a great deal of importance to aesthetics or aesthetic production. This seems to stem from the worth that commodities are assigned through the identities they are able to provide. With the proliferation of information and modern communication technologies, the world seems to have now entered, – or found utility in – a cultural economy. Here markets have moved beyond the capacity of states to manage them, and units of economic production have been reduced to a more individual scale. The economy at a certain level becomes so subordinate to individual taste and choice that it becomes reflexively marketized, and because "these markets are perfunctory they do not succumb to physical boundaries" (Lash and Urry 1994).

In short, they have become reflexively globalized. The leading sectors in this process are those whose commodities are themselves symbols – the mass media, entertainment, and sports industries. This is particularly important in any televised sporting spectacle as we see a star-centred type of investment in leading athletes who possess heroic, almost mythic qualities. This has become a standard feature of pre-game speculation and post-game analysis in sports journalism, which is a key mechanism in the marketing and selling of the event. We find resonance of this type of theorizing in the work of Roland Barthes (1972, 109–10), in which everything can be a myth provided it is conveyed by a discourse.

Precisely because of this type of economy, many human myths or mythical figures acquire qualities that transform them. They become emblems and/or icons; that is to say, they become essences that can be represented by signs. Thus, they may symbolize an abstraction, an idea, or a collectivity that can recognize itself and that can be recognized by others in the form of that sign. This sign then becomes "integrated into commodity production as capitalism produces fresh waves of ever more novel-seeming goods (from clothing to airplanes), at ever greater rates of turnover" (Jameson 1984, 55). As Jameson further explains: "[This] now assigns an increasingly essential structural function and position to aesthetic innovation and experimentation. Such economic necessities then find recognition in [institutional supports] of all kinds available ... from foundations and grants to museums and other forms of patronage" (56). Thus, a show business producer, sports team owner, or sports commissioner cannot simply order as many Tom Cruises, Julia Roberts, Ronaldos, Wayne Gretzkys, Shaquille O'Neils, Tiger Woodses, or Ricky Martins as he or she might like. The unique characteristics of such stars markedly surpass the scope of the far more numerous capable run-of-the-mill performers.

With this in mind, we must return to the concept of economic rent. Bear in mind that the entire monetary compensation that organizations pay individuals with unique abilities is an economic rent.[7] In the aforementioned examples, the payment is a pure economic rent. Athletes are inputs – factors of production – in this process.[8] The available quantity of such a factor does not vary when its market price changes. When demand for a service is weak, the factor's total return – its rent – will be small. Conversely, when demand for a service is strong, the factor's total return will be large. Thus, the return to a factor fixed in the long run, a factor such as a unique talent, is determined solely by the strength of consumer demand for the final good that factor produces. I leave the discussion of economic rents and factors of production for later; for now, let us just say that not all athletes have unique abilities. Therefore, not all athletes are paid a pure economic rent; and, in the sports sector, unique talents are paid pure economic rents.

In addition to economic rent, hockey teams and the NHL produce contests that they market to spectators and viewers and/or listeners through the electronic and print media. The audiences to whom the NHL offers television and radio networks can be considered commodities for sale in the media marketplace (Leslie 1995; Levitt 1983). Recall that athletes are inputs and factors of production in this process. This means that a team's demand for the services of a player is derived from the market demand for its output – athletic contests. This point bears repeating: the value to a sports organization – such as the NHL, the NFL, or any other sports franchise – of the services provided by the athletes it hires is derived from the demand sports fans exhibit for the events these inputs produce. All other things being equal, the payments athletes receive for their services are positively correlated with fans' demand for professional sporting events.

However, as I pointed out earlier, much of what informs this view fundamentally engages neoclassical economic theory. One crucial point that is missing from this view is that of labour power. Neoclassical economic theory constantly confuses labour with labour power and, thereby, blinds its followers to the nature of the most critical transaction of the capitalist economic system – the exchange of labour power. The exchange of labour power takes place between formal equivalents: the worker and the capitalist meet in the market on the same equal terms as do other traders. However, the real content of the transaction is power and subordination. One party places her or his capacities (and, therefore, her- or himself) at the disposal of the other. The substitution of labour for labour power covers up the crucial aspect of wage labour, suggesting that athletes are paid for what they do (productivity), measured in terms of physical output of revenue. It creates the inaccurate impression that the object traded on the labour market is external to the athlete and not an integral aspect of her or his personality, predisposition, and capacities.

CONTROL, CORNERING AND MANIPULATION: THE TALE OF COMMERCIAL SPECTATOR SPORTS

What is also crucial with regard to understanding the fragility of the NHL vis-à-vis its individual and collective power bases and legitimacy is the realization that all major professional teams and individual sports are organized into leagues or associations. Forming a league or an international organization with periodic competitions appears to be a prerequisite for the financial success (or at least stability) of any sport. Prior to the appearance of leagues and regular competitions such as the Stanley Cup Playoffs, hockey teams played each other on an informal, ad hoc basis. The NHL and any other major-league spectator sport are by nature cooperative bodies; at one level each team's success depends on the success of the other teams in the league and on the success of the league or organization as an institution. The goal of the cooperative behaviour is to maximize the combined wealth and success of the teams in the league or organization. Off the field, team owners, competitors, and commissioners of leagues regard each other and their athletes as colleagues rather than as adversaries – or at least they should. Together, they try to maximize their wealth and success by maximizing revenues and controlling costs (among other things). Also, in their business operations, member clubs of a league are not so much competitors as partners or participants in a joint venture (Flynn and Gilbert 2001). Whereas ordinary business may view the failure of a competitor with equanimity or even satisfaction, the members of a sports league, association, or organization does not.

Nevertheless, leagues such as the NHL do much more than create a set of common opponents. Their activities also include – or should include – deciding on revenue-sharing arranging, staging championship-style tournaments, creating a framework for the entry of new players and teams into the league, and conducting marketing companies. For instance, groups like the Professional Golfers' Association and the United States Tennis Association perform much the same function for the more individually based sports that leagues such as the NHL fulfill for team franchises. Much if not all of the success of such organizations depends on their market position, and, overwhelmingly, this involves monopoly. This has enormous implications for an organization's dominion, whether it be a national or an international league or association. This is because, fundamentally, the monopoly structure provides a terrain of survival for all capitals involved. This institutional form is not limited to the sports industry but, rather, is reflective of much of the form that capital in general has taken – establishing or reinforcing a structure that ensures the survivability of a minimum threshold of participating capitals (i.e., franchises, teams, individuals, etc.).

In this sense, the sports league – or, in this case, the NHL – also commands a "monopsony." In other words, it is the sole employer and is thus able, on a general level, to direct the cost of the average price of athletic labour power. This establishes a foundation from which all participating capitals are able to draw athletic prowess. At another level, and in contrast to the monopoly/monopsony taking place at the level of the league, there is a monopoly mechanism utilized *within* competitive leagues as some kind of national or even global sports structure. At this level the competition among capitals is more direct. Despite an average cost of athletic labour power, powerful capitals (i.e., franchise owners, teams) attempt to control talent utilization by negotiating extraordinary contracts, determining salaries for specific athletic functions based upon potential/expected return.

MONOPOLY/MONOPSONY

Population, local sporting tradition, accessibility of venue, comfort of seating arrangements, weather, game time, and popularity of individual athletes all influence revenue, but the most important determinant is the existence or absence of competition. Without competition, promoters can charge as much as they want for as many seats as they want to sell. Also, once a league has established itself, it is almost impossible to displace it from its dominant position. For instance, during the 1960s and 1970s, several new leagues were created in an attempt to challenge the established monopolies of the NHL, the National Basketball Association (NBA), and the National Football League (NFL). These challengers quickly folded or simply merged with already existing leagues, ultimately reinforcing the market monopoly.

To be sure, major-league spectator sports leagues such as the NHL resemble a natural monopoly. The monopoly position explains, in part, a major spectator sports league's power over cities. The profits shown by franchises in cities such as New York, Los Angeles, and Toronto dramatically increases the number of cities bidding to be a home for a franchise as cities and countries see opportunities to create new revenue streams (e.g., tourism) and to generate international attention. In effect, major-league spectator sports teams or franchises are viewed as assets that major leagues such as the NHL can auction off to the highest bidder, much like a valuable painting.

As the number of competing bidders rise, the price of the asset is driven upward. At its limit, the price of the asset approaches the expected profits (or utility) that asset can provide. The original owner of the asset (in this case, a team or franchise) captures all its value, just as the monopolist attracts all consumer surplus through the all-or-nothing demand curve. The team's or franchise's monopoly position is highlighted by the fact that cities and countries wishing to host them must, with little direct competition, purchase the right from a producer. Moreover, cities that consider bidding on franchises also face the constraint that they cannot purchase part of a team and, thus, face an all-or-nothing decision. Finally, the winning city may be overly optimistic about the benefits that host cities can accrue, or it may be led by the auction process to overbid for the right to host a team or franchise. In sum, the major spectator sports leagues represent a very challenging problem for potential host cities: those that would like to host a franchise face a monopolist offering an all-or-nothing scenario within an environment in which costs and benefits are both highly uncertain (Zimbalist 1998).

This example would suggest that "all rent is based on the monopoly power of private owners of certain portions [spaces?] of the globe" (Harvey 2002, 2). Monopoly rent originates because certain actors can actualize an increased income over a long period of time by virtue of an especially saleable item over which they exercise exclusive or extensive control. Nowhere is this more evident than with the control of athletic contests like the NHL and its regular season and playoffs. Social actors, entrepreneurs, owners, commissioners – whatever or whomever they may be – control the special quality of the sporting event, which, because of its uniqueness, enables them to extract monopoly rents from those desiring to use it. The monopoly price creates the rent, and the bidder is willing to pay a premium for the use of the event. This would be considered an indirect use of the event because we are not talking about something tangible that is being traded (e.g., land) but, rather, about a commodity or service that is produced through its use.

Sports organizations such as the NHL have sought to create and protect monopolies in the cities in which they operate and to bargain collectively for broadcast revenue. For the most part, it is these monopolies – and not athlete salaries – that account for the high prices and fat profits in commercial sports.

Monopsony is essentially the mirror image of monopoly. Whereas monopolists derive their power from being the only seller and use this power to drive up the price of what they sell, monopsonists derive their power from being the sole consumer and use their power to drive down the price of what they buy. Like a monopolist, a monopsonist does not have any competition and is the sole buyer of a good or service. Firms that sell their goods or services in a monopsonistic market can sell them to no one except the monopsonist. A monopsonist and a monopolist are identical in one respect: both restrict the quantity of transactions. A monopolist cannot force consumers to buy at the higher price, and a monopsonist cannot force producers to sell at the lower price. The monopsonist has market power over the input market and so can pay lower or higher wages as production necessitates. The effect, in practice, is that employers are in a position to set wage and salary levels because there are no alternative employers in that field of work.

Monopsony power was once – and to some extent still very much is – one of the cornerstones of professional sports. Until the 1970s, most sports leagues held monopsony power through specific language in the standard player contract. This was known as the "reserve clause." The reserve clause effectively bound players to the team that held their contracts for as long as the teams desired their services. As a whole, professional sports leagues were, for the longest time, in the enviable position of having both monopoly power over fans and monopsony power over players. Almost since the NHL's inception, the franchise owners operated as though the League were a virtual monopsony. Ever since the NHL emerged in the 1930s as hockey's only "major league" (having driven its competitors in other parts of North America out of business), NHL owners have enjoyed a monopsony position as the only significant buyers of professional hockey talent. This was the situation in professional hockey, with the brief exception of the 1970s when the World Hockey Association (WHA) offered employment choices and, therefore, salary competition. Until then, NHL owners had effectively controlled the hockey labour market through the reserve clause. Once again, this placed

NHL owners in an enviable position since there were no other buyers of hockey labour and disgruntled players had nowhere else to turn. However, in the 1960s, US court rulings against the validity of the reserve clause in baseball established an important legal precedent. In the other sports, the brief existence of competitive leagues (the American Football League and the WHA), together with the threat of anti-trust suits from players when these leagues merged with their erstwhile rivals, persuaded the surviving leagues to negotiate looser controls on player mobility.

However, the major factor in the achievement of greater player mobility in North American professional sports has been collective bargaining and the growth of strong player unions. Until the late 1980s, the NHL Players' Association (NHLPA) was led by Toronto lawyer Alan Eagleson, who had a cosy relationship with the NHL executive. Eagleson would ultimately be accused of failing to adequately represent players' interests on a series of financial issues; and, indeed, during the 1980s, NHL salaries had certainly fallen below those paid in the other major-league sports. Following Bob Goodenow's replacement of Eagleson as head of the NHLPA and a new initiative on the part of the NHLPA and player agents to publicly publish player salaries, NHL salaries rose dramatically to levels akin to those of the other major sports (even though NHL revenues remained markedly lower). It is worth noting that hockey players had begun to use the services of agents and that the latter were collectively discussing how their clients' salaries could be systematically maximized through arbitration and free agency.[9] What is also worth noting is that, after 1989, the terms and conditions for free agency (i.e., when players are eligible to move and when a player's former club is entitled to compensation) became central issues in collective bargaining negotiations between the NHL and the NHLPA.

The wealthiest owners, meanwhile, sensing large rewards in marketing and merchandising (as well as competitive success) if star players could be secured, began to spend unprecedented amounts for the services of hockey players.[10] The sums of the early 1990s seem paltry by current standards; but for a league that was still surviving mainly on gate revenues, what's important to understand is that multi-million-dollar salaries and long-term contracts were gambles by owners who were in a monopoly/monopsony position with regard to a different kind of future – a future that promised new revenues from expansion, from more lucrative television contracts, from luxury boxes, and from merchandising and endorsements. Star players were the first beneficiaries, clearly; but free agency became a predictable point in an established player's career – a point at which he could expect a large raise. Moreover, with a system of "qualifying offers" set at 110 percent, and an arbitration system that established comparable salaries for players posting comparable statistics (whether their teams had large revenues or limited ones), the salaries of journeyman players also began to escalate rapidly, and owners found themselves negotiating from positions of weakness. Essentially, the NHL was feudal in its management-labour relationship. A liberalization of this labour had to take place. This, then, was the "business model" that owners determined to "fix" through a salary cap.

CARTELIZATION

The essential operating element of commercial sports is the league, not the franchise. To maximize the respective sporting enterprise, entrepreneurs must first maximize joint profits. Cartelization, a derivative form of monopoly, exists because two teams or a small number of athletes (relative to the existing supply) are necessary in order to stage the contest that generates the greatest possible revenue. Revenues can be enhanced if teams or individuals cooperate in setting and enforcing rules, advertising, and other arrangements. As interest in the contest is considered to vary directly with the uncertainty of the outcome, sports leagues and organizations usually attempt to equalize playing talent among member clubs and organizations through a wide range of arrangements designed to give weaker teams or competitors a promising chance. Some of the major leagues perform this function by offering "development" funds to competitors from smaller or weaker competing nations or regions. In short, most leagues have some arrangement for revenue sharing in order to equalize the ability of franchises to purchase players. But no league has achieved complete revenue equalization – a circumstance that seems to explain why, historically, teams in the richest markets have dominated.

ABSTRACT/FREE WAGE LABOUR

It is precisely through the institutional form of monopoly/monopsony and cartel that owners and commissioners can reorganize the production of athletes so as to increase the productivity and intensity of the athlete's labour. Here, those controlling the sporting event can maximize the movement from productive capital to commodity capital. Furthermore, this reorganization would have the effect of decreasing the dependence of production on the labour of skilled and, hence, higher paid athletes or workers, thus increasing the dependence on regular run-of-the-mill athletes who will to do anything to get their break in marquee competitions or the "big leagues." Many have complained about the homogenization of styles and the cheapening of talent as leagues have broadened the pool of athletes available for their respective sport. The apparent blandness and insipidity characterizing sports today can be considered both directly and indirectly related to this institutional form of capital organization.

At the same time, sports promoters discovered the limits of cartelization many years ago. Historically, collusion among sports franchises and organizations has been less than perfect. Owners, coaches, trainers, and general managers want to win on the pitch, rink, or field, and a winning team or athlete tends to earn more revenue than a losing team or athlete. This condition has created a contradictory dual movement that has caused much of the labour-capital problems characterizing not only the NHL but also major-league spectator sports in general. Just as the homogenization of styles and skill has broadened the pool of employable athletes, so capital has reserved the big contract for superstars, who are seen as revenue accumulators. Ironically, by understanding how monopoly competition works, we can see exactly how the struggle over the control of athletic output between organizations and owners, on the one hand, and athletes, on the other, transpires. By awarding value to specialized athletic labour power, as well as by increasing the supply of athletic workers, owners have inadvertently necessitated a struggle on the part of athletes and their agents over the price they can command. Increasingly, athletes begin to view their talents in abstract terms amenable to contract discourse – for sale to the highest bidder. Increasing the pool of players has tended to effectively increase the potential of athletes to see themselves as collectively providing a service and/or commodity. The greater the pool, the greater the potential for unionization or organizing on the part of athletes. This increasingly evident struggle determines not only the extent to which athletic labour processes are shaped by the profit imperatives of capital but also the crucial implications for the wage and rights struggle occurring in the sports sector.

Here is a potential source of instability for sports leagues and team franchises. Contradictorily, while sports leagues such as the NHL attempt to stabilize their stranglehold over athletic labour, competing capitals within these associations engage in destabilizing practices associated with the systemic need to drive for accelerated profits. One need look no further than the inability of the NHL to come to terms on a revenue-sharing agreement or the de facto veto of seven of the league's owners.[11] This, in turn, strengthens the labour-capital tension in professional and amateur sporting structures. In attempting to reproduce and maintain their position of dominance, the NHL and its team franchises contribute to their own instability.

MEDIA DEPENDENCE

A professional sports league or sporting event is not a natural product. It is a wholly artificial entity created and kept alive by rules developed for that purpose. The media plays a key role in marketing spectator sports, advertising games, exaggerating the significance of performances, suppressing criticism, and supporting the owners in their struggles with the players and player unions. Such ideological support should not come as a surprise. Sporting events around the world generate massive interest. This is a fact that has not been lost on television broadcasters. In recent years, there has been a global explosion in the airtime allotted to sports events. Changes in the business of broadcasting sports have been moving at a tremendous pace, at times exceeding any attempt at analysis. However, we can identify some significant occurrences vis-à-vis the NHL.

Hockey has always been a successful television product in Canada, with CBC's long-running *Hockey Night in Canada* attracting large nationwide audiences and becoming, over the years, something of a national institution (Gruneau and Whitson 1993). However, in the United States, hockey has historically been a regional sport at best, largely limited to the northeastern and Great Lakes states in its popular appeal. When the NHL first expanded in the mid-1960s, it succeeded in securing national network television deals in the United States, first with CBS (1968–72) and then with NBC (1973–75). However, each of these contracts was terminated by the network because of disappointing audience ratings, and NHL hockey would not appear on a US network again until the 1990s. Sports specialty channels on cable (such as ESPN and, in Canada, TSN) began to develop profitable niche markets in the early 1980s. However, where other sports – and not only the major-league team sports but also, for example, golf – succeeded in developing national audiences in the United States, hockey remained regional in its appeal and, hence, in its revenue potential. Moreover, although cable and satellite television now contribute significantly to the revenues of many sports in the United Sates, pay-per-view (i.e., paying to watch single events) has not caught on to anything like the extent it has in Europe. Speculating as to the reasons for this is beyond the scope of this chapter, but one outcome is that US hockey operators who have tried to develop pay-per-view as a new revenue stream have been disappointed in the results. Finally, where the NFL and the NBA have succeeded in centrally controlling their television exposure (and, thus, in increasing the value of television rights), the NHL and MLB have left member teams with the rights to develop their own regional cable audiences. This has meant large advantages for teams in major metropolitan markets (e.g., New York Rangers, Toronto Maple Leafs) and for teams owned by cable television interests (e.g., Atlanta Braves, Colorado Avalanche) but slim pickings for teams based in smaller cities surrounded by dispersed rural populations (e.g.,

Edmonton, Calgary, and Pittsburgh). In short, the gap between rich and poor clubs is widening, and when the wealthiest clubs get so much of their revenue from *their own* media contracts (whether local cable contracts or the independent media deals made by widely followed clubs like the Toronto Maple Leafs), it is almost impossible to get them either to share these revenues or to be very concerned with the fate of their small-market competitors.

Much if not all of what has been described here has to be seen in the context of the increased involvement in sports of global telecommunications corporations (the Murdoch and Disney/ESPN empires) and their efforts to gain control of hugely popular sporting content. In the NHL, the agenda has been to turn a predominantly regional sport into one that attracts North America-wide and potentially global audiences, and to capitalize on the full potential of subscription television. Innovations in the technology of direct-to-home television, whether this is through digital cable or satellite transmission, coupled with the forced liberalization of broadcast regulations have presented challenges to traditional national broadcast networks, including public broadcasters. They have also produced staggering revenue opportunities for new kinds of television providers and for professional sports leagues. However, to date, the NHL has not been successful in taking advantage of these developments. Hockey, despite its roots in North America, the preeminent commercial zone in the world, cannot seem to expand beyond its original base in Canada and the northeastern United States. So why has the NHL directed its energies towards the American market rather than towards the European market? After all, in Scandinavia and countries such as Russia, the Czech Republic, Slovakia, Germany, Switzerland, France, and Italy, hockey has considerably more history than it does in the southern United States.

The answer seems to rest in the new patterns of sports consumption both for spectators at events and for television fans. These patterns are qualitatively different from the patterns that once characterized sports throughout the world, and this has served to reinforce the production and the aggressive marketing of merchandise. In this regard, the growth of the sports clothing business and the interpenetration of the world of fashion and sports have made images of sports part of the currency of everyday life. In fact, these images may well be more central than ever before.

Casual fashion and street wear have now become largely dominated by sports-derived styles. The effects of this are complex and far-reaching. For example, although few people play American sports in Europe (i.e., gridiron football, baseball, etc.), and TV audiences for these sports have declined, the merchandising of their products has boomed. The American company NFL Properties, which licenses the manufacture and sale of gridiron products in Europe, had a turnover of 220 million pounds in 1994 (Williams 1994). By this token, the example of the recently retired NBA basketball player Michael Jordan, who achieved near mythical status in the United States and throughout the world, becomes significant (LaFeber 1999). Jordan was seldom if ever seen playing his sport on national television stations throughout the world; yet, he has become famous. Much of this fame is a result of his fronting the global advertising campaign for the sporting goods manufacturer Nike. Jordan seems to have become massively popular because of his appearance in ads and because his name and image have been heavily promoted and stylized through the particular brand of sporting goods known as "Air Jordan." His global fame is also closely tied to a wide range of endorsements reputed to have earned the ex-basketball player around $58 million a year – or eight times the salary he earned as a player for the Chicago Bulls. Interesting in this regard is Jordan's appearance for the United States at the Barcelona Olympics, where he was wearing Reebok's brand name (Reebok, of course, being Nike's rival). Here, we clearly see an example of the sports sponsors demanding the kind of brand allegiance that has traditionally been the preserve of the nation-state (Williams 1994).[12]

When it comes to the question of the merchandizing and licensing of hockey, the NHL clung to its status quo far longer than did the other big league sports in North America. Whereas NFL football, MLB baseball, and NBA basketball aggressively marketed their "product" in the hope of expanding revenues and the number of new fans, the NHL barely promoted the game outside of its loyal and dedicated fan base. This was the approach of Bill Wirtz, the long-time owner of the Chicago Black Hawks and it seemed to be the blueprint followed by the NHL until the end of John Ziegler's tenure as commissioner in the early 1990s. In fact, the Original Six owners saw no need to seek the big television deals and related advertising revenue that other major-league North American sports had been exploiting since the early 1960s. Television or televised events had been revolutionizing the business and economics of major-league sports in North America, and, as the broadcasting of baseball, football, and basketball games grew, so did the revenue for franchises in their respective leagues. Most important, as teams began to compete financially, this development set in motion a process that made generating lucrative secondary sources of revenue not only possible but also necessary.

As the ease of televising sports matured (particularly at the expense of radio broadcasts) in the late 1960s and 1970s, this established larger audiences to which commodities could be sold. More important, the increasing emphasis placed on televising the event produced a greater emphasis on targeting audiences to which networks could match specific advertisers. Nowhere was this more evident than with regard to beer companies and beer consumption as the demographic of beer consumers expanded with the expansion of televised sport.[13] As the demand for advertisers to place their products "on air" grew, so did the price that networks could charge advertisers and, in turn, the price that major-league sports could charge the networks. By the early 1990s, televised revenue in North America constituted more than one-half the total revenue of major-league baseball and basketball and almost two-thirds the revenue of NFL football. Hockey was left lagging far behind.

Once again, it was not until the 1988 sale of hockey superstar Wayne Gretzky from the Edmonton Oilers to the Los Angeles Kings that this condition dramatically changed. This transfer signified the beginning of a new marketing and commercial expansion era in the NHL – one that took flight with the exit of the "old guard"[14] and that witnessed an unprecedented corporatization, Americanization, and geographic shift in the sport of hockey.

In attempting to get fans of hockey to become consumers of the sport and its accessories, the NHL (shortly after the Gretzky sale) solicited the assistance of the Walt Disney Company and Blockbuster Video. After the entrance of these two corporations into the NHL (Disney with the Anaheim Mighty Ducks and Blockbuster with the Florida Panthers in 1992–93), the merchandizing of the NHL began in earnest. Though the NHL was very far behind the other major-league North American spectator sports, five years following the Gretzky move to Los Angeles sales of licensed NHL apparel grew tenfold, from $100 million to $1 billion (Silver 1996, 31). Much of this could be attributed to the strategic use of the various entertainment commodities in Disney's arsenal to promote and give visibility to the game of hockey. Nowhere was this more evident than with the Disney movie *The Mighty Ducks*.

However, it was Wayne Gretzky's star power that motored the process of merchandising along. Gretzky earned close to $12 million in fees and royalties from the 1993–94 season, which, after adding his salary of $11.6 million, pushed his annual income to almost $24 million (Silver 1996, 31). Endorsements for a Finnish hockey equipment manufacturer pushed this small company (which, for the most part, made sticks) from fifteenth in the world in 1979 to number one in 1989. Other NHL stars quickly jumped on the bandwagon as endorsement opportunities multiplied. This was seen as the motivating factor behind Mark Messier's move (an instrumental linemate of Gretzky's with the Edmonton Oilers' five-time Stanley Cup championship team) to the New York Rangers shortly after Gretzky's move to Los Angeles, along with the emerging junior star Eric Lindros's refusal to play for the Quebec Nordiques and, instead, to hold out for a contract with a large American city (Philadelphia) team that offered significant endorsement opportunities. Both Messier and Lindros understood the amount of money that could be made by being front and centre of the new commercial ethos that was permeating the NHL. Nonetheless, none of this seemed to have caught on in the lucrative American spectator-sports market.

The increasing emphasis on style and surface appearances in sports is not merely a symptom of a new condition of postmodernity; rather, it is a product of the commercial and global restructuring of the broadcasting industry and popular culture, all of which stems from the surplus value of the athlete's labour combined with the actual processes involved in making the merchandise. Within this new global context, sports have had a new economic circumstance forced upon them by the arrival of modern cable and satellite television. This has produced enormous tensions between older traditions of support and a new independent entrepreneurial ethos. Part of the impact of television, the rise of sponsorship, and the growth of the sports business has been to produce conflicting notions of supporters, fans, and customers. Who, in fact, are the fans and customers? Since the live spectator has been greatly outnumbered by the television viewer, sponsorship has become central, and if the sponsors are paying for the event, they must, at least implicitly, be the customer. Television produces audiences, which it sells to advertisers, thus transforming the latter into the customers, with the television audience being merely the product. This seems to be especially the case with regard to sports coverage as its format has been increasingly dictated by the demands of advertisers. In the history of sports, sporting events have only recently been interrupted by breaks for television commercials. This development alters the flow and outcomes of matches.

The conquering of sports by broadcasting, marketing, and advertising networks means, clearly, that there is no longer a neat distinction between the sports event and the promotion of the sports event. Following this development, we must ask ourselves, does the clothing promote Michael Jordan or does Michael Jordan promote clothing? Do the Olympics promote Nike, Adidas, Reebok, and so on or vice versa? This raises an interesting case study. In this sense, securing the mega-star is as important a process for competing capitals as it is for participating states. Producing and then securing the superstar synonymously enables pecuniary commercial promotion. It is the activities of the commercial media that secure the conditions under which stardom is promoted on every front. The media guarantee the inevitable *existence* of superstars, but it is up to competing capitals and states to determine who exercises stardom at any given time. The media help to ensure the conditions under which every athlete can potentially realize her or his value in the marketplace. All that is required is one mega-star with extensive symbolic value to catalyse this process. Thus, media not only underwrite sports as big business but also accentuate the fragility of big-business sports.

PUBLIC SUBSIDY

Capital accumulation by the NHL and its franchises is greatly facilitated by the state. For the state, underwriting sports production must be viewed as both a responsibility and an opportunity. On the responsibility side, it enforces League monopolies by allowing exemption from antitrust legislation. Schools, universities, and community recreation programs train athletes for careers in sports and socialize non-athletes to be consumers; tax laws permit the depreciation of players, the deduction of sports losses from other business (primarily in the United States), and the deduction of ticket purchases as a business expense. Local governments provide the necessary facilities to rear and nurture young athletes at below market rents. The provision of facilities is particularly important. Athletic development owes a large debt to government policies that promote physical education aimed at building sport facilities of any kind.

On the opportunity side, the state claims returns on economic development derived from sporting enterprises, just as it would from the encouragement of any economic development within its borders. The major league expansions of the 1960s and the early 1970s in North America were part of a similar trend occurring in the greater economy as exercises in revenue creation through franchising. Indeed, expansion in major-league sports in this period coincided with the unprecedented growth of franchising in other businesses (such as McDonald's, Burger King, and Dairy Queen) and the eclipse of many kinds of independently operated local businesses at the hands of nationally promoted, brand-name goods and services. Expansion in major-league sports was thus entirely consistent with postwar developments in commerce, which saw leading retailers in the United States and Canada move into booming suburban locations, with local manufacturers being either taken over or marginalized by heavily promoted national brands. All these phenomena contributed to the standardizing of consumer opportunity and continued the undercutting of local and regional differences. The arena of public subsidies intrudes at the level at which civic and regional authorities feel an ever-increasing need to offer infrastructure and other incentives to attract new businesses – or just to keep existing ones.

Nowhere is this condition more clear than in the current controversy over minor hockey in Canada, particularly in the Greater Toronto Hockey League and the major metropolitan area of Toronto – the world's biggest hockey community. Individual entrepreneurs have found ways to acquire pecuniary control of minor hockey organizations and feeder leagues – a system designed for and by volunteers and parents and whose purpose is to enable boys and girls to play hockey in publicly financed facilities, thus ensuring that hockey continues to be as affordable a public amenity as, say, the public library or public courts. However, these individual entrepreneurs have not only been able to procure a high degree of profit from the creation of revenue through exorbitant increases in fees for young hockey players, but they have also considerably raised the cost of participation for a largely middle-class constituency. These individuals then go on to play in more senior leagues (and perhaps professional leagues), and, ultimately, it is the parents who make the initial financial investment in the development of the athlete and not professional hockey leagues and franchises. Thus, it is the state and the commons that have underwritten the production of the athletes.

CONCLUSION: PROPOSALS FOR CHANGE

Most proposals for change within the realm of NHL hockey have been put forth within the context of offering opportunities for capital accumulation to large investors, opportunities for major advertisers to reach huge audiences, and opportunities for the best players to make huge sums of money. With enormous sums at stake, these different groups have increasingly put their own interests ahead of the interests of the game, regardless of the interests of the fans. This should not be surprising; however, it seems that many fans find it hard to surrender the idealistic belief that sports are, or at least should be, different from other commodities that are produced and sold in the marketplace.

Underpinning this resistance is a notion that some areas of life, like sports, should not be "infected" by the logic of profit and growth (which structures other areas of economic activity) and the instrumental rationality that follows from this logic.

Resistance to the commodifying pressures in sports is widely framed as nostalgia, perhaps because criticism of the major-league sports industry is rarely extended to encompass a broader critique of current patterns of economic life (never mind being couched in "political" terms). However, no matter how well this description seems to fit, "it ... fail[s] to distinguish between nostalgia as recollections ... and a sincere ... longing for times past, and the ... corporate exploitation of nostalgia, with all the kitsch this entails" (Kaye 1996, 87). Very rarely do people seriously entertain the possibility that, however selective or wistful their ideas of the past, their hopes for the restoration of an "authentic pastime" express a legitimate perception that something is wrong with major-league sports in general and with the NHL in particular, along with society's current relationship to it. What is needed is a historical understanding that allows us to situate the transformations in sports discussed here within larger transformations in global capitalism and to apply this understanding to thinking about possible futures. This may enable us to make greater sense not only of events like the NHL lockout but also of the economic transformations that are reshaping our society. And this, in turn, may enable us to begin to respond to them more effectively.

One alternative proposal would be to obtain a more effective and equitable revenue-sharing arrangement among competing team franchises. While this would open up issues of restrictions on athletes, the intended benefits for the sport at large would be seen in the form of balanced competition, greater financial security for weaker teams, and profits and salaries that would reflect an owner's and athlete's real worth to the greater society. Better revenue sharing would permit an increase in the number of leagues, teams, and associations as entry conditions and prohibitive costs would be curtailed. This would also limit, or perhaps discourage altogether, the phenomenon of "musical franchises" and ruinous competition for prestigious international competitions such as the Olympics.

Such proposals, however, demand some kind of national or international regulatory agency or restrictive state involvement. These agencies would resemble the type of regulatory agency that state administrations have for food, drugs, safety, and broadcasting rather than the type of hierarchical league association that the NHL already has in place and in which the same parties (i.e., owners) who are directly involved in profit maximization are also those responsible for regulatory duties. This would mean that monopolies would have to be broken up and that advertiser control would have to be seriously curbed. Given the current messianic control of public discourses that aggressively celebrate the role of markets and consumer choices in the delivery of a better life, there seems to be little popular support for this proposal and, thus, little likelihood of its happening any time soon.

Another radical proposal would involve removing profit from sports altogether. Since sports are in many ways a fundamental part of culture, and since communities contribute excessively to the development of the athletes and the facilities that pro-leagues and global sports organizations exploit, sports should be the property of the community. Organizations structured along non-profit and revenue-sharing lines would go a long way to repatriating and reinvigorating sports at all levels. However, such a scheme would demand a serious evaluation of capitalist ideology not only in relation to sports but also in relation to economic and political power.

NOTES

1 For instance, Anthony King makes the point that a football fan's relations with his or her club is a special one. Although at one level it is monetary, it is far more complex than the "unidimensionality of the market transaction. The close identification that the fans have with the club, and the fact that they are an integral part of the very commodity which the new directors seek to sell, suggests that the fan's relations to the club cannot be adequately theorized within the confines of conventional economic understanding. Football is a curious product, fans extraordinary consumers" (King 1997, 236). It is only logical

that the above sentiment be extended to almost all major league spectator sports.

2 A quick listen or quick read of any of the sports talk radio stations or dailies in the Toronto area quickly revealed the general sentiment that these locked out players were knaves, ingrates who were violating some public trust, men without principles, men who would be struggling at a "regular job" but for the opportunity accorded to them by the joint venture that is the NHL. See "Don't weep for NHL or players," *Toronto Star*, 15 September 2004. Of course, this kind of subservience on behalf of the Canadian sport media is nothing new (Cruise and Griffiths 1991).

3 Some suggest that sports fans deal with the predicament of the commercialization of sports by tuning out the contradictory information. For instance, fans and media commentators recognize and resent the fact that the commercialization of sports has enriched athletes, but they tune out the fact that it has also enriched owners and promoters (Morrison 1996; Lobmeyer and Weidinger 1992; Curry and Jiobu 1991). However, these authors attribute this fan discontent with ignorance in the workings of the market. I would submit that it is more an expression of the ideological predisposition towards labour, particularly in the United States. In short, it is an example of how popular discourses produced around sport either sustain or challenge the new economic and political orthodoxies of our age. It is arguable that these industries have helped generate popular consent for the current gospel of free trade, re-regulated markets, economic competitiveness, and the privatization of public goods and services (Gruneau and Whitson 1993).

4 I make this qualification because, more and more, the conditions of labour and the class positionality of the increasing number of workers engaged in sports activities and production is a worthy consideration. One must remember that the labour side of the sports industry has increasingly been made not just of athletes or the creators of the spectacle but also of the transmitters of the event in the media and elsewhere. We need to consider the broader set of underlying tendencies that are part of the integration of sports with modern marketing. That is, we need to consider cross-ownership and cross-marketing by large integrated corporations, which also have substantial interests in related leisure and entertainment businesses: the credit industry; the tourism industry; the fast-food, alcohol, and soft drink industries; sports and leisure-wear

equipment; gambling; audio-visual technologies such as cameras, television, video recorders, CD players, VCRs, DVDs, personal home computers, and cable television, along with cell phones; and, rather conspicuously of late, libido enhancement drugs such as Viagra. All of these businesses employ significant numbers of people.

5 Four pivotal events come immediately to mind when presenting the subject of agency among athletes. First is the baseball strike of 1972, which marked a turning point in the relations between players and owners in every professional sport. This was the first major-league spectator sport strike to affect regular season games, and it also marked the maturation of the Major League Baseball Player's Association. Second is Title IX, perhaps the most important measure ever undertaken to promote gender equity in sports. In 1972, a group of college women in Florida filed suit against the Association for Intercollegiate Athletics for Women's ban on scholarships for women. The result was a major change in the structure of athletic resources for women's intercollegiate athletics. Some even ascribe the success of the Women's National Basketball Association and the US Women's World Cup soccer team directly to Title IX. It has not, however, been universally praised as many claim that Title IX has denied opportunities to as many people as it has helped. Third is the significant spill-over effect that general social movements have had on sports. For example, the lobbying for the exclusion of South Africa from international competition. In 1964, after intense pressure, the International Olympic Committee withdrew its invitation to South Africa to participate in the Olympics. Fourth is the 2004 NHL lockout. This was the first time in any major-league spectator sport that a regular season was fully cancelled due to a labour dispute.

6 From the athlete's perspective (especially the amateur Olympic athlete), there is much more at stake than playing for a contract or medals. The commercial value of a gold medal in some events is a six-figure sum, which comes in the form of endorsements, speaking engagements, and appearance fees. In the case of the Olympics, the endorsement value of a bronze medal is less than half that of a gold; thus, in the absence of explicit wages, there is a consequential incentive structure to a rank-order tournament. Tara Lipinski, who retired from amateur skating at the age of fifteen, is an example of just how valuable a gold medal can be. After winning her medal, Lipinski agreed to participate in the

Campbell Soup Champions on Ice Tour for a salary of several million dollars per tour. A more applicable example would be the multi-million-dollar, five-year deal that the seventeen-year-old prospect Sidney Crosby signed with the Reebok athletic wear company.

7 Admittedly, I am utilizing a rather conventional definition of economic rent. Once again, for the sake of clarity, I understand economic rent as "the difference between the return made by a factor of production and the return necessary to keep the factor in its current occupation" (Bannock, Baxter, and Davis 1992, 129).

8 Few services or goods are produced by means of one input. Typically, firms employ many different factors of production and consider relative factor prices, product market conditions, and an input's marginal effect on output. This is obviously true of any league or professional sports team – the NHL and its clubs notwithstanding.

9 For instance, in hockey, there is a standard player-agent contract between player and agent. This was introduced when the NHLPA began its agent certification program in 1996 (Mason and Slack 2001, 169).

10 With the Gretzky transfer, the NHL player salary structure changed dramatically. Owners, who sensed large marketing and merchandising rewards if they could secure star players, began an unprecedented spending spree for the services of players – particularly star players. Gretzky's transfer to Los Angeles, one the largest media markets in the United States, propelled the wages paid to hockey players to a position relative to the exorbitant wages paid to other major North American professional sports players. One after another, the more ambitious teams and the more talented players lined up to spend and cash in. For instance, Mario Lemieux, a player who could easily rival Gretzky in terms of skill and market power, renegotiated with a smaller market team in the Pittsburgh Penguins for $2 million a year. Brett Hull, a highly skilled forward, would follow with the St Louis Blues in obtaining a $7 million contract for four years. After this, the genie was out of the bottle and the NHL could no longer attempt to control player utilization by negotiating contracts and determining salaries from a position of strength. Every team with a superstar seemed obliged to rewrite contracts. By the beginning of the 1990–91 season, the Detroit Red Wings renegotiated with their superstar Steve Yzerman for an increase of $1.3 million dollars;

Patrick Roy, the clutch goalie for the Montreal Canadiens, increased his net pay by $1.2 million; Boston Bruin Ray Bourque resigned for an increase of $1.194 million; Paul Coffey was lured to Pittsburgh for an extra $1.15 million; Chicago Blawk Hawks followed suit by signing their star defensive player Chris Chelios for $1.1 million; and Scott Stevens moved as a free agent to St Louis for a $1.217 million (Dowbiggin 2003).

11 The big seven are the profit centres of New York, Detroit, Dallas, Colorado, Philadelphia, Toronto, and New Jersey (see Bruce Dowbiggin 2003).

12 Arguably, Jordan's soccer counterpart has been the mediocre English footballing creation/sensation David Beckham. Beckham and Adidas have negotiated massive deals with his club Real Madrid of Spain.

13 As the demographic of beer drinkers and the demographic of sports consumption are almost one and the same, beer consumption and sports seem to be a marriage made in heaven. In the United States, white middle-class males aged eighteen to thirty-four make up almost 22 percent of the population, and they drink 70 percent of the beer consumed. However, what is most important to understand is that the vehicle of sports event seems to be the most efficient delivery system through which this demographic can be reached. Beer companies have long understood this and have even purchased teams in order to gain this access (Gorman and Calhoun 1994; Sullivan 1992, 161–83).

14 The issue of the old guard is of particular interest when it comes to discussing the history of the NHL. From the 1930s until about the mid-1960s, NHL hockey was dominated by the Norris family and their associates and successors. At the time, Chicago-based Jim Norris, the multi-millionaire grain and shipping baron and one of the United States' richest men, owned or controlled four out of six NHL franchises. Roughly between the years 1966 and 1990, the NHL was dominated by the Norris-groomed trio of Bill Wirtz (owner of the Chicago Black Hawks) John Ziegler (president of the NHL), and Alan Eagleson (players' agent with a virtual monopoly of player affairs). It would not be an exaggeration to describe this lot as a feudal dynasty as it appeared to survive a succession of threats from rebellious players, outside owners, and minor leagues. This order seemed to "change" somewhat with the

arrival of Bruce McNall, the new owner of the Los Angles Kings, in the mid-1980s and with the movement of Gretzky and a couple of NHL franchises to the sun belt. There are several books chronicling this situation (see Cruise and Griffiths 1991; Houston and Shoalts 1993; Conway 1995).

References

INTRODUCTION

Arnold, Matthew. 1994 [1869]. *Culture and Anarchy*. rep. New Haven, CT: Yale University Press.

Canadian Museum of Civilization "'Rocket' Richard, the Legend – The Legacy." Available at: http://www.civilisations.ca/hist/rocket/rocket1e.html (viewed 6 April 2007).

Gruneau, Richard, and David Whitson. 1993. *Hockey Night in Canada: Sport, Identities, and Cultural Politics* Toronto: Garamond Press.

Kidd, Bruce. 1970. "Canada's 'National' Sport." In *Close the 49th Parallel Etc.: The Americanization of Canada*. Ed. Ian Lumsden, 257–74. Toronto: University of Toronto Press.

Kidd, Bruce, and John Macfarlane. 1972. *The Death of Hockey*. Toronto: New Press.

Metcalfe, Alan. 1987. *Canada Learns to Play: The Emergence of Organized Sport, 1807–1914*. Toronto: McClelland and Stewart.

Morton, W.L. 1972 [1961]. *The Canadian Identity*. Toronto: University of Toronto Press.

Richards, David Adams. 2001 [1996]. *Hockey Dream: Memoirs of a Man Who Couldn't Play*. Toronto: Anchor Canada.

Sport History Review. 2006. 37: 1. Guest ed. Andrew C. Holman.

Symons, Thomas H.B. 1975. *To Know Ourselves: The Report of the Commission on Canadian Studies*. Ottawa: Association of Universities and College of Canada.

Whitson, David, and Richard Gruneau, eds. 2006. *Artificial Ice: Hockey, Culture, and Commerce*. Peterborough: Broadview Press.

CHAPTER ONE

Bouchier, Nancy. 2003. *For the Love of the Game: Amateur Sport in Small-town Ontario, 1838–1895*. Montreal and Kingston: McGill-Queen's University Press.

Cosentino, Frank. 1973. "A History of the Concept of Professionalism in Canadian Sport." PhD diss., University of Alberta.

Field, Russell. 2002. "Passive Participation: The Selling of Spectacle and the Construction of Maple Leaf Gardens, 1931." *Sport History Review* 33 (1): 35–50.

Gruneau, Richard, and David Whitson. 1993. *Hockey Night in Canada: Sport, Identities, and Cultural Politics*. Toronto: Garamond Press.

Howell, Colin D. 2001. *Blood, Sweat, and Cheers: Sport in the Making of Modern Canada*. Toronto: University of Toronto Press.

Kidd, Bruce. 1996. *The Struggle for Canadian Sport*. Toronto: University of Toronto Press.

Lansley, Keith. 1971. "The Amateur Athletic Union of Canada and Changing Concepts of Amateurism." PhD diss., University of Alberta.

Macdonald, Robb. 1992. "The Battle of Port Arthur: A War of Words and Ideologies within the Canadian Olympic Committee." *Proceedings of the First International Symposium for Olympic Research, International Centre for Olympic Studies*, 135–52. London: University of Western Ontario.

Metcalfe, Alan. 1983. "1937: The Demise of Amateurism in Canada." In *The University's Role in the Development of Modern Sport: Past, Present, and Future*. Proceedings of the FISU Conference-Universidae '83 in Association with the tenth HISPA Conference. Ed. Sandra Kereliuk, 308–15. Edmonton: s.n..

– 1992. "Power: A Case Study of the Ontario Hockey Association, 1890–1936." *Journal of Sport History* 19 (1): 5–25.

Morrow, Don. 1989. "A Case Study in Amateur Conflict: The Athletic War in Canada, 1906–1908." In *Sports in Canada: Historical Readings*, ed. Morris Mott, 201–19. Toronto: Copp Clark.

Morrow, Don, and Kevin Wamsley. 2005. *Sport in Canada: A History*. Don Mills: Oxford University Press.

Pudas, Albert, 1935–1936. Playoff and Olympic Scrapbook, dated 5 March 1935. Northwestern Ontario Sports Hall of Fame, Thunder Bay, Ontario.

Savoie, Marc. 2000. "Broken Time and Broken Hearts: The Maritimes and the Selection of Canada's 1936 Olympic Hockey Team." *Sport History Review* 31 (2): 120–38.

Wong, John. 2003. "Sport Networks on Ice: The Canadian Experience at the 1936 Olympic Hockey Tournament." *Sport History Review* 34 (2): 190–212.

CHAPTER TWO

Bobknows. 2005, 7 May. Unrealistic Expectations. Message posted to http://www.slam.canoe.ca/mb2/messages/slam/688.html (viewed 12 May 2005).

Cruise, D.C., and A. Griffiths. 1991. *Net Worth: Exploding the Myths of Pro Hockey*. Toronto: Viking.

Kidd, B., and J. Macfarlane. 1972. *The Death of Hockey*. Toronto: New Press.

LaRose, S. 2005, 7 July. Sidney Crosby to Play in Europe, Bypass NHL? Message posted to http://www.riderfans.com/showthread.php?t=22115 (viewed 15 July 2005).

Gruneau, R., and D. Whitson. 1993. *Hockey Night in Canada: Sport, Identities and Cultural Politics*. Toronto: Garamond Press.

Mason, D.S. 2002. "'Get the puck outta here!'" Media Transnationalism and Canadian Hockey Identity." *Journal of Sport and Social Issues* 26 (2): 140–67.

Purdon, M. 2000, 28 January. "Opinion – Canada's National Shame: The NHL Doesn't Live Here Anymore." *Digital Times/Kamloops News Online*. Available at: www.cariboo.bc.ca/news/Pastjan28/NHL.html (viewed 12 October 2004).

Rempel, A., and R. Van Leewan. 1996. "The Great White Fight." Available at: www.geocities.com/Hollywood/Lot/5619/jets.htm (viewed 12 October 2004).

Scherer, J. 2001. "Globalization and the Construction of Local Particularities: A Case Study of the Winnipeg Jets. *Sociology of Sport Journal* 18 (2): 205–30.

Silver, J. 1996. *Thin Ice: Money, Politics, and the Demise of an NHL Franchise*. Halifax, NS: Fernwood.

Stevens, J. 2003. "The Development of Hockey in Canada: A Process of Institutional Divergence and Convergence." In *Putting It on Ice*.

Vol. 2: *Internationalizing "Canada's Game,"* ed. C. Howell and
M. Vance, 51–64. Halifax: Gorsebrook Institute.

Whitson, D., and D. Macintosh. 1993. "Becoming a World-class City:
Hallmark Events and Sport Franchises in the Growth Strategies of
Western Canadian Cities." *Sociology of Sport Journal* 10 (3): 221–40.

CHAPTER THREE

Arac, Jonathan. 2003. "Toward a Critical Genealogy of the US
Discourse of Identity: *Invisible Man* after Fifty Years." *boundary 2*
30 (2): 195–216. Available at: *Project Muse*, EP 1–12 (viewed
17 December 2003).

Bakhtin, Mikhail. 1981. "Epic and the Novel." In *The Dialogic
Imagination: Four Essays by M.M. Bakhtin*, ed. Michael Holquist,
trans. Caryl Emerson and Michael Holquist, 3–40. Austin: University
of Texas Press.

Canada's Team of the Century: 1972 Canada vs. USSR. 2002. Produced
and directed by Robert MacAskill, nineteen hours, Universal Studios,
DVD.

Coupland, Douglas. 2002. *Souvenir of Canada*. Vancouver/Toronto:
Douglas and McIntyre.

Earle, Neil. 1995. "Hockey as Canadian Popular Culture: Team Canada
1972, Television and the Canadian Identity." *Journal of Canadian
Studies* 30 (2): 107–23.

Ferguson, Will. 1997. *Why I Hate Canadians*. Vancouver: Douglas and
McIntyre.

Frosh, Stephen. 2002. "The Other." *American Imago* 59 (4): 389–407.

Gwyn, Richard. 1996. *Nationalism without Walls: The Unbearable
Lightness of Being Canadian*. Toronto: McClelland and Stewart.

Hockey Canada. 1973. *Twenty-seven Days in September: The Official
Hockey Canada History of the 1972 Canada/USSR Series*. Canada:
Hockey Canada and Prospect.

Laplanche, Jean. 1999. *Essays on Otherness*. Trans. J. Fletcher. London:
Routledge.

Légaré, André. 2002. "NUNAVUT: The Construction of a Regional
Collective Identity in the Canadian Arctic." *Wicazo Sa Review* 17 (2):
65–89. Available at *Project Muse*, EP 1–14 (viewed 17 December 2003).

Ludwig, Jack. 1974. *Hockey Night in Moscow*. Richmond Hill, ON: Pocket-Penguin.

MacGregor, Robert M. 2003. "I Am Canadian: National Identity in Beer Commercials." *Journal of Popular Culture* 37 (2): 276–86. Available at *Project Muse*, EP 1–8 (viewed 17 August 2005).

Macintosh, Donald, and Donna Greenhorn. 1993. "Hockey Diplomacy and Canadian Foreign Policy." *Journal of Canadian Studies* (28) 2: 96–112.

Macskimming, Roy. 1996. *Cold War: The Amazing Canada-Soviet Hockey Series of 1972*. Vancouver: Greystone/Douglas and McIntyre.

Manning, Erin. 2000. "I AM CANADIAN [sic]: Identity, Territory and the Canadian National Landscape." *Theory and Event* 4 (4): n.p. *Project Muse* (6 November 2003): EP 1–29.

Richards, David Adams. 1997 [1988]. *Nights Below Station Street*. Toronto: McClelland and Stewart.

Robidoux, Michael A. 2002. "Imagining a Canadian Identity through Sport: A Historical Interpretation of Lacrosse and Hockey." *Journal of American Folklore* 115 (456): 209–25.

Wagman, Ira. 2002. "Wheat, Barley, Hops, Citizenship: Molson's 'I Am [Canadian]' [sic] Campaign and the Defense of Canadian National Identity through Advertising." *Velvet Light Trap* 50: 77–89. Available at *Project Muse*, EP 1–14 (viewed 17 August 2005).

CHAPTER FOUR

Coady, Lynn. 2002. *Saints of Big Harbour*. New York: Mariner Books.

Dunning Eric, and Norbert Elias. 1986. *Quest for Excitement: Sport and Leisure in the Civilizing Process*. Oxford: Blackwell.

Gaston, Bill. 1998. "Your First Time." In *Sex is Red*, 53–64. Dunvegan, ON: Cormorant Books.

Gruneau, Richard, and David Whitson. 1993. *Hockey Night in Canada: Sport, Identities, and Cultural Politics*. Toronto: Garamond Press.

Guttmann, Allen. 1992. "Chariot Races, Tournaments and the Civilizing Process." In *Sport and Leisure in the Civilizing Process: Critique and Counter-critique*, ed. E. Dunning and C. Rojek, 137–60. London: Macmillan.

Huizinga, Johan. 1955. *Homo Ludens: A Study of the Play Element in Culture*. Boston: Beacon Press.

Jarman, Mark. 1997. *Salvage King, Ya! A Herky-Jerky Picaresque.* Vancouver: Anvil Press.

Jennings, Bryant, Dolf Zillmann, and Arthur A. Raney. 1988. "Violence and the Enjoyment of Media Sports." In *MediaSport*, ed. Laurence Wenner, 252–65. London and New York: Routledge.

Liebling, A.J. 2004 [1956]. *The Sweet Science.* New York: North Point Press.

London, Jack. 1953. "A Piece of Steak." In *Best Stories of Jack London*, 73–88. Garden City, NY: Garden City Press.

Lorenz, Konrad. 2002 [1966]. *On Aggression.* Trans. Marjorie Kerr Wilson. London and NY: Routledge.

MacLennan, Hugh. 1989. "Fury on Ice." In *Riding on the Roar of the Crowd: A Hockey Anthology*, ed. David Gowdey, 4–16. Toronto: Macmillan.

MacGregor, Roy. 2002. *The Last Season.* Toronto: Penguin.

Paci, Frank. 1999. *Icelands.* Canada: Oberon Press.

Pronger, Brian. 1990. *The Arena of Masculinity: Sports, Homosexuality, and the Meaning of Sex.* New York: St. Martin's Press.

Quarrington, Paul. 1994. *King Leary.* Toronto: Doubleday.

Robidoux, Michael A. 2001. *Men at Play: A Working Understanding of Professional Hockey.* Kingston: McGill-Queen's University Press.

Robinson, Laura. 1998. *Crossing the Line: Violence and Sexual Assault in Canada's National Sport.* Toronto: McClelland and Stewart.

Scanlan, Lawrence. 2002. *Grace under Fire: The State of Our Sweet and Savage Game.* Toronto: Penguin Canada.

Schiller, Friedrich. 1962. *Über die ästhetische Erziehung des Menschen in einer Reihe von Briefen.* In *Sämtliche Werke 5*, ed. Gerhard Fricke and Herbert G. Göpfert, 570–669. Munich: Carl Hanser.

Spariosu, Mihai. 1991. *God of Many Names: Play, Poetry, and Power in Hellenic Thought from Homer to Aristotle.* Durham and London: Duke University Press.

Suits, Bernard. 1978. *The Grasshopper: Games, Life, and Utopia.* Toronto: University of Toronto Press.

Sutton-Smith, Brian. 1997. *The Ambiguity of Play.* Cambridge, MA: Harvard University Press.

Wann, Daniel L., Merrill J. Melnick, Gordon W. Russell, and Dale G. Pease. 2001. *Sport Fans: The Psychology and Social Impact of Spectators.* New York: Routledge.

Woods, Hanford. 1997. "The Drubbing of Nesterenko." In *Our Game: An All-star Collection of Hockey Fiction*, ed. Doug Beardsley, 244–59. Toronto: Polestar.

CHAPTER FIVE

Berger, Carl. 1997. "The True North Strong and Free." In *Canadian Culture*, ed. Elspeth Cameron, 83–102. Toronto: Canadian Scholars Press.

Dopp, Jamie. 1999. Getting Off a Good One. *Mattoid* 54: 46–57.

Dryden, Ken. 1983. *The Game*. Toronto: Macmillan.

Dryden, Ken, and Roy MacGregor. 1989. *Home Game: Hockey and Life in Canada*. Toronto: McClelland and Stewart.

Fischler, Stan. 1984. *Hockey's 100*. Don Mills: Stoddart.

Gaston, Bill. 2000. *The Good Body*. Dunvegan, ON: Cormorant.

Gruneau, Richard, and David Whitson. 1993. *Hockey Night in Canada: Sport, Identities, and Cultural Politics*. Toronto: Garamond Press.

Jarman, Mark Anthony. 1997. *Salvage King, Ya! A Herky-Jerky Picaresque*. Vancouver: Anvil.

Leacock, Stephen. 1994 [1912]. *Sunshine Sketches of a Little Town*. Toronto: McClelland and Stewart.

Miller, J. Hillis. 1990. "Narrative." In *Critical Terms for Literary Study*, ed. Frank Lentricchia and Thomas McLaughlin, 66–79. Chicago and London: University of Chicago Press.

Quarrington, Paul. 1994 [1987]. *King Leary*. Toronto: Doubleday.

CHAPTER SIX

Anderson, Benedict. 1983. *Imagined Communities: Reflections on the Origins and Spread of Nationalism*. London: Verso.

Atwood, Margaret. 1972. *Survival: A Thematic Guide to Canadian Literature*. Toronto: Anansi.

Backcheck: Hockey for Kids. http://www.collectionscanada.ca/hockey/kids/024003–3500-e.html.

Barzun, Jacques. 1954. *God's Country and Mine*. New York: Little, Brown.

Billman, Carol. 1986. *The Secret of the Stratemeyer Syndicate: Nancy Drew, The Hardy Boys, and the Million Dollar Fiction Factory*. New York: Ungar Publishing.

Bouchard, David, and Dean Griffiths. 2004. *That's Hockey*. Victoria: Orca Book Publishers.

Cochrane, Tom. 1988. "Big League." EMI.

Connors, Tom. 1973. "The Hockey Song." *Stompin' Tom and the Hockey Song*. EMI.

Cordukes, Laura. 1992. Sports Fiction: The Jock and the Library Do Have Something in Common! *CM: A Reviewing Journal of Canadian Materials for Young People*. 20 (1). Available at: www.manitoba.ca/outreach/cm/cmarchive/vol20no1/sportfiction.html.

Dixon, Franklin W. (John Button). 1939. *The Twisted Claw*. New York: Grosset and Dunlap.

Downie, Gordon. 1992. "Fifty Mission Cap." Perf. The Tragically Hip. *Fully Completely*. MCA Records.

– 1998. "Fireworks." Perf. The Tragically Hip. *Phantom Power*. Sire/WEA.

Frye, Northrop. 1971. *The Bush Garden: Essays on the Canadian Imagination*. Toronto: House of Anansi.

Grace, Sherrill E. 1991. "Comparing Mythologies: Ideas of West and North." In *Borderlands: Essays in Canadian-American Literature*, ed. Robert Lecker, 246–62. Toronto: ECW Press.

Greenwald, Marilyn S. 2004. *The Secret of the Hardy Boys: Leslie McFarlane and the Stratemeyer Syndicate*. Athens: Ohio University Press.

Gruneau, Richard, and David Whitson. 1993. *Hockey Night in Canada: Sport, Identities and Cultural Politics*. Toronto: Garamond Press.

Haliburton, Thomas Chandler. 1845. *The Attaché, or, Sam Slick in England / by the author of Sam Slick, the Clockmaker*. New York: Dick and Fitzgerald.

Hendy, Jim. 1933. "Hockey Brothers." *Sport Story Magazine*, 10 February, 85–8.

Henighan, Stephen. 2002. *When Words Deny the World: The Reshaping of Canadian Writing*. Erin: The Porcupine's Quill.

Huizinga, J. 1970. *Homo Ludens: A Study of the Play Element In Culture*. Boston: Beacon Press.

Jenkinson, Dave. 1998. Roy MacGregor. *CM: A Reviewing Journal of Canadian Materials for Young People*. Available at: http://www.umanitoba.ca/cm/profiles/mcgregor.html (viewed 29 September 2007).

Johnson, Deidre. 1993. *Edward Stratemeyer and the Stratemeyer Syndicate*. New York: Twayne Publishers.

Keeline, James D. 2000. The Writings of Leslie Charles McFarlane (1902–1977). Available at http://www.keeline.com/McFarlane (viewed 25 September 2005).

LePan, Douglas. 1987. *Weathering It: Complete Poems 1948–1987*. Toronto: McClelland and Stewart.

MacGregor, Roy. 1985. *The Last Season*. Toronto: Penguin Canada.

McFarlane, Leslie. (as Franklin W. Dixon). 1927a. *The Hardy Boys: The Secret of the Old Mill*. New York: Grosset and Dunlap.

– (as Franklin W. Dixon). 1927b. *The Hardy Boys: The Tower Treasure*. New York: Grosset and Dunlap.

– 1931. "A Canadian Eldorado." *Maclean's*, 15 December, 12–13, 61.

– 1933a. "Throwing Down McCloskie." *Sport Story Magazine*, 25 March, 22–32.

– 1933b. "The Wrist Shot." *Sport Story Magazine*, 10 April, 77–86.

– 1936. "Softy at Center Ice" *Sport Story Magazine*, 1st April, 88–106.

– (as Franklin W. Dixon). 1945. *The Hardy Boys: The Short-wave Mystery*. New York: Grosset and Dunlap.

– 1966. *McGonigle Scores!* Toronto: McClelland and Stewart.

– 1972. *Fire in the North*. Cobalt: Highway Bookshop.

– 1975a. [1936]. *The Dynamite Flynns*. Toronto: Methuen.

– 1975b. *Squeeze Play*. Toronto: Methuen.

– 1976a. *Breakaway*. Toronto: Methuen.

– 1976b. *Ghost of the Hardy Boys*. Toronto: Methuen.

– 1996. *A Kid in Haileybury*. Cobalt: Highway Bookshop.

– 2005. *Leslie McFarlane's Hockey Stories*. Ed. Brian McFarlane. Toronto: Key Porter.

– 2006. *Leslie McFarlane's Hockey Stories 2*. Ed. Brian McFarlane. Toronto: Key Porter.

Moxy Früvous. 1994a. "Gulf War Song." *Bargainville*. Warner Music Canada.

– 1994b. "King of Spain." *Bargainville*. Warner Music Canada.

Ott, Bill. 2004, "The Secret of the Hardy Boys: Leslie McFarlane and the Stratemeyer Syndicate." *The Booklist* 100 (17): 1503.

Patell, Cyrus R. K. 1993. "Baseball and the Cultural Logic of American Individualism." *Prospects* 18: 401–63.

Prager, Arthur. 1971. "Edward Stratemeyer and His Book Machine."
  Saturday Review, 10 July, 15–17, 52–3.

Richler, Mordecai. 2002. *Dispatches from the Sporting Life*. Guilford:
  The Lyons Press.

Rober, Eric. 1933. "Rink Jinx." *Sport Story Magazine*, 25 January, 2–19.

– "A Second Generation: Chatting with Brian McFarlane, Author of the
  New Mitchell Brother Series ... and Leslie McFarlane's Son. *Bayport
  Gazette*. Available at: http://www.bayportgazette.com/bg/14/bg_14_4.html
  (viewed 25 September 2005).

Trillin, Calvin. 2001. "Paper Baron." *The New Yorker*, 17 December,
  62–71.

"What's Canadian about Canadian Children's Literature? A Compendium
  of Answers to the Question." 1997. *Canadian Children's Literature*.
  87/23 (3).

Young, Neil. 1972. Old Man. *Harvest*. Reprise.

Young, Scott. 1952. Scrubs on Skates. Toronto: McClelland and Stewart.

– 1953. Boy on Defense. Toronto: McClelland and Stewart.

– 1963. A Boy at the Leafs Camp. Boston: Little, Brown and Company.

CHAPTER SEVEN

Allen, Oliver E. 1990. *New York, New York: A History of the World's
  Most Exhilarating and Challenging City*. New York: Atheneum.

Barth, Gunther. 1980. *City People: The Rise of Modern City Culture in
  Nineteenth-Century America*. New York: Oxford University Press.

Black, Robson. 1913. "The Theatrical Field in Canada." *New York
  Dramatic Mirror*, 8 January, 4.

Botto, Louis. 2002. *At This Theatre: 100 Years of Broadway Shows,
  Stories and Stars*. New York: Playbill Books and Applause Theatre and
  Cinema Books.

Bush, Gregory. 1993. "'Genial Evasion' in the Big Time: Changing
  Norms of Respectability within an Expansive Urban Culture." *Journal
  of Urban History* 19 (3): 121–38.

Cauz, Louis. 1977. *Baseball's Back in Town*. Toronto: Controlled Media
  Corporation.

Chach, Maryann, Regan Fletcher, Mark E. Swartz, and Sylvia Wang.
  2001. *The Shuberts Present: 100 Years of American Theatre*. New
  York: Harry N. Abrams and The Shubert Organization.

Cohen, Lizabeth. 1990. "The Mass in Mass Consumption." *Reviews in American History* 18 (4): 548–55.

Cross, Harry. 1925. "Garden Is Opened in a Blaze of Color." *New York Times,* 16 December, 29.

Dendy, William, and William Kilbourn. 1986. *Toronto Observed: Its Architecture, Patrons, and History.* Toronto: Oxford University Press.

Dilse, Paul. 1989. *Toronto's Theatre Block: An Architectural History.* Toronto: Toronto Region Architectural Conservancy.

Dryden, Ken. 1983. *The Game: A Reflective and Thought-provoking Look at Life in Hockey.* Toronto: Macmillan.

Erenberg, Lewis A. 1984 [1981]. *Steppin' Out: New York Nightlife and the Transformation of American Culture, 1890–1930.* Chicago: University of Chicago Press.

Field, Russell. 1993. "On the Waterfront: Toronto's Professional Baseball Heritage." *Dugout* 1 (1): 4–11.

– 2002. "Passive Participation: The Selling of Spectacle and the Construction of Maple Leaf Gardens, 1931." *Sport History Review* 33 (1): 35–50.

Fishwick, Nicholas. 1989. *English Football and Society, 1910–1950.* Manchester, UK: Manchester University Press.

Gruneau, Richard, and David Whitson. 1993. *Hockey Night in Canada: Sport, Identities and Cultural Politics.* Toronto: Garamond.

Guttmann, Allen. 1986. *Sports Spectators.* New York: Columbia University Press.

Hall, M. Ann Hall. 2002. *The Girl and the Game: A History of Women's Sport in Canada.* Peterborough, ON: Broadview Press.

Hardy, Stephen. 1981. "The City and the Rise of American Sport: 1820–1920." *Exercise and Sports Sciences Reviews* 9 (1): 183–219.

– 1997. "Sport in Urbanizing America: A Historical Review." *Journal of Urban History* 23 (6): 675–708.

Henderson, Mary C. 1973. *The City and the Theatre: New York Playhouses from Bowling Green to Times Square.* Clifton, NJ: James T. White and Co.

– 1997. *The New Amsterdam: The Biography of a Broadway Theatre.* New York: Hyperion.

Hill, Jeffrey. 2003. "'The day was an ugly one': Wembley, 28th April 1923." Unpublished paper.

Hill, Jeff, and Francesco Varrasi. 1997. "Creating Wembley: The Construction of a National Monument." *Sports Historian* 17 (2): 28–43.

Jancovich, Mark, and Lucy Faire, with Sarah Stubbings. 2003. *The Place of Audience: Cultural Geographies of Film Consumption*. London: British Film Institute.

Jenish, D'Arcy. 1992. *The Stanley Cup: A Hundred Years of Hockey at Its Best*. Toronto: McClelland and Stewart.

Johnes, Martin. 2002. *Soccer and Society: South Wales, 1900–1939*. Cardiff: University of Wales Press.

Kidd, Bruce. 1996. *The Struggle for Canadian Sport*. Toronto: University of Toronto Press.

Kilbourn, William. 1993. *Intimate Grandeur: One Hundred Years at Massey Hall*. Toronto: Stoddart.

Levine, Peter. 1992. *Ellis Island to Ebbets Field: Sport and the American Jewish Experience*. New York: Oxford University Press.

Lindsay, John C. 1983. *Turn Out the Stars before Leaving: The Story of Canada's Theatres*. Erin, ON: Boston Mills Press.

– 1986. *Royal Alexandra: The Finest Theatre on the Continent*. Erin, ON: Boston Mills Press.

McFarlane, Brian. 1994. *Proud Past, Bright Future: One Hundred Years of Canadian Women's Hockey*. Toronto: Stoddart.

McKinley, Michael. 2000. *Putting a Roof on Winter: Hockey's Rise from Sport to Spectacle*. Vancouver: Greystone Books.

Morrison, Andrew Craig. 1974. *Opera House, Nickel Show, and Palace: An Illustrated Inventory of Theater Buildings in the Detroit Area*. Dearborn, MI: Greenfield Village and Henry Ford Museum.

Nasaw, David. 2002 [1993]. *Going Out: The Rise and Fall of Public Amusements*. Cambridge, MA: Harvard University Press.

Olsheski, Constance. 1989. *Pantages Theatre: Rebirth of a Landmark*. Toronto: Cineplex Odeon Corporation and Key Porter Books.

Quarrington, Paul. 1999. "Introduction." In *Maple Leaf Gardens: Memories and Dreams, 1931–1999*, ed. Dan Diamond, 5–42. Toronto: Maple Leaf Sports and Entertainment.

Rickard, Maxine, with Arch Oboler. 1936. *Everything Happened to Him: The Story of Tex Rickard*. New York: Frederick A. Stokes Co.

Riess, Steven A. 1999. *Touching Base: Professional Baseball and American Culture in the Progressive Era*. 2nd ed. Urbana and Chicago: University of Illinois Press.

Russell, Hilary. 1989. *Double Take: The Story of the Elgin and Winter Garden Theatres*. Toronto: Ontario Heritage Foundation and Dundurn Press.

Saddlemyer, Ann, ed. 1990. *Early Stages: Theatre in Ontario, 1800–1914*. Toronto: University of Toronto Press.

Saddlemyer, Ann, and Richard Plant, eds. 1997. *Later Stages: Essays in Ontario Theatre from the First World War to the 1970s*. Toronto: University of Toronto Press.

Selke, Frank, with H. Gordon Green. 1962. *Behind the Cheering*. Toronto: McClelland and Stewart.

Shubert, Howard. 2002. "The Changing Experience of Hockey Spectatorship: Architecture, Design, Technology, and Economics." In *Putting it on Ice*. Vol. 1: *Hockey and Cultural Identities*. Ed. Colin Howell, 59–63. Halifax: Gorsebrook Research Institute.

Smythe, Conn, with Scott Young. 1981. *If You Can't Beat 'Em in the Alley*. Toronto: McClelland and Stewart.

Stern, Robert A.M., Gregory Gilmartin, and Thomas Mellins. 1987. *New York, 1930: Architecture and Urbanism between the Two World Wars*. New York: Rizzoli.

Sullivan, Neil J. 2001. *The Diamond in the Bronx: Yankee Stadium and the Politics of New York*. New York: Oxford University Press.

Taylor, Rogan. 1991. "Walking Alone Together: Football Supporters and Their Relationship with the Game." In *British Football and Social Change: Getting into Europe*, ed. John Williams and Stephen Wagg, 111–29. Leicester: Leicester University Press.

Taylor, William R. 1988. "The Launching of a Commercial Culture: New York City, 1860–1930." In *Power, Culture, and Place: Essays on New York City*, ed. John Hull Mollenkopf, 107–33. New York: Russell Sage Foundation.

Thompson, John Herd, with Allen Seager. 1985. *Canada, 1922–1939: Decades of Discord*. Toronto: McClelland and Stewart.

Tippett, Maria. 1990. *Making Culture: English-Canadian Arts Institutions before the Massey Commission*. Toronto: University of Toronto Press.

Waddington, Ivan, Dominic Malcolm, and Roman Horak. 1998. "The Social Composition of Football Crowds in Western Europe." *International Review for the Sociology of Sport* 33 (2): 155–69.

Walton, John K. 2003. "Football, Fainting and Fatalities, 1923–1946." *History Today* 53 (1): 10–17.

The Weather Vein. 1926. (Carrier Engineering Corp.) 6 (2): 23–8.

White, G. Edward. 1996. *Creating the National Pastime: Baseball Transforms Itself, 1903–1953.* Princeton, NJ: Princeton University Press.

White, Philip and Brian Wilson. 1999. "Distinctions in the Stands: An Investigation of Bourdieu's 'Habitus,' Socioeconomic Status and Sport Spectatorship in Canada." *International Review for the Sociology of Sport* 34 (3): 245–64.

Wilkins, Charles. 1999. "Maple Leaf Gardens (and How It Got That Way)." In *Maple Leaf Gardens: Memories and Dreams, 1931–1999,* ed. Dan Diamond, 45–57. Toronto: Maple Leaf Sports and Entertainment.

Wong, John. 2001. "The Development of Professional Hockey and the Making of the National Hockey League." PhD diss., University of Maryland.

CHAPTER EIGHT

Bird, P.J. 1988. "Professional Football and Injuries." Available at: http://www.hhp.ufl.edu/keepingfit/ARTICLE/profootball.htm. (viewed July 2005).

Carrier, Roch. 1997 [1979]. "The Hockey Sweater." In *Our Game: An All-Star Collection of Hockey Fiction.* ed. Doug Beardsley, 15–17. Victoria: Polestar.

Festinger, Leon. 1964 [1956]. *When Prophecy Fails: A Social and Psychological Study of a Modern Group That Predicted the Destruction of the World.* New York: Harper and Row.

Friedman, D. 2001. "ABA Numbers Paint a Very Different Picture." *Basketball Digest* 28 (7). Available at http://findarticles.com/p/articles/mi_moFCJ/is_7_28/ai_74437533?tag=content;col1 (viewed 12 March 2009).

Harrison, Richard. 2004. *Hero of the Play.* 10th anniversary edition. Toronto: Wolsak and Wynn.

McKinley, Michael. 2000. *Putting a Roof on Winter: Hockey's Rise from Sport to Spectacle.* Toronto: Douglas and McIntyre.

SLAM! Sports: Hockey. 2004. "SLAM! Hockey Poll: What Is Your Mood as the NHL Lockout Is Close to Wiping Out the Whole Season?"

Available at: http://cgi.canoe.ca/htbin/survey?poll=slamo41124&
pollresult.html (viewed 24 November 2004).

World Hockey Association. 2005. "History." Available at: http://www.
worldhockeyassociation.net/history/ (viewed 15 March 2005).

CHAPTER NINE

Abley, Mark. 1998. "A Street of Villages: Sainte-Catherine Street Diverts,
Detains, and Entertains." *Canadian Geographic* 118 (3): 64–5.

Baum, Gregory. 1991. "Catholicism and Secularization in Quebec." In
The Church in Quebec. Ottawa: Novalis.

Bélanger, Anouk. 2000. "Sports Venues and Spectacularization of Urban
Space in North America: The Case of the Molson Centre in Montreal." *International Review for the Sociology of Sport* 35 (3): 378–97.

Coates, Colin M., and Cecilia Morgan. 2002. *Heroines and History:
Representations of Madeleine de Verchères and Laura Secord*. Toronto:
University of Toronto Press.

Di Felice, David. 1999. "The Richard Riot: A Socio-historical Examination of Sport, Culture, and the Construction of Symbolic Identities."
MA thesis, Queen's University.

Falardeau, J.C. 1964. "The Role and Importance of the Church in
French Canada." In *French Canadian Society*, ed. M. Rioux and
Y. Martin, 342–57. Toronto: McClelland and Stewart.

Le fantôme de Forum. 1996. Quebec: SRC.

Gordon, Alan. 1997. "Contested Terrain: The Politics of Public Memory
in Montreal, 1891–1930." PhD diss., Queen's University.

Goyens, Chrystian, Allan Turowetz, Jean-Luc Duguay. 1996. *Le Forum
de Montreal: La fierté pour toujours, 1924–1996*. Montreal: Les
Edition Effix, Inc.

Hobsbawm, Eric. 1983. "Introduction: Inventing Traditions." In *The
Invention of Tradition*, ed. E. Hobsbawm and T. Ranger, 1–14.
Cambridge: Cambridge University Press.

James, C.L.R. 1963. *Beyond a Boundary*. London: Hutchinson.

Koshar, Rudy J. 1994. "Building Pasts: Historic Preservation and Identity
in Twentieth-century Germany." In *Commemorations: The Politics of
National Identity*, ed. John R. Gillis, 215–38. Princeton: Princeton
University Press.

Lowenthal, David. 1989. *The Heritage Crusade and the Spoils of History*. Cambridge: Cambridge University Press.

McKay, Ian. 1992. "Tartanism Triumphant: The Construction of Scottishness in Nova Scotia, 1933–1954." *Acadiensis* 21 (2): 5–47.

Riley, Susan. 1980. "Serenity with a Touch of Anger." *Maclean's*, 26 May, 19.

Slater, Don. 1997. *Consumer Culture and Modernity*. Cambridge, UK: Polity Press.

Sperber, Jonathan. 1992. "Festival of National Unity in the German Revolution of 1848–1849." *Past and Present* 136: 114–38.

Trevor-Roper, Hugh. 1983. "The Invention of Tradition: The Highland Tradition of Scotland." In *The Invention of Tradition*, ed. E. Hobsbawm and T. Ranger, 15–41. Cambridge: Cambridge University Press.

Vamplew, Wray. 1988. *Pay up and Play the Game: Professional Sport in Britain, 1875–1914*. New York: Cambridge University Press.

Walden, Keith. 1989. "Speaking Modern: Language, Culture, and Hegemony in Grocery Window Displays, 1887–1920." *Canadian Historical Review* 70 (3): 285–310.

Wyatt, Nelson. 2000, 18 May. Sovereignists make a few advances since 1980 loss. *Canadian Free Press*.

Zukin, Sharon. 1991. "Disney World: The Power of Façade/The Façade of Power." In *Landscapes of Power: From Detroit to Disney World*, 217–50. Berkeley: University of California Press.

CHAPTER TEN

Bannock, G., R.E. Baxter, and E. Davis. 1992. *The Penguin Dictionary of Economics*. 5th ed. Harmondsworth, Middlesex, UK: Penguin Books.

Barthes, R. 1972. *Mythologies*. Selected and Translated from French by Annette Lavers. New York: Hill and Wang.

Conway, R. 1995. *Game Misconduct: Alan Eagleson and the Corruption of Hockey*. Toronto: Macfarlane, Walter and Ross.

Cruise, D., and A. Griffiths. 1991. *Net Worth: Exploding the Myths of Pro Hockey*. Toronto: McFarlane Walter and Ross.

Curry, T., and R. Jiobu. 1984. *Sports: A Social Perspective*. Englewood Cliffs, NJ: Prentice Hall.

Dowbiggin, B. 2003. *Money Players: How Hockey's Greatest Stars Beat the NHL at Its Own Game*. Toronto: McClelland and Stewart.

Ehrenberg, R., and R. Smith. 1988. *Modern Labor Economics*. 3rd ed. Glenview, IL: Scott, Foresmand and Company.

Flynn, M.A., and R.J. Gilbert. 2001. "The Analysis of Professional Sports Leagues as Joint Ventures." *Economic Journal* 111 (469): F27–46.

Gorman, J., and K. Calhoun. 1994. *The Name of the Game: The Business of Sport*. New York: John Wiley and Sons.

Gruneau, Richard, and David Whitson. 1993. *Hockey Night in Canada: Sport, Identities, and Cultural Politics* Toronto: Garamond Press.

Hamermesh, D., and A. Rees. 1984. *The Economics of Work and Pay*. 3rd ed. New York: Harper and Row.

Harvey, D. 2002. "The Art of Rent: Globalization, Monopoly and the Commodification of Culture." In *Socialist Register 2002: A World of Contradictions*, ed. Leo Panitch and Colin Leys, 93–110. Halifax, NS: Fernwood.

Houston, W., and D. Shoalts. 1993. *Eagleson: The Fall of a Hockey Czar*. Toronto: McGraw Hill Ryerson.

Jameson, F. 1984. "Postmodernism, or the Cultural Logic of Late Capitalism." *New Left Review* 146: 53–92.

Kaufman, B. 1989. *The Economics of Labour Markets and Labour Relations*. Orlando, FL: The Dryden Press.

Kaye, H.J. 1996. *"Why do ruling classes fear history?" And Other Questions*. New York: St Martin's Press.

King, A. 1997. "New Directors, Customers and Fans: The Transformation of English Football in the 1990s." *Sociology of Sport Journal* 14 (3): 224–40.

LaFeber W. 1999. *Michael Jordan and the New Global Capitalism*. New York: W.W. Norton.

Lash, S., and J. Urry. 1994. *Economies of Signs and Space*. London: Sage.

Leslie, D.A. 1995. "Global Scan: The Globalization of Advertising Agencies, Concepts and Campaigns." *Economic Geography* 71 (4): 402–26.

Levitt, T. 1983. *The Marketing Imagination*. Boston: Beacon.

Lobmeyer, H., and L. Weidinger. 1992. "Commercialism as a Dominant Factor in the American Sports Scene: Sources, Development, Perspectives." *International Review for the Sociology of Sport* 27 (4): 309–27.

Mason, D.S., and T. Slack. 2001. "Industry Factors and the Changing Dynamics of the Player-Agent Relationship in Professional Ice Hockey." *Sport Management Review* 4 (2): 165–91.

Morrison, R.J. 1996. "Sports Fans, Athletes' Salaries, and Economic Rent." *International Review for the Sociology of Sport* 31 (3): 257–69.

Scoville, J. 1974. "Labour Relations in Sport." In *Government and the Sports Business*, ed. R. Noll, 185–220. Washington: The Brookings Institute.

Silver, J. 1996. *Thin Ice: Money, Politics, and the Demise of an NHL Franchise*. Halifax: Fernwood.

Sullivan, N.J. 1992. *The Diamond Revolution: The Prospects for Baseball after the Collapse of Its Ruling Class*. New York: St. Martin's Press.

Williams, J. 1994. "The Local and the Global in English Soccer and the Rise of Satellite Television." *Sociology of Sport.* 11 (4): 389–91.

Zimbalist, A. 1998. "The Economics of Stadiums, Teams and Cities." *Policy Studies Review* 15 (1): 17–29.

Contributors

JULIAN AMMIRANTE teaches Canadian politics and Canadian public policy at Laurentian University at Georgian. He is a big fan of hockey but not of the NHL.

JASON F. BLAKE is a lecturer in the English department at the University of Ljubljana (Slovenia). A revised and updated version of his doctoral dissertation, "Ice Hockey as a Cultural Symbol in Canadian Prose," is forthcoming with University of Toronto Press. He is the secretary of the Central European Canadian Studies Association. Outside of hockey and theories of play and sport, his research interests include the pianist Glenn Gould, the novelist Philip Roth, and Slovene-English translation issues.

ROBERT H. DENNIS is a doctoral candidate and teaching fellow in the Department of History at Queen's University. His previous publications include work on offshore oil and gas development in British Columbia and Newfoundland and Labrador. He holds a SSHRC doctoral fellowship, which supports his dissertation research on the relationship between Roman Catholicism and the Canadian left from the 1930s to the 1940s.

JAMIE DOPP is an associate professor of Canadian literature at the University of Victoria. He has published a variety of articles on Canadian fiction, poetry, and culture as well as one novel and two books of poems. In 2004, during a very rare cold spell in Victoria, he stayed up all night to build a backyard ice rink and managed to have three blissful days of outdoor hockey with his family.

RUSSELL FIELD is an assistant professor in the Faculty of Kinesiology and Recreation Management at the University of Manitoba. He has a PhD from the University of Toronto, where his doctoral project examined the design of ice hockey facilities, the composition of the crowd, and the nature of spectator experiences in New York and Toronto in the 1920s and 1930s.

GREG GILLESPIE is an associate professor in the Department of Communication, Popular Culture, and Film at Brock University in St Catharines, Ontario.

RICHARD HARRISON is the award-winning author of *Hero of the Play*, poems told in the language of hockey: the first book of poems to be launched at the Hockey Hall of Fame (in 1994). His poetry, essays, and commentaries on the game have been internationally published in books of essays and poetry, and radio and television, most recently on CBC's *Hockey: A People's History*. He teaches creative writing, English literature, and the graphic novel at Mount Royal College in Calgary, Alberta.

ANDREW C. HOLMAN teaches Canadian and US History at Bridgewater State College in Bridgewater, Massachusetts. He is the author of several scholarly articles on hockey and Canadian history and is co-writing (with Stephen Hardy) *The Coolest Game? A History of Ice Hockey* (forthcoming, University of Illinois Press).

CRAIG HYATT is an assistant professor in the Department of Sport Management at Brock University, St Catharines, Ontario. His research focuses on sports fans who fall outside the existing sport fan models: fans who have lost their favourite teams through franchise relocation, switch loyalties from one team to another, and reject the obvious local option in order to cheer instead for distant teams.

BRIAN KENNEDY is associate professor of English at Pasadena City College. He is the author of *Living the Hockey Life* (Folklore Publishing, 2009) and *Growing Up Hockey: The Life and Times of Everyone Who Ever Loved the Game* (Folklore Publishing, 2007). He is also co-editor (with Mona Field) of *The People and Promise of California* (Pearson Longman, 2008). His academic interests include contemporary British and Commonwealth literature. He has published articles on Virginia Woolf, Henry James, Mikhail Bakhtin, and other topics.

KAREN E.H. SKINAZI studies immigrant and ethnic American literature and is currently working on a project that focuses on literary communities across the Canadian-American border. Her recent publications include "'As to her race, its secret is loudly revealed': Winnifred Eaton's Revision of North American Identity" in the Summer 2007 issue of *MELUS* and "Through Roots and Routes: *On the Road*'s Portrayal of an Outsider's Journey into the Meaning of America" forthcoming from the *Canadian Review of American Studies*. She is an instructor at the University of Alberta.

JULIE STEVENS is an associate professor in the Department of Sport Management at Brock University in St Catharines, Ontario. Her research interests include change management and capacity in non-profit sport organizations. She is the co-author of *Too Many Men on the Ice: Women's Hockey in North America* (1997). Her hockey research examines the institutional development of the Canadian hockey system, women's hockey identity, and governance issues related to the female game. She played varsity hockey at Queen's University, coached elite girls' teams, and is an active member of her women's recreational team.

Index